Among Friends

*A consultation with Friends
about the condition of Quakers
in the U.S. today*

AN EARLHAM SCHOOL OF RELIGION REPORT

TABLE OF CONTENTS

AMONG FRIENDS IS THE REPORT of a national consultation with U.S. Quakers carried out on behalf of the Earlham School of Religion. The project was conducted by Crane MetaMarketing Ltd. of Atlanta, Georgia, and overseen by ESR's Board of Advisors.

A complex picture of U.S. Quakerism emerges in *Among Friends*: weaknesses and strengths, obstacles and opportunities. This portrait shows Friends thriving in some places, stalled in others. Leadership is a central concern: the need for it, the difficulties of providing it, the possibilities for nurturing it. We believe the study is the most comprehensive look at Quakers in the United States ever conducted. We are eager to share the results with all who are interested, and eager to encourage wide discussion of the report.

The call for the consultation was issued by the ESR faculty, by ESR's Board of Advisors, and by the Earlham Board of Trustees. Forty years ago, before ESR was founded, Wilmer Cooper crisscrossed the United States asking Friends whether Quakerism needed a seminary, and if so, what its aims and programs should be. Today ESR is a vital and spirited place. Since 1960, however, there have been major changes in the Religious Society of Friends and in the nature of seminary education. We thought the time was ripe for ESR to consider again how its programs could best serve the needs of all Quakers.

Understanding ESR's best contribution requires understanding Quakerism in the United States today, its current situation and needs. Thus, these three questions have been at the center of the national consultation.

> 1) *What is the current situation of the Religious Society of Friends? What are the main strengths, and what are the main challenges before us at the present time?*

> 2) *More specifically, what is the situation with regard to leadership? Are we finding the leaders we need, and are they being prepared for leadership roles as well as they might be?*

> 3) *What are the potential contributions that the Earlham School of Religion can make to meet these needs and challenges in the preparation of leaders?*

The report is based on focus groups, interviews, and letters. There were 24 focus groups conducted last fall and winter in 22 locations across the United States, from North Carolina through Indiana to the Pacific Northwest, from Los Angeles through Wichita to New England. We invited about a dozen people to each focus group, hoping that six to 10, an ideal size for a such a group, would be able to participate. In total, 210 Quakers participated in this way. Our consultants conducted broad-ranging telephone interviews with an additional 31 individuals. Finally, we placed an ad in *Quaker Life* and *Friends Journal* inviting all who were interested to write letters. In response we received 14 thoughtful essays.

In selecting those to invite to focus groups or interviews, we worked closely with the clerks and superintendents of Yearly Meetings. We asked them to suggest Quakers with broad experience and understanding: leaders among Friends. We worked hard to include Friends of every orientation: evangelical and universalistic; orthodox and conservative (and neither); EFI, FGC, FUM, and other. On a number of dimensions we also tried to gather a good mix of participants, for example men and women, well seasoned and more recently arrived, older and younger, those in larger Meetings or churches and those in smaller, those in paid positions and those not. We could not possibly include every leader in the Religious Society of Friends, but we did include a broadly representative group. A profile of the 210 focus group participants is featured as an appendix to the report.

Accompanying the report is a thematically organized compilation of quotations, *Quaker Voices*, drawn from the focus groups and interviews.

At ESR we will be using the report during this academic year (1999–2000) as the beginning point of a planning process to make sure ESR's programs are responsive to the needs of Friends. In addition, we will be sponsoring some gatherings around the country over the next several months (and encouraging other discussions) to consider the report and discern how we might make the most of our strengths and opportunities.

We selected Crane MetaMarketing Ltd. to conduct the research and write the report because they had shown in previous work a capacity to understand communities of faith broadly similar to Quakers—their hopes and commitments, their struggles and their worries. Because they are not Friends (though tender to our beliefs and practices), we hoped they would be more readily accepted and respected among all branches of Friends. I would like to thank everyone at Crane, especially

Patti Crane, Jennifer Joseph, and Ginger Pyron for their matchless ability to listen carefully to what Friends have to say, and to synthesize hundreds of pages of transcripts and letters into a coherent and insightful report. Their task was made much harder (and their skill all the more to be appreciated) because what we Friends have to say is complex, sometimes contradictory.

At Earlham, Keith Esch allowed us to draw on his talents and experience among Friends to oversee the process we used to identify participants in the consultation. With conscientious support from Mary Ann Weaver, he also made arrangements for the focus groups. Kirsten Bohl lent invaluable assistance at the very beginning and again at the end as we moved the report towards publication.

We are grateful to many clerks and superintendents of the Yearly Meetings and to a number of other Friends for their assistance in identifying participants in the focus groups. The Board of Advisors of ESR provided crucial insight and support throughout this project. Many members of the Board of Advisors as well as a few alumni of ESR served as hosts for focus groups. We appreciate their assistance and hospitality.

We are especially indebted to those who wrote letters, and to all who participated in the focus groups and interviews. It is their thoughtful contributions that form the substance of the report.

The national consultation was made possible by a gift from Howard and Gussie Mills, members of Western Yearly Meeting in Indiana, graduates of Earlham College and long-time friends of ESR. Howard is currently vice chair of the Earlham Board of Trustees. I am extraordinarily grateful to Howard and Gussie for their support and advice throughout this project.

Douglas Bennett, President
Earlham
September, 1999

FROM ASIA BENNETT, one of the "weighty Friends" we interviewed for Earlham School of Religion's national consultation, our CRANE team received some generous words of encouragement:

> *This is a good effort. Just going through the process of asking people what they think is helpful. I hope you get more material than you know what to do with! It's great to see some fresh energy.*

Fresh energy. Those two words, we believe, capture the intention, the spirit, and the outcome of this national consultation. With a keen appreciation for the significance of Earlham's choice of a non-Quaker group to conduct the consultation, our CRANE team approached its task with profound respect. Lacking any agenda other than to learn and to understand, we visited, listened, questioned, and finally—after months of absorbing information—began to synthesize.

During the entire process, Friends throughout the United States and beyond shared willingly and eloquently their observations, experiences, disappointments, and hopes. Many also shared a quiet gratification: "We haven't talked this way as a group before," some said. Others simply told us, "Thanks for listening."

As we took in Friends' perceptive and thoughtful remarks, we felt a responsibility not only to document our general findings but to feed back to ESR in greater detail the wide-ranging commentary that gradually filled our notebooks and cassette tapes. We also yearned to pass along some of the inspiring stories we heard about Quaker faith in action, and—amid the undeniable struggles of Friends today—about Quaker efforts that undoubtedly are working well.

By the end of our gathering and sifting, Asia Bennett's wish had come true: Our wealth of material was more than we could manageably assimilate into the formal report. In response, we created *Quaker Voices*— a supplementary document that we had not anticipated, and thus a document that we never mentioned to all the Friends who attended our groups and received our calls. To protect the confidentiality we had promised, we attributed no quotations and also removed details that might identify the speakers.

Like Wilmer Cooper, scouting the vast Quaker landscape 40 years ago to see whether a seminary among Friends was even a feasible undertaking, our CRANE team met idealists as well as skeptics; we heard support as well as admonition. But just as Wil's forthright and penetrating study opened the way for a new institution to arise, perhaps this year's national consultation can help open the way for an existing institution to recharge.

During our months of candid discussions with a range of Friends, we noted one particularly optimistic indication: Friends still have passionate hopes and suggestions for what ESR can become. Not everyone is entirely happy with the school, but no one believes that the experiment has reached its conclusion. The potential, we believe, is enormous.

In its relatively short history, the Earlham School of Religion has generated expectations, praise, criticism, and requests. All of those responses are likely to continue. But whether one approves of ESR or disparages its efforts, one must admit that this still-young seminary has accomplished something quite remarkable: Among all branches of Friends, it has established a living legacy of theologically astute graduates who care deeply about the Quaker movement and the Quaker testimonies—and who, like ESR itself, are working toward a vital Quaker future.

For our entire CRANE staff, the task of acting as a channel for new dialogue between ESR and its wide constituency has been not only a challenge and an eye-opener, but a privilege. We hope that, with fresh energy, Friends will continue the conversation.

Patti Crane
Jennifer Joseph
Ginger Pyron
Crane MetaMarketing Ltd.
Atlanta, Georgia

THE RELIGIOUS SOCIETY OF FRIENDS BEGAN in England in the 1650s in the seeking of a young man named George Fox. Discouraged by his encounters with a succession of religious authorities, he came to the powerful insight that God was directly accessible to all who would seek Him. "There is one, even Christ Jesus, who can speak to thy condition," he realized.

The Religious Society of Friends spread to America in its first generation. Fox himself visited early Friends in the colonies. William Penn established a Quaker community, a "Holy experiment," in Pennsylvania. Other Friends settled in the Carolinas, Virginia, New York, New England, and elsewhere.

Fox and other early Friends adopted an unusual form of worship: gathering together in silence for divine instruction. When moved to speak, a Friend rises and shares her message with others. Today some Friends have programmed elements in their worship (hymns, a prepared message, prayers, readings from the Bible), and others continue in a wholly unprogrammed manner, but most Friends worship has periods of waiting in silence upon God.

Friends believe there is that of God within each of us. A number of testimonies—orientations to action—emerge directly from this fundamental understanding. Because there is a divine spark within each of us, for example, Friends have a deep leading towards human equality. In line with this, Friends were early and vigorous advocates for the abolition of slavery and for recognizing the full equality of women. And because there is something divine within each of us, Friends have a testimony of peace that leads toward pacifism. Friends often refuse to serve in the military, at times choosing jail rather than conscription. Said George Fox, "I live in the virtue of that life and power that takes away the occasion of all wars."

Friends' belief in that of God within each of us also contributes to an understanding of the manner in which Friends organize themselves. Local Meetings (similar in size and purpose to mainline Protestant congregations) gather weekly for worship, and monthly for business. Business itself is understood as a form of worship, with an emphasis on waiting upon the Spirit for guidance towards decision making in unity. Local Meetings are sometimes referred to as Monthly Meetings, after the scheduling of these worshipful business sessions. In turn, Monthly

Meetings may affiliate with each other to form Yearly Meetings—large gatherings of Friends (roughly geographical in nature) that meet annually for worship and business.

Despite the common framework of Friends' understandings sketched above, there is considerable diversity among the beliefs and practices of individuals and groups of Friends. A series of schisms (and some healings) in the 19th century has led to the existence today of three main branches of Friends: those affiliated with Friends General Conference (FGC), Friends United Meeting (FUM), and Evangelical Friends International (EFI). It is important to note that some Monthly and Yearly Meetings are affiliated with none of these branches, or with more than one. From universalistic to Christ-centered—many different approaches to worship and witness are represented among Friends.

Quakers have also created a dense thicket of other organizations: the American Friends Service Committee (AFSC), Friends Committee on National Legislation (FCNL), and Friends World Committee for Consultation (FWCC) are just a few. Their functions are various: from lobbying to outreach to communication among Friends. In addition, Quakers have created and continue to support a multitude of retreat centers (Pendle Hill, Quaker Hill), schools, colleges, seminaries, and retirement homes. Many of these organizations are under the care of one or more Yearly Meetings, Monthly Meetings, or other assemblages of Friends.

Our hope is that the consultation report that follows will give newcomers to Quakerism a sense of what is on the hearts and minds of Friends today, especially with regard to leadership. If you find that you would like to learn more about the Religious Society of Friends, we would recommend this beginning bibliography:

Howard Brinton, *Friends for 300 Years* (Wallingford, PA: Pendle Hill Publications, 1952, 1964).

John Punshon, *Portrait in Grey: A Short History of Quakers* (London: Quaker Home Service, 1984).

Thomas Hamm, *The Transformation of American Quakerism; Orthodox Friends, 1800–1907* (Bloomington: Indiana University Press, 1988).

We hope you will find, as you browse through the report that follows, many occasions for reflection and engagement in the company of Friends.

Among Friends

We commit ourselves to listening carefully
to what Friends across the country have to say.

CALL FOR A NATIONAL CONSULTATION, 1998
EARLHAM SCHOOL OF RELIGION

~

FOR A GROUP THAT OFTEN HAS CHARACTERIZED itself as "silent"
or "quiet," the Religious Society of Friends shows a remarkable talent
for speaking up.

Beginning with our two-day visit to Earlham School of Religion
in December 1998, continuing through 24 focus groups in 22 cities
throughout the country, and culminating in 14 written essays as well as
31 telephone interviews with individual Friends both in the U.S. and
abroad, the national consultation sponsored by Earlham School of
Religion has generated willing and abundant comment.

Our CRANE team, though predisposed to admire this historically
transformative religious movement, gained an increasing respect
for Friends—a respect gently flavored with exasperation—as the consultation progressed. Whether participants arrived well prepared or
slightly mystified, all joined eagerly in the discussions and offered
observations noteworthy for both thoughtfulness and candor.
Many of those observations appear in *Quaker Voices*, a collection
of representative (but by no means exhaustive) responses.

Our occasional exasperation arose from the awareness that
perceptions within our groups and interviews so often echoed—
uncannily, sometimes almost word for word—those that Wilmer
Cooper recorded 40 years ago in his 1959 feasibility study. As people
described for us the strengths, challenges, and leadership needs of
today's Religious Society of Friends, we heard much that we had
encountered already in Appendix II of Cooper's *The ESR Story*.
"In 40 years, has so little changed?" we asked ourselves.

But among Friends, at least one thing *has* changed—and is still changing. Little by little the Earlham School of Religion, founded in 1960 as an unabashed experiment, has engendered awareness, criticism, and applause; dialogue, frustration, and hope. Almost a microcosm of modern Quaker achievements and concerns, ESR reflects much that is both commendable and disquieting in the Society of Friends. The good news, however, is that the experiment isn't finished. The revelation continues. And like the Friends themselves, Earlham School of Religion is listening.

It is imperative that ESR resist the temptation
to function within its own comfort zone
as an institution without reference to its larger calling
as a mover and shaker within the Society of Friends.

A FRIEND

~

AS AN INSTITUTION FOUNDED EXPLICITLY to prepare Quaker
leaders, Earlham School of Religion can neither function nor be understood outside of its Quaker context. ESR exists not on an island of its
own aims and aspirations, but in the midst of watchful, needy, volatile,
and often clashing constituents: in other words, among Friends.

These Friends—a peculiar people, as they themselves acknowledge—
defy glib description. From the various forks and branches of their
weathered family tree, they all staunchly bear the family name, even
while regretting or even actively disparaging the divergent leanings of
their more distant kin. But who are these Friends, really? What keeps
the Quaker family strong and vital? On behalf of ESR, we asked.

Among the hundreds of Friends who answered, we found more
consistency of response than we might have expected. The Religious
Society of Friends' current strengths, as participants described them,
fall into several broad categories:

> **the past:** our 350-year-old heritage and culture; our
> good reputation; the influential work we've done,
> despite our small numbers; our schools

> **distinctive Quaker teachings:** an individual, direct,
> and experiential relationship with God; a transformed
> life that bears witness to that relationship; the Inner

Light; the existence of "that of God in each person"; continuing revelation; the sacredness of all life; "There is one, even Christ Jesus, that can speak to thy condition."

the traditional Quaker testimonies: peacemaking, concern for social justice, equality of all persons, simplicity in living, personal integrity

specific Quaker practices: listening in the silence, simplicity in worship, the gathered Meeting, Meeting for Business as Worship, Meeting for Education as Worship, corporate decision making, clearness committees, "every member a minister"

Friends themselves: a wide variety; people who care for each other; the salt of the earth; plain speakers; people who keep trying to work together; beneath all the divisiveness, "brothers and sisters in Christ"; our dedicated pastors; our elders

traits of the Quaker movement and community: relevant, refreshing, open, a haven for seekers, tolerant, welcoming, prophetic, revolutionary, authentically Christian, courageously self-critical

This list of strengths sounds comprehensive and hardy—a set of virtues quite adequate, one might think, to support and sustain even a geographically diffuse and theologically tangled Society. Enumerating these attributes and telling us the stories of their own Quaker experiences and commitment, people in our groups often looked modestly proud, quietly contented. Although participants typically minimized the impact and power of their conscientiously lived faith, we frequently felt awed by the realization that, Friend by Friend, these "Valiant Many" not only are making a difference: they're quite capable—if fully galvanized—of making a world.

But when we asked participants about the weaknesses or challenges that Quakers face, we heard a much longer list, sobering in both its scope and seriousness. Because the broad points of that list comprise many smaller ones, we quote in each section below a handful of representative remarks from across the spectrum of Friends.

We don't know who we are.

General issues: we've lost our identity; we're confused; we can't articulate who we are; we represent too broad a theological spectrum; our beliefs are too loose to convey; when new people come, we have nothing clear to tell them; we "navel-gaze"; we think too much and conclude too little

"The Society of Friends is so broad and so open. It's hard to see what we believe or stand for."

"With our heady cognitive gymnastics and splitting hairs, we waste energy for doing divine work."

"We're reluctant to take a firm stand, to identify with something. But if we allow that vacuum to exist, everyone else gets to define who we are."

"Friends hesitate to declare their faith; we think too much. We need to get out of our heads and into raw Spirit."

"As a Society, we've lost our identity. We're not training people about what Friends believe, so new people bring their own 'baggage' and then want to change us."

"One group of Friends hardly are Christians anymore; the other have lost much of the Quaker identity by identifying with evangelical churches that grow faster than ours do."

"It's gotten to the point that Quakers can believe anything they want. But if we let go of our Christian heritage, we'll lose the power of our witness."

"Some people are confrontational or even antagonistic, implying, '*I* have the right kind of Quakerism.' Others are so eager to please and so wishy-washy, they don't know *what* they stand for."

"Sociological studies show that evangelical organizations' health lies in clear self-understanding. They know where they stand. Liberal Quakers, on the other hand, have no idea. It's like the old joke: 'Welcome to

Friends. These are our beliefs. But if you don't like these, we have others.'"

"We have little common theology. Some of us are grounded in Christian faith while others are immersed in wicca, Zen and a variety of other sects. We do not engage this issue and it weakens us."

Even if we knew, we couldn't tell people—or wouldn't.
General issues: our fear of proselytizing, our natural reserve, our low self-esteem; we're sometimes embarrassed to invite others, reluctant to tell people about Friends; some Meetings won't even use the word *God*

"Some people are so scared to talk to others about what we believe. They don't see the difference between sharing your faith and dragging someone to Meeting in a headlock!"

"I heard about a Meeting whose sign was parallel to the road—no one who passed by could see it! After 15 years, they finally changed the sign's location."

"The world *needs* the message of Friends—it's hungry for that message. But we're not able to get it out."

"Because our faith is experiential, we're not good at teaching how to do it. We have to begin to use words."

"George Fox said, 'Walk low to the earth, and be wary of notions.' But maybe we walk *too* low. Where's the balance between self-aggrandizement and articulating who we are?"

"Our opaqueness is killing us."

"Someone in our Meeting was worried that maybe we shouldn't even put our phone number in the telephone directory because we're not supposed to proselytize."

"The religions doing well now are the loud, big religions. I don't know how Quakers can call attention to themselves in such a climate."

"Culture mavens walk around and tell us what is 'Quaker' and what is not. For example, it's 'not Quaker' to advertise the Society of Friends and recruit members. Who told them that? It's false."

"Driving to a recent conference at Earlham, I saw on highway 40 a sign for ESR. But there was no sign at all for ESR as I came into Richmond—though there was a big sign for Bethany. That's so Quaker-like. The Quaker tradition seems one of diffidence, an unwillingness to promote ourselves. I tease about our being the 'Secret Society of Friends.' We'd love to have more people—but sometimes we don't understand that they need to know where we are!"

"A Baptist minister asked me for my denomination, and when I told him he said, 'I pass your meetinghouse every day, but we don't hear much about you Quakers.' I think this says it all."

"We hide whatever modest light we possess under a large bushel basket."

We can't get along.

General issues: the theological diversity of Friends; fragmentation within the Society; tensions beneath the surface, sometimes open confrontation; our self-righteousness, fear, intolerance, and lack of trust; our inability to come together on foundational things; we're a peace church, but we don't practice peacemaking among ourselves

"We do fine when it comes to accepting Buddhists and Jews—but we don't accept each other."

"The branches of Friends have grown so far apart. We don't respect one another. And what do we have in common? No one can answer that well."

"We're self-righteous—either from cultural smugness or from the zeal of the converted."

"I fear that the extremes on either end will pull us apart; on both sides, there's a fear of contamination."

"Jesus Christ said, 'A kingdom divided against itself can't stand.'"

"We give so much time and energy to internal conflict."

"We love the people who agree with us—especially us liberal Friends. And we're very open to gays, but condemn people who condemn gays. We're at a stuck point."

"In our diverse and fragmented condition, contemporary Quakerism hardly makes a credible witness to the testimonies, and thus their power and influence both within the Quaker family and in society is largely dissipated."

"Some Evangelical Friends refuse to take part in dialogue; they say they have lost faith by talking to other Friends. There's a tension: liberal Friends want to sit around and talk, and evangelicals want to proselytize and evangelize the world."

"The tension among Friends troubles me; it's such a clash. There's a lack of appreciation for others' points of view."

"Universalists want to deny Christ. Some evangelicals want to deny Quaker heritage and the testimonies— but without those, a person might as well become a Nazarene."

"A lot of Quakers think that they've got it about right, and that if the world would accept their way, everything would be hunky-dory."

We're not what we used to be.

General issues: our dwindling numbers, few seasoned Friends, our "lost generation of elders"; we're not educating our children well in Quaker ways; we've become too rich and comfortable; we no longer challenge our members or hold each other accountable; we've forgotten how much we need each other; we're not living up to our potential

"We have been shrinking in numbers and influence for a long time and I believe that's a direct function of the loss of our spiritual center."

"We've forgotten the difference between church and the world. We enjoy our wealth and comfort; it's easy to come and 'do church.'"

"Historically, Quakers were on the forefront of revolutionary thought. That's not so now."

"When we educate the children, we back off because we don't want to influence them too much. We end by not teaching them anything."

"We're terribly stagnant. We've hidden the key to our treasure because we don't want to lose it."

"I'm concerned by how much *all* of us have capitulated to today's culture, taken on its tone and color."

"We talk about simple living, but very often it turns out to be Volvo simple living. We crank up the peace testimony when there's a war."

"I don't think there are any people who are the identified storytellers in the Society of Friends anymore—like the elders and overseers used to be."

"We've lacked the courage to tackle seriously the consequences of living in the U.S. at this time."

"We've allowed our truths to become stale. God is alive; Christ has risen."

"Liberals can become dry, losing charisma and energy. For Evangelical Friends, the dangers are dogma and exclusion."

"I think Universalist Friends can learn a lot by looking to programmed, Christocentric Friends for leadership. We're seriously in danger of secularization. We're getting a lot of people in who are afraid of telling kids even about God or the Bible, let alone Christ. So our kids aren't learning things that some Quakers—and other Christians—know."

"We've become too individualistic, too economically privileged. We may have lost our capacity to speak prophetically."

"I knew the Society of Friends as a child from a different point of view. That's when the older Friends were still around who were venerable, sometimes wealthy, but simple in their demeanor—humble but often powerful people who were very traditional, who would not have dreamed of showing up in bare feet at a Quaker Meeting."

"I think that theological education is extremely important for Friends. Many of our Meetings are very small, and virtually no theological education takes place, in that formal way of Sunday School. A lot of Quaker young people aren't getting that kind of education."

"In so many ways we have bent to be like the church and culture around us. We want to accommodate everyone, and at times this rings as shallow or untrue."

In fact, we may not be anything special at all.

General issues: without a strong Quaker stance, we lack distinctiveness; we've gravitated to the lowest common denominator of Protestantism; we're like an organization for social concerns; to ourselves and to others, we're uninteresting or virtually invisible

"Talking about 'Quaker values' sounds to me like something from the liberal wing of the Democratic party. Why can't we use the word *religious?* People say it's because we don't want to proselytize."

"I believe conventional Friends churches will continue to wither, because we're too much like everyone else, and we do it less well."

"The Mennonites do a much better job of challenging young people."

"If we lose our distinctiveness, we might as well be Methodists or anything else. Why have the Religious Society of Friends if it's not distinctive?"

"We could be Unitarians or Unity people or liberal Jews; it's hard to tell."

"We have an inferiority complex, which we wear with some pride."

"Today in many parts of the world we could be looked upon nearly as humanists; some have even suggested taking the word *religious* out of the Religious Society of Friends."

"A few years ago, I heard a presentation at ESR about Friends pastors, which said that 90 percent of their service is exactly the same as that of pastors in any other denomination. That comment met howls of protest, but it's transparently true. Maybe even more than 90 percent."

"It's almost embarrassing to me as a Quaker: We're just like the rest of the world, in a sense. Look at what's happening in the Balkans, in Africa: People with tribal differences can't get along with each other. Quakers can meet in a conference for a few days and be nice to each other, but when you dig a little deeper, you find we're not ready to give up our own understanding of what we're doing and try to accommodate ourselves to what others believe and how they practice their faith."

"Unprogrammed Meetings feel rather like Unitarian or Buddhist gatherings; some pastoral Meetings feel like Holiness churches."

We're out of touch.

General issues: we lack a strong connection with our heritage and even with Christ; with each other, too, we're distant—we don't check out our leadings with each other, we don't speak frankly in Meeting, we don't know each other well, we don't visit; some Meetings are isolated; we're also out of touch with the larger world: ethnically, internationally, financially

"We're moribund, removed from the world."

"We elevate our practice above Christ."

"Tolerance has escalated to the point where there is no substance; we engage in 'nice speak.'"

"Once someone from out of town, a person of color, stopped in to worship with us. Our greeter at the door asked, 'Are you lost? Do you need directions?'"

"Both programmed and unprogrammed Friends need more traveling ministry between the two. I've learned a great deal from unprogrammed Friends."

"We want to be nice, rather than truthful; we're always avoiding conflict."

"In being committed to conflict resolution, we often find ourselves avoiding conflict amongst ourselves."

"The ordinary Quaker in the pew often has very little knowledge of the other branches."

"Through a settled disposition about cultural orientation, the Religious Society of Friends has attracted a bunch of ne'er-do-wells who are not thinkers. Often in reaction to other religions or from no religious tradition at all, they prefer vagueness. They're suspicious of money, wealth, and power, so they've marginalized every successful business person who is a member of the Society of Friends."

"In the last 50 years unprogrammed Friends, due to the influence of historical factors as much as anything else, have bought into a white, liberal, educated, middle-class culture that has never re-examined itself and has never adjusted to the realities of life—and they love preserving it. There's no mistake about why we don't have many black members, for example: It has absolutely nothing to do with anything but that protective white middle-class culture. It reflects the narrowness of our culture and our constituency."

"EFI has very much internationalized itself. I think FUM and FGC haven't quite figured out how to do that. But EFI recognizes that the majority of their contingency are non-American and they've set up structures with regions in different parts of the world and given them positions and leadership—trying to simply coordinate them and put North America alongside them, not on top of them."

"FUM is now much more actively reaching out to places like Cuba and Kenya and saying, 'Let's work at understanding one another, at relating as equals, at trying to get out of the dependency models of the missionary era'—or out of the later era, which said that decisions are made in the U.S. and we will try to let you know what we have decided.

That's not a terribly healthy model for people who are bright and committed and maybe have more parts of the Quaker message figured out than the Americans do."

"People now have their satellite TVs, they have their radios, travel more and are seeing other forms of Christianity on TV…and there are these groups with all this joyous worship and off-the-wall music—all this spontaneous spirituality—and our young folk are just going to stream off to these Nazarene and Baptist and Independent and Charismatic churches. And Quakers are never going to compete. Yet I think there is a crying need out there for exactly what Friends do have to offer."

"We have not managed to grow. In California…the Religious Society of Friends continues to fail in attracting those of other races and ethnicities. We also seem to be a haven for intellectuals and the upper classes. Is our faith welcoming to those who work with their hands, who don't have college degrees, or who work in business?"

And maybe we're not going anywhere.
General issues: we're complacent, sitting on our laurels; we're without focus and vision; we have little sense of the future possibilities for Friends

"Our vision of what Christ asks of us is much too limited. We've settled for individualistic religion."

"We don't hand on our tradition well, so we can't move forward."

"I worry that we're too intent on preserving our heritage. If God sent a message and it didn't look like our heritage, we might not be willing to receive it."

"If we disappear, who'll say things about peace and simplicity?"

"Among Friends, there's a confusion between careful seeking and plain inertia."

"We sit on our laurels too much and get bogged down in our past. We have a good history, but where are we today? Where are we going with it?"

"We evangelicals don't know what to do beyond the Great Commission. Are we just trying to get everyone into heaven? Or is there a reason to become a Christian and be a disciple? Our faith in Christ is to change us so that we redeem our culture, not just get into heaven. Sometimes we seem to have no goals beyond evangelism."

"We settle for so little from God."

"Quaker culture rules in the eastern unprogrammed tradition, and it's a silly, pedantic, uninspired, rather marginal culture that determines everything about how you behave as a Quaker—including the color of the car you drive and the type of clothes you wear. But more importantly, it precludes us from doing some of the most important things like evangelism or outreach, which the culture says we 'don't do' but the faith says you definitely do. We've really gotten that badly wrong and as a result, we're disappearing."

"I think Quakerism itself is facing a crisis as it goes into the 21st century. Who is it? What is it? Where is it going? Why is it?"

"When Friends say the word *Christ*, they can mean extraordinarily different things. And they all want to be respectful to each other—so courtesy is well served but the Quaker integrity sometimes is not. And we all know that this isn't going anywhere."

"We do not know where our 'movement' is going."

Clustered here, without a parallel presentation of the many appreciative and optimistic remarks we also heard about Quakers, such comments may seem unfairly weighted and disproportionately bleak. Certainly we recognize that Friends United Meeting, Friends General Conference, Evangelical Friends International, Friends World Committee for Consultation, Friends Committee for National Legislation, American Friends Service Committee, and countless other groups work tirelessly and creatively—and, we understand, with some success—to foster Quaker identity, growth, unity, and service.

Despite those admirable efforts, however, and despite the constant stream of eloquently discerning speeches, articles, books, seminars, and conferences on the current state of Quakerdom and astute suggestions for its improvement, the Society remains both polarized and equivocal. Granted, our question to Friends invited complaint; even so, we found the intensity of the overall response disturbing. In the speech of people not given to exaggeration, recurring words like *stagnant*, *stale*, *stuck*, and *moribund* land with a thud of finality. A huge religious denomination could either absorb or tackle such consternation; for the Friends, relatively small in number and lacking a centralized administration, such a widely distributed and emphatically articulated discouragement carries fairly heavy significance.

Listening, as Friends well know, is not merely a helpful exercise. Among Friends, the message heard—whether in the silence, amid programmed worship, or during attentive, Spirit-led conversation— can point the way to new thought, new action, and renewed vitality. Thanks to the candid messages of Friends during this national consultation, evaluating both the strengths and the struggles within Quakerism today, Earlham School of Religion stands on the threshold of just such a renewal.

*ESR needs to stand in the paradox
and be a meeting ground for Friends.*

A FRIEND

~

THAT AFTER 350 YEARS THE RELIGIOUS SOCIETY OF FRIENDS
is still standing—and represents a spiritual approach at least nominally
intact—speaks powerfully of George Fox's original vision, the faithfulness of Friends over the centuries, years of assiduous work toward unity,
and perhaps a pervasive streak of Quaker stubbornness. On all of those
counts many other religious groups have fallen short, as today's plethora
of splintered denominations can attest.

Comparison with other denominations, however, is not the point
here. Friends need to be true to their own distinctive heritage and
potential. For all Friends now, the critical question is not "How can we
reach accord?" or even "How can we expand our numbers?" but *How can
we go forward?* Still standing is one thing; *standing still*—an all-too-easy
alternative—is another.

Hearing a number of Friends describe the Society as "resting on
its laurels," we marveled at the centuries-long momentum of Quaker
accomplishments—a momentum built, certainly, by goodness, integrity,
and conscientious labor. The Society's sterling reputation and steady
human-investment returns may continue to keep Friends viable
indefinitely. In the meantime, though, the Society of Friends might
consider forsaking its tendency toward figurative "rest" for something
more invigorating: *stance.*

The question "What do Friends stand for?" as we have seen, elicits
myriad responses (and sometimes, no response at all). In a group that
encourages its members to cultivate a direct, individual, and largely
private relationship with the Divine—even though corporate experience

confirms and enhances that relationship—*perhaps no final response to this question is possible.* For the consideration of FUM, FGC, EFI, and all Friends, we pose another option: The elusive, ineffable *what* of Quakerism may be, simply, a *why.*

Why do I *choose to worship among Friends?* each person can ask. We believe that the answer—rather, the thousands of different answers—paradoxically can create a kind of unity. For those gifted at definition and conclusion, the *why* may reside in precise statements of belief; for those whose gifts lie in seeking and wonder, the why might be a continually unfolding discovery. And in fact, if the secret heart of each person everywhere were suddenly disclosed, we would find in every organized group—religious or not—just such a diversity of motivation. The Society of Friends, as it currently stands, may never resolve its internal disagreements about *what.* But by boosting a heartfelt and mind-satisfying *why,* it can affirm its people, reinforce its purposes, and continue productively on its way.

If the Society decides to forgo the search for a conclusive *what* and instead to acknowledge and celebrate each Friend's *why,* can Quakerism then move forward? We suggest that a crucial element remains ambiguous: the *how.* Among Friends, addressing that *how* means approaching the thorny, daunting question of leadership.

Every participant in ESR's national consultation, we imagine, has passed through the mental labyrinth that this question represents: rummaging in the works of Fox and Barclay, following tortuous trails of reasoning, alternating between frustration and hope, and likely arriving again exactly where the path began. As we reviewed our own circuitous exploration of Quaker "leadership," we charted these lines of thought:

Our leadership comes from God.

> "Quaker heritage says that people get guidance from Christ, God, Light; and the Meeting is a place where that guidance can come through."

> "Leadership is not just about technical skills. It's about living obediently to the calling of the Holy Spirit—the Leader."

In our churches, pastors are the leaders—sort of.

"Quakers have always been against 'hireling ministers.'"

"Pastoral leadership in the Quaker movement is an add-on. It creates tension."

"John Punshon clarified George Fox's words about hireling ministers: Fox was talking about people hired by the state."

"[Many unprogrammed Friends], as far as I can tell, will never overcome their cultural inhibitions about having paid clergy. Now there are some religious and theological reasons as well that are worth taking a look at, but mostly it's 'we'll never pay anybody to do that; we're all ministers.'"

"Friends never really corporately approved of the pastoral arrangement; it oozed in, Meeting by Meeting. And so a standard discipline was never developed—or a standard understanding of the pastor's role."

But there aren't enough well-prepared ones.

"The bar we set is awfully low, so sometimes we get pastors who haven't done the real work of figuring out what it is to be a Quaker."

"In our Meetings, are we looking for a pastor, or for a Quaker who's a pastor? If non-Quakers lead our congregations, we'll lose our foundation."

"In desperation, Meetings sometimes hire a pastor without training; then they don't have the leadership they need to grow and move forward."

"It seems to me that some pastors I encounter don't know what to do. They don't know what it means to lead a congregation. It's like 'Where am I supposed to go with all these people?'"

"We are often ambiguous about the role and value of leadership. Too many Friends Meetings have come to rely on non-Quaker-trained pastoral leadership whose preparation for and experience in ministry are at variance with Quaker faith and practice."

"We need leaders with a good background in what the Religious Society of Friends is all about, plus actual experience of spiritual life in one's own self."

"For a while there was a perception that people were not being prepared well at ESR to do pastoral service. They didn't have good administrative skills, didn't have good preaching skills, and didn't really know how to equip people and draw people into service."

And being a Quaker pastor isn't necessarily very gratifying.

"I saw two recent surveys of U.S. pastors' salaries— and on both lists, Quakers were at the bottom."

"Low salaries signify low value. Our pastors don't carry any clout."

"The problem is that once we pastors land in a church, the people don't want to help. They say, 'That's *your* job.'"

"Our leaders are frustrated, because they're not allowed to lead. I see them leave and look for other places."

"Compared to other denominations, we don't pay our people well."

"Our pastors' situation isn't new: I saw a tract from 1900 titled *Will we starve our Quaker pastors?*"

"Since we offer no retirement benefits, we have some retired men and their wives who are suffering."

"We're poor employers; we don't think through the economic lives of our leaders. We just assume that because you're a Quaker employee, you will work 80 hours a week and accept half the pay."

"Who would choose to go into the pastorate, when our pastors are overworked and underpaid?"

"Leadership in a Quaker organization is just a very hard thing to do. When we do get good people in those roles, the tendency is for them to burn out or get cut down in a fairly short period of time. I know very few people who have managed to take on those kinds of roles and be effective for more than seven or eight years; and if you last three or four you have done well."

"We are experiencing a leadership drought because of pastors' low salaries, burnout, and stress."

"It appears to me that within a very short time after placement, each pastor or Yearly Meeting executive becomes captive to traditional patterns of operation within the arena of their assigned responsibility, and any hope of effecting change or of igniting fires soon dies. This means that their energies are expended in a routine that provides for a maintenance operation with no overarching, widely shared vision to connect to or to steer by."

But other Friends lead, too: clerks, teachers, elders, organizational heads. And we need them.

"I want *leadership* not to mean just pastors. It's too easy to defer to a pastor for leadership. If we as Friends do that, we're not living up to our own gifts."

"I think we've failed. In looking for pastors, we've brought in *preachers;* what we needed was Christian educators."

"We need people who can give us the heart to move us to courageous action."

"We deeply need visionaries."

"I understand why we stopped having elders and overseers; but without a leadership class, so to speak, it's very difficult to communicate our values."

"We have a lost generation of elders—a number of older people who've never taken on that role."

"In our Meeting the people aged 70 to 85 represent the best. Where spiritual leadership is concerned, we've missed a couple of generations."

"There is no disciplined ministry in our [unprogrammed] Meetings, except that which is provided oftentimes by graduates of ESR who actually know something about the Bible, about Quaker history, about theology, and can give some content....So the spoken ministry is generally poor, and there's absolutely no attention in our Meetings to the pastoral function, so sick members are often totally ignored."

"We have had pastors for about 100 years now, and now we have 'paid staff' in Meetings and churches, too. On top of that there are superintendents and 'general secretaries' who assume leadership. While these are not supposed to be leadership by government, I submit that they are *de facto* governments of our Yearly and Monthly Meetings. In addition to this corps of hireling ministers are the academes and Quaker celebrities who create leadership from the 'top.'"

"Our most serious deficiency is a glaring scarcity of trained and active Quaker thinkers and scholars."

Actually, anyone can lead — if they want to.

"Leadership could include pastors, and it should — but it also should include clerks and anyone with gifts. We have to challenge one another not to let the terms *pastor* and *leader* be synonymous and exclusive."

"Once we point out someone as the leader, it cripples our capacity to become leaders ourselves."

"Everyone has the potential to use their gifts, down to the smallest child in our Meetings."

"If we have a pastor, members participate less."

But we aren't doing a good job of cultivating new leaders.

"I came to this local Meeting with a substantial background, but no one tapped me to lead."

"We say we don't want the pastor to be the leader— but we do expect the pastor to do all the work. We've not done a very good job of educating people about the responsibilities of leadership."

"Our generation lacks ownership. We should teach people to be Quaker *now*, not to wait for a certain level of knowledge or maturity."

"We need to identify people who have the call to ministry, then initiate the process to draw them out."

"Our Meetings aren't doing a good job of finding people to lead; we need to grow our own."

"A great concern from my point of view is the absence of people in the 30–45 range from our ranks. They are often very active locally, but not at all on the organizational level. If those folks aren't involved, and if our Meeting doesn't have clergy, we have no persons who are good models for that age group. In the last 50 to 100 years the elders have disappeared as well. There are no networks of those people."

"What's being done to identify and track potential leaders, potential students for ESR, for Friends positions around the country in Meetings and organizations? It's important to do that sort of thing— to have a sense of who's coming along. We need something like a talent pool, a resource of knowledgeable and capable people to attract to positions of teaching, administering, working for organizations, guiding the work of others."

And anyway, we don't really accept authority very well.

"We're anti-leader. We beg people to take positions, then undermine them. That's very serious."

"We have an ambivalence about leadership: We want leaders, but don't know how to relate to them."

"As a Society, we're super-critical of people who lead, so we get leaders who pander to our comfort zone."

"We have a 300-year-old phobia of charismatic leaders."

"As a group, we distrust strong leaders; and that repels them."

"We're very tough on our leaders, very critical."

"We burn out our leadership; we give people positions of responsibility but no real authority, because we're not willing to let them make mistakes."

"We don't give our leaders the tools they need, and we don't back them up when they stumble—yet we want them to do a lot."

"It's the 'hired man' syndrome: Our attitude is 'You're working for us,' not 'This is a person of God who has something valuable to say.'"

"Even the jokes we've made around this table today are anti-leadership jokes. We've got to stop that."

"Using *Quaker* and *leadership* together is an oxymoron."

"Quakers want leadership, but they don't want leaders. They want things to be managed, they want people to take responsibility, but they are frankly allergic to people exercising authority. That's the crux of the leadership problem for unprogrammed Friends."

"Meetings previously subjected to the ministry of poorly educated ministers often will not accept new ideas from seminary-trained pastors when pastoral changes are made."

"Meetings want pastors but are leery of leadership, and the prophetic function tends to become buried under a mountain of pastoral duties."

Then, too, it depends on what you mean by "leadership."

"I wish pastors could be bridge builders, equippers."

"We need to distinguish leadership from management—which is about just caretaking what *is.*"

"We've defined our leaders as 'pastors'—so we only record people who fit that mold."

"Being the leader is more than being in charge."

"Leadership is not a position: It's influence, given by other people. It has to be earned."

"We need fewer leaders and more Quakers."

"A *minister* is the facilitator of a Meeting; *leadership* means helping each person develop his or her ministry. What if we called it 'servant leadership,' or 'discipleship'?"

"*Leadership* is a problematic word, because it implies status. Could we call it something else? 'Servant leadership' helps a little."

"To me, leadership is more than servanthood. It's about helping others recognize and use their gifts."

"I'd define leadership as developing human potential."

"The leader has to see that practical things get done, but also has to have vision."

"We want training in how to elicit the sense of the Meeting, how to uncover Spirit as it speaks to a group in unity. Not many Friends today understand what 'leadership from the Spirit' means."

"The best spiritual leadership points us to Christ. I think that servant leadership characterizes the Friends' view of leadership; it means evoking from other people their sense of what God is saying and gathering in ideas and helping to articulate them in a way that others can conncct with."

"Leadership is an influence-relationship among leaders and followers who intend real changes that reflect their mutual purposes. That's the kind of leadership among Quakers at their best."

"I've come to understand that being a pastor is serving a people, living with them, helping them marry and have children and die; being with them while they struggle with life and their doubts and their fears."

"If Friends have grown up in Kenya or elsewhere in Africa or in Bolivia in a tribal culture, they expect strong leadership and they expect their personal self-definition to derive from their membership in the tribe."

"We have people who 'do things' but we don't have leadership."

"The skills of leadership can be learned, but leadership is truly a gift from other persons."

Our leaders don't make decisions; that's a corporate process.

"It's not for a leader to decide. Every person's voice is important."

"We don't have one person who decides, and we don't vote, either. We just try to get a sense of the meeting."

"Too often, Quakers want to be so non-threatening, we end up not making decisions at all."

"Decision making has to do with letting go; it's a willingness to come out with a new idea. That's hard to do."

But our leadership really should come from God.

"People should follow not the leader, but God: not Moses, but the cloud that led him."

"We forget to ask God what to do."

"We believe that God calls and equips ministers. So where does formal study fit in? *Credentialing*— which is absolutely necessary for pastors—holds ambiguity for many Friends."

"As I see it, this [range of Quaker 'leaders'] abdicates a founding principle of Friends—that leadership and ministry belong to Christ, and we are witnesses of what He does in our midst. It is not our job to 'find leadership.' That is God's job. To me, it is more than semantics to say that 'God selects the leadership and we record the fact.'"

Maybe we need a new model.

"I see the pastor model fail a lot in my ministry, when I unthinkingly embrace Protestant and Catholic models of pastoral leadership. Quakers are a whole different wrinkle."

"There's the commune model—that's one possibility. People in communes rotate the work."

"Our Quaker culture has taken on a corporate image, and the church has to be a corporation that follows the business model, which means that more professional training is expected. We're caught between the early Quaker understanding of gathered people, and the church model of a corporate structure that puts on a good religious performance."

"No religion stays the same; it needs to evolve. George Fox had a good message, but his wasn't the only way."

"We need help with visionary leadership—to point us in a direction so we can follow. We need to link arms and pull together."

"What we do in church looks surprisingly like the workplace: we invest some people with authority and let them do it, instead of vigorously seeking God's will and acting on it."

"If our leading is supposed to come from God, pastors are in opposition to that; we need a new way."

"It seems like our vision of no distinction between clergy and laity would spawn a broad movement of leadership within a local setting."

"We evangelicals are falling short in leadership because we don't know what to do except to convert people. So we look around at different models and see who is growing the fastest—who can convert the most people and get them in our churches."

"I proposed the model of team ministry with a part-time paid pastor and a ministry team pulled from the Meeting; the team rotates once every two years, so many members would serve by appointment. But even that was too much for [my unprogrammed Meeting]."

"A study said that in the future, a congregation will need 200 people to be able to afford a pastor. So we have to learn to look at pastoring in different ways."

"In this church we emphasize the mentoring concept of leadership training—being on the front line with someone else, or helping someone wrestle with life. To me, having the opportunity to sit one with another is a leadership experience."

"I think we really could use a revival of the traveling ministry. It would have to be a new style, of course, to be appropriate to the time and the culture. In the old style, it meant a person who simply feels a deep concern to travel and to visit and to spend unhurried time with people, to 'hold opportunities' with them. I wish we had scores of people traveling around like that."

"In a lot of our churches, there's a prejudice that the only person who can preach on a Sunday is a paid pastor. That doesn't need to be a given. We have fallen prey to other models of ministry than Friends models. One of the things that intrigued me about ESR early on was the hope that we might find models for ministry that served our heritage and our modern situation creatively. Maybe we haven't worked at it creatively enough."

"I would like to see a version of Quaker leadership which paid some particular attention to the possibilities of emerging 'voices' out of the communal worship silence. What could it mean for a way of leadership propelled by the Spirit, by God, but that originated from the Silent Meeting Quakers?"

"Local Meetings cannot grow unless they are willing to change the way they relate to the world around them and to do that, they need leadership with skills in conflict resolution, community development and bridge building."

"I tend to view religious leadership from the age-old perspective of a necessary duality consisting of priests and prophets. We need to have spiritual leaders who help us all know, respect, and understand our belief structure — the priests. Equally important is our need for spiritual leaders who point out the inadequacies of the existing structures while also providing the vision that can take us nearer to the Commonwealth of God — the prophets."

"I am inclined to think that the pastor's role as defined historically is not the kind of leadership that is really needed for the century now dawning. Much of a pastor's time is consumed in pastoral and priestly functions which could be shared by members of the Meeting.

That would release the employed minister to devote his/her efforts to serve as a specialist in community development, specifically identifying the areas where there is need for community, equality, conflict resolution, integrity, and compassion. Much time could be devoted to equipping the membership through creative biblical studies and the application of Quaker testimonies, helping members identify their gifts, and engaging them in appropriate ministries."

Almost inevitably, the discussion comes full circle. Over the past few months we found that every focus group, almost every interview, and quite a few written responses addressed a number of these points. With perspicacity and deep concern, Friends stated the issues, identified the problems, and recommended solutions. Underneath all the comments—and often directly—we heard loud and clear the message that Quakers, as more than one Friend put it, "are hungry for leadership." "Our church longs to see a creative leadership developed somewhere," said one Friend. Another person cautioned, "It's true there's a great hunger, but there's also a great resistance to being told how to do it."

Particularly as ESR prepares to consider institutional changes, a new leadership model for Quakers—perhaps even with some new vocabulary—may be worth pursuing. The distinctive *how* of Friends, as we understand it, takes place in two ways: 1) through a direct, life-transforming relationship with God and 2) through specific Quaker practices such as silent worship, corporate decision making, and activities related to the testimonies. The Society's *leaders*, then, are the people who facilitate one or both of those broadly understood experiences. Certain people who are gifted and/or called to such facilitation may choose to enhance their facility through education or professional training.

Because the Quaker DNA precludes any docile submission to self-proclaimed authorities (even the innocuous "follower" gene, we've learned, appears rarely in Friends), the Society's "leaders" continually must operate from a position of humility, and the "followers" continually must work at letting go their own inherent resistance to being led. Training in group dynamics and conflict resolution—for both the leaders and the leadees—can help. But then, so can continual introspection and, of course, more talking and writing about the problem.

We think that there's a more Quakerly way to frame and practice Friends leadership, one that arises from the peculiarly Quaker use of the word *leading*. Relative newcomers to the Society's vocabulary ourselves, we can't presume to have a full understanding of Quaker terms. But from the still uncluttered (if not actually blank) slate of our perspective, we think of a "leading" in this way:

a) a Quaker leading can proceed from the One to one, and subsequently from one to many (possibly taking a temporary detour of one to one).

b) alternatively—and sometimes simultaneously—it can proceed from the One to many, then trickle down from many to one or, in other words, from many to each.

All leadings, then, involve three essential participants: the One Source, each individual "one," and the corporate "many" who help test and confirm the leading, support the one(s) feeling led, and perhaps participate in a resulting action. Since we can't fault the Source, and since the "many" simply consists of individuals together, and since no individual person(s) can claim to be singled out for the authoritative reception or transmission of truth, the responsibility for receiving and conveying God's messages ("following through," we might say) falls clearly upon this one and this one and this one *ad infinitum:* that is, on *each individual Friend.*

This, we realize, is not a new idea; but considered afresh, it could inspire a new framework for Friends leadership.

One Friend described Quaker leadings this way: "We're really individualistic—it's a whole theological position: Each person has access to divine leading. According to the tradition, you bring a leading to your Meeting and test it; if you find support, you move on it. For some people, it becomes an invitation to individual action or decision-making."

That inclination to act on one's own, however, could become an unexpected source of strength. Throughout the Society of Friends, we heard people say, *Our leadership isn't working as well as it could; we've followed non-Quakerly models, to our detriment; let's look at new models; let's work together.* Only occasionally, however, did we hear evidence that within Friends Meetings or churches, people other than designated "leaders" are asking themselves, *Instead of relying on others, what can* I *do to help?*

In some scattered pockets of Quakerism, that very process is happening—and it's working. One resourceful Christian "leader," for example, while choosing pastoral training, decided early on that the responsibility for his future livelihood lay not with a congregation's resources but within himself: "While I was at ESR I learned auto mechanics on the side, so I wouldn't have to depend completely on pastoring for money. I released *myself* for ministry." Even more urgently needed than such pastoral foresight, though, is individual *members'* assumption of such responsibility. "In our church," a Friend in Indiana told us, "the pastor's coming hasn't made us sit back and wait for leadership. Every member really is a minister. Where there's a need, people pitch in and meet it."

We learned about one unconventional pastoral Meeting where such participation is standard operating procedure:

> "In our Meeting, we don't have any standing committees. If one person sees a job that needs to get done, like storm windows, that person finds another person to help and they get the storm windows made. And usually it is not even mentioned until somebody notices there are storm windows. It's been like that here for over 10 years. Two men by themselves painted the entire church on the outside. It took all summer, but they never mentioned it. They just did it.
>
> Pretty consistently, that's the way work gets done in our Meeting. If somebody thinks that a certain educational class needs to happen, they find someone else with the same leading and the two of them do it. There's a real emphasis here on the leading of the Holy Spirit in individuals and in the Meeting as well."

During a phone interview, a Friend told us that his pastoral Meeting is "revamping the whole membership idea," practicing a new "covenant" relationship. "There are some things that you commit to the group and some things that the group commits to you," he explained. "And that relationship is renewed and affirmed annually."

Furthermore, the group is working to de-emphasize the pastoral role, considering how it can best equip every member to be a minister and specifically to hear God's call. Recently the church held a "ministry fair" in which various ministries of either the church or the Yearly Meeting set up booths and made presentations about their work. The Friend continued, "People could see everything from an unwed mothers shelter, to a right sharing of world resources, to our mission activities in Bolivia and Peru."

Another Friend, clear across the country, described an epiphany that forever changed her view of Quaker leadership:

> "Once, years ago, when I was talking with another Friend and bemoaning our lack of leaders, I said, 'Where are the strong people who used to be here to guide me?' He said, 'There's just you and me, kid.' That brought me up short. It's true: We *all* have that responsibility. Friends *talk* a lot about every person being a minister, but we don't internalize it. And we don't activate ourselves to offer the ministry we're each capable of. We tend to look to someone else for that."

One person's realization of her own responsibility. Another person's recognition of a task to be done. A church's determination to meet needs—or to educate its members about hearing God's call to ministry. A pastor's resolve not to be a victim of circumstances. Today's Friends, we believe, don't need to follow; like the people in these few stories, they need to *follow through*. That's behavior that the DNA clearly can support.

What if such behavior began to spread? What if it infused the entire Society of Friends? Here's the sequence we can imagine: Individual Friends, not passively or autocratically *held accountable* but actively *choosing accountability*, begin to feel more important, more useful, more engaged. Pastors and other "leaders" begin to feel helped and lightened; freed from an unrealistic burden of duties, they can tend to the details of administration or can pursue their much-needed gifts of preaching, caring, teaching, eldering, mentoring. Newcomers quickly learn from others' example, if not from explicit words, that "belonging" among Friends carries an expectation of willingly shared tasks. And the entire Society flourishes.

Under such circumstances, too, the word "leader" gradually gives way to potentially more accurate terms. (*Equipper* offers one possibility, though its no-nonsense efficiency hardly suggests the careful nurture and discernment that the role requires. *Enabler*, we fear, probably could not surmount its firm association with the problems of co-dependency. *Servant leader*, which certainly comes closer to the Quakerly sense of the task, not only is cumbersome but already enjoys wide use within some Protestant models that many Friends consider inappropriate for Quaker practice. We've been intrigued by such terms as *influencer*, *facilitator*, even *mover*.) Consequently, the word *leading* is released to resume its rightful place among Friends, not only as a long-cherished experience but also as a privilege—one that calls for the serious, joyful responsibilities of listening, standing, and following through.

Over the years, Earlham School of Religion has sought ways to meet the needs of Quaker leadership: Instruction. Scholarship. Dialog. Community. And ESR, like a new patch on an old garment or like new wine in old wineskins, must continue to do as much as it can. But when a garment is badly frayed, or when a wineskin is noticeably strained, what happens next? Amid the fragmentation and divisiveness that still plague the Religious Society of Friends, how much can ESR realistically hope to accomplish?

Is it time for old wineskins and old garments to be made new? Perhaps the School's next message to Friends—much like Friends' ongoing message to the School—could be that simple, potent, and so very Quakerly question: *What canst thou say?*

*The greatest success of Earlham School of Religion
might prove to be its contributions to building up
in the next generation of Quaker leaders an understanding
of their faith that does not rely on the conflicts of the past,
because its student body transcends them.*

JOHN PUNSHON,
PORTRAIT IN GREY: A SHORT HISTORY OF THE QUAKERS

~

TRADITIONALLY SPEAKING, Friends meet for various reasons: to worship, to do business, to educate children, to be gathered. The various branches of Friends, however, usually fail to meet each other's standards; only once in a while do they meet head-on, and very rarely indeed do they meet each other halfway.

An ESR alum recalls, "I remember some times during my stay at ESR when our diversity was causing some significant problems. People would come together to get a sense of clarity about how to spend money for programming, how to define ourselves, and how to define what Friends have to offer. Our differences were so great that creative work would grind to a halt."

But on those rare occasions when members of today's multi-branched Quakerism do meet somewhere near the center—usually during an absorbing project rather than a discussion—something miraculous can happen. And according to some stories we heard, it does.

Several people mentioned, for instance, Marge Abbott's productive, inspiring work in literally and figuratively bringing together women from historically opposite Quaker viewpoints. We heard about other examples of amity: adult education programs, FWCC conferences, some efforts of particular Yearly Meetings to bridge differences among local Meetings, and the Richmond consultations that Wil Cooper and others held in years past. "I hope that FUM will also continue to be a place where those exchanges can occur," said one Friend.

John Punshon explained that a few decades ago, some bridging happened quite naturally. In the '40s, he told us, most Friends maintained the peace testimony; and when large numbers of disparate Friends found themselves in public service together during the war, they realized that they actually had a great deal in common. Consequently, after 1945 a number of people working their way up through Friends organizations held a broader understanding of Quakerism than the version they might have learned as a child or at their Yearly Meeting.

One of the most intriguing stories of Quaker cross-pollination came from a person who described the exchange he and a distant Friend have arranged between their two Meetings' young people. "At YouthQuake our kids always connect with their kids," he said, "so last summer they sent 10 kids out to our youth Yearly Meeting sessions, and this summer we're sending some out to theirs. It has been a real dynamic relationship, with lots of interplay between who we are—Christ-centered Quakers— and who they are as unprogrammed Friends. We share our faith experiences and really learn from one another."

Someone else told us a story from the recent past, about two Friends who favored opposite sides of a particularly heated issue and often got into open confrontation during Meeting. One day they ended up working together on a Habitat for Humanity project, building a house. "They had to work really close, hammering nails and doing other tasks," said our storyteller. "At the next Yearly Meeting, we had a session on this issue that was really getting acrimonious. The clerk called for a period of silence—and out of that came a reconciliation between those two people, with one apologizing and asking forgiveness of the other. It showed how working together on a common project can sometimes overcome our differences."

During a phone interview, another Friend confirmed that last point: "No matter what part of the tradition we come from, when we work together we always do better and come closer to being comfortable with one another."

All of these stories suggest that when Friends come together to *do things*—rather than to explore or dispute their differences—their highest shared vision easily surfaces. In that theory we see a possible key to future directions for both the Society of Friends and Earlham School of Religion. For that key to prove the extent of its usefulness at ESR, however, the School must begin to generate widespread, positive, and accurate public awareness.

Friends' opinions of Earlham School of Religion, we've learned, follow paths as divergent as Friends themselves.

A surprising number of people we met declared themselves almost totally ignorant of ESR's mission and activities, and others admitted that their understanding of the School is sketchy. "I don't know much about it," we heard among Friends throughout the country, even some who live not so far from Richmond. "Our people don't really know ESR, even though it's in our geographical boundaries," one person admitted. "It has a limited impact on our Yearly Meeting; it's almost a non-factor." "There's no publication of ESR scholarship, so we're not aware of what ESR offers or does," said another. From a pastoral Friend at some distance from the School, we heard, "My sense of ESR is kind of vague. It seems like the things I've heard are that they have a strong sense of equipping people for the ministry, not necessarily paid ministry. It sounds like they're doing a good job of trying to investigate and balance both branches of Quakerism. But I don't really know."

Digging for more information, we often asked directly (albeit ungrammatically), "Who is ESR for?" The answers, much like the Friends who spoke or wrote them, came from all over the map.

> "Who is ESR for? I don't know."

> "I see it as primarily for the Religious Society of Friends with a particular call to train pastors, but with a broad concept of ministry."

> "During a survey for ESR, I called a conservative Friend in Iowa who said, 'We know that ESR is only for pastors, and we don't have one. So this doesn't apply to us.'"

> "I'm concerned it's just a preacher factory."

> "At this point, all the Quakers I know who go to ESR are women—they're all searching. I think the men there want to be preachers, and the women want to be ministers."

> "It's mainly for unprogrammed Friends."

> "I identify it with FUM, and I know FUM isn't open to me as a gay person."

"I've been on the periphery of ESR since its founding. It has catered to the needs of the people who've gone there. The Meetings of Western and Indiana Yearly Meeting haven't sent the candidates who should've gone."

"ESR is for people with questions, not answers. People can ask the questions there with safety—questions they didn't have permission to ask at other places."

"ESR's original role was to train pastors, Now less and less pastors go there."

"ESR is for middle-of-the-road Friends: mostly programmed, mostly those with garden-variety liberal Protestant theology."

"It's more right-wing, more evangelical; only for people going to pastor."

"The main thrust at ESR seems to be feminist theology, from what people say."

"ESR grads are either vague, soft, or accept homosexuality as normal."

"ESR people are extreme about homosexuality; they're loving the sinner more than hating the sin."

"ESR is where sick people went to get well."

"I think only 10 to 15 percent of the people there are Quakers."

"There are no opportunities at ESR for someone like me. I guess it's just for professionals, not ordinary members."

"ESR is a place for seekers, not for training leadership."

"It's for all Friends, if they're willing to do the intellectual and personal work."

"ESR is for lots of folks."

"It's for more people than people know it is."

These and other impressions, taken together, showed us an ESR somewhat maligned, somewhat overpraised, and regrettably indistinct. Opinions of the School's academic and spiritual quality (reflecting several disjunctive periods in the School's relatively brief history) varied widely, too: We met many constituents well satisfied with the institution, via either firsthand experience, secondary observation, or third-hand report; we met some who felt disappointed. Bitter criticism came from only a few—like the Friend who told us, "There's *nothing* ESR could do to bring back the interest of my church. They asked me to tell you that."

Diversity of opinion, of course, is neither unexpected nor problematic; no matter what changes ESR chooses to make in its curriculum or programs, some people will applaud, some will disapprove, and some will simply shrug. We were intrigued, though, to hear substantial evidence that over the years ESR (both deliberately and involuntarily) has served as a meeting ground: a place where Friends of all stripes reliably collide with new ideas and undergo that inescapable element of growth, *change.*

> "The ESR community was very important: the conversations we had, the diversity of theologies and histories, and just sitting around together in the library or at Common Meal or playing ping pong. I got a real awakening of interest in the Bible and an understanding that you didn't have to be a fundamentalist to appreciate the Bible."

> "ESR was a very different model of a seminary from the conventional model; to me—20 years ago—it felt as if its focus was as much about being a community of faith that lived and learned together as it was about being an academic institution. Which doesn't mean that academics weren't taken very seriously. I was pushed hard by some very fine teachers and still draw regularly on my training in scripture and church history and theology."

> "I went to ESR not knowing what to expect—and the diverse community there came as a shock. It forced me to discover for myself the Source of spiritual authority, instead of just accepting what I'd learned at Philadelphia Yearly Meeting."

"A lot of Philadelphia Yearly Meeting types went to ESR as non-Christians and came out Christians."

"I came to ESR as a fundamentalist, even though some leaders had tried to talk me out of going. The atmosphere there was really stimulating; I had fun getting to know unprogrammed Friends and others—a delightful mix of people. In Old Testament, I was flailing around, and Gene Roop gave me extra material to read. He let me struggle until I came to change on my own. It was a fabulous experience; I wouldn't trade it."

"When I was at ESR, it was powerful; you couldn't get out of there with your prejudices intact."

"I came out of an evangelical church and my roommate at ESR was from Pacific Yearly Meeting. He had books on Eastern spirituality and I had my books on the defense of the virgin birth. But we became great friends, and he gained a new appreciation for the Bible and I became a little less doctrinaire. That's the kind of thing that can happen at ESR at its best."

"It's amazing how many unprogrammed, vaguely formed folks have come to the ESR community and found Jesus."

"I can't think of any Christ-centered Quaker that went away from ESR feeling ambiguous. But I know folks whose lives have been transformed there."

"Part of the work at ESR is about being open to be changed; that involves stretching the intellect. Some Friends, though, only want their prejudices confirmed—and it's not just the evangelicals, either."

"There's really no place like it in the world where people come together from different groups of Quakers and bring both their background and strengths but also questions and contribute to the larger community. For instance, someone said to me the first couple of weeks I was there, 'So you're an evangelical. What's it like? I've never met one.' And that was an opportunity to say, 'Here are what things are like and this has been my experience.' And the person asking that question has become a lifelong friend."

"ESR was a transformational experience for me. What it taught me—and I don't always live it out— is the difference between defining myself and defending myself."

"The students who come back to us from ESR sometimes have a better balance because they are more familiar with or comfortable with some more liberal theology."

"It was incredibly valuable for me to be with people who came from different backgrounds. I was with a group in constructive theology where there were four of us who met at the local diner: one from Iowa, one from EFI, and an unprogrammed Friend from California, and me. And it was so funny to see the four of us come to a more central place and even switch places. It was just a microcosm of what took place at ESR. I learned to do ministry there rather than just getting a piece of paper. I learned to do that just by living with my fellow students and being a part of people's lives."

"What I liked about ESR for unprogrammed Friends is that we went out there and were changed rather dramatically. Our liberal theology and politics were competently challenged. We got into the Bible and into disciplined theological reflection and we ended up, many of us, revising and deepening our understanding."

"I would say that ESR is not for everyone. I would not recommend it for someone from my own tradition who doesn't have a strong understanding of what they believe. So, if a person graduating from George Fox is a new Christian or a new Friend…at ESR they will be stretched beyond that. But I would recommend ESR for more courageous and resilient folks."

A Friend we met by phone shared his vision:

> "I see on both ends of the Quaker spectrum a fearfulness towards what they perceive at the other end of the spectrum. [That tension] requires a willingness to risk and be teachable among the different varieties of Friends. You need to be clear and secure in what your own faith is, while at the same time really trying to hear and appreciate what gives life and hope to people whose perspectives within the Quaker family are different. Certainly ESR is a place that I've taken hope in, because it is a meeting place for people of the different stances within Quakerism to meet and learn together—and to learn from each other."

Although ESR's basic mission statement contains no reference to hoped-for change or growth among its students, that objective—for any educational institution—goes without saying. And for Quakers, indeed for all Christians, the *transformed life* is the final litmus test of faith. An evangelical Friend spoke eloquently to that point:

> "In the Religious Society of Friends overall, you have a lot of Quaker Meetings that are small and dwindling. One important thing is not just church growth—how we make ends meet and that kind of thing—but the spiritual core of Quaker experience, the conviction that God changes people's lives.…The most significant factor in a Meeting's health and growth is its spiritual tone: Are people being *changed* by the Meeting for Worship and during the week? I think that's the most pressing question for Quakers in the world. And that has always been Quakers' strength.
>
> I think ESR could be a leader in the world in that vein, to believe that God is at work even in the academic venture: that the academic venture is a spiritual quest, so that the goal is not simply to produce a rational reflection on a topic…but the hope that something will happen even beyond the academic performance."

Among Friends, is it time to think in new ways about the word *meeting?* Whether Friends sit in a pew or in a semicircle—or both;

whether they open themselves to the Light or to Christ or to each other—or all of those; and whether, together, they worship or talk or just do things—separately or in combination or in sequence: *meeting necessitates change.* One person meets Christ, hears God's call, glimpses truth; and life is never again quite the same. The Holy Spirit, assorted nomenclature notwithstanding, sweeps through a worshipful assembly of Friends; subsequently hearts are lifted and solutions miraculously arise. At ESR or through any other venue, a variety of Friends bend their efforts toward a shared purpose; and somewhere in the larger world the light of peace and justice shines a bit more brightly.

Can Friends meet and stand? Can Friends also meet and change? And what can ESR do to help? Some of the answers, we believe, may lie in a new way of framing the question.

While working with this national consultation, we ran across a metaphor that spoke to us of meeting and change. A homily written by Dorotheos of Gaza, a sixth-century monk, introduces the image of a perfect circle, traced by a compass around a single point:

> "Let us suppose that this circle is the world and that God himself is the center: the straight lines drawn from the circumference to the center are the lives of human beings.…Let us assume for the sake of the analogy that to move toward God, then, human beings move from the circumference along the various radii of the circle to the center. But at the same time, the closer they are to God, the closer they become to one another; and the closer they are to one another, the closer they become to God."*

Metaphors, of course, don't present fact; they merely offer us new ways to see. Human beings' approach to God is rarely so tidily direct as a radius might suggest, and our individual radii themselves are altogether too likely to overlap in less than comfortable ways. In any real *meeting*, however—person-to-God, person-to-person, person-to-idea—something happens. Something changes. And something, invariably, moves.

---

*Quoted in Roberta C. Bondi, *To Love as God Loves: Conversations with the Early Church* (Philadelphia: Fortress Press, 1987), p. 25

We cannot duplicate the original Quaker story.
We can, however, seek to better understand the process
by which our forebears became an incendiary fellowship.
Before they sought to change the world,
they were themselves transformed.

A FRIEND

~

EVERY NOW AND THEN SOMEONE GENTLY reminded us: "The Religious Society of Friends is not a denomination. We are a *movement*." In other words, "We're not just a name, a designation, or a sect; we're a happening, a group that represents progress and change. Although the label 'Quakers'—people who quake before the Lord—originated in ridicule, it has proven prophetically resonant with our larger purpose. Through the centuries, quietly yet radically, we Quakers have caused some upheaval."

History, we know, supports that claim. Yet some Friends have described the group as *stagnant, stale, stuck, moribund,* creatively *grinding to a halt,* tending toward *inertia.* One person who wrote to us listed among Quakerism's challenges "the fading hope to be an effective movement for change." With decreasing and aging numbers of Friends, youth education programs that vary widely in quality and content, and momentum-sapping internal discord, from what source can Quakers draw new vitality?

From all we can tell, Friends' hope—though perhaps fading—is not dead. In a focus group, someone spoke up passionately: "If we could break through our bonds of worn-out tradition, we could become radical counterculture people all over again." "I think there's still movement among Friends," agreed someone during a phone interview. "I don't expect that our problems are going to be easily resolved, but I think we still have a valuable witness for the world."

While Friends have been off in separate corners, however, some of that witness may have begun finding other passageways. So thinks one person we interviewed:

> "There is a crying need out there for exactly what Friends have to offer. The peace testimony, for example: In the wake of Littleton, folks ought to be just streaming to Quaker communities, who have for 350 years been talking about peace and conflict resolution. Look across the United States and see the deep interest in the voluntary simplicity movement; we've had it for 350 years! Look at the deep concern about racial and gender equality; we've been talking about that for 350 years, too. Meditation, silence, reflection—look at the stuff that's popular out there these days. So why aren't people beating a path to our door?"

A tirelessly optimistic Friend believes the time is ripe for Quaker renewal:

> "When I look at what we've taught over the years, I think, 'This is hot stuff.' It's a message of scriptural common sense—and it could be deeply joyful. I dream of great changes for us. There's a group of people out there now, some of whom maybe aren't even Friends yet, who are radically discontented with the old structures but have recovered some of the excitement of being Christian. I think big changes will happen even if we don't officially nurture that excitement— but our business is to figure out how to nurture it, without occluding it with the old arguments."

And the excitement? What is it, exactly? Here's one Friend's definition: "There's definitely a hunger in our society for *experiential spirituality*. It's not just about joining a club; it's about really experiencing the movement of the Spirit. And I think that's a strength of Quakerism."

As we listened, we found ourselves agreeing with the Friend who succinctly declared, "Something has got to happen in the Religious Society of Friends." That "something," we think, may well *include* growth or even *cause* growth, but growth itself cannot be the goal.

Individually, organizationally, and institutionally, Friends need to work again toward a witness that will speak—simply and radically—as perhaps only Quakers can. One person suggested that growth is the reward of faithfulness; if so, with a newly vibrant faith and witness, the numbers within the Society of Friends will multiply.

Such a mission, of course, requires the full-scale participation of ESR.

Here's the good news: Among Friends, we found an expansive vision of the various roles ESR might fill. Rather than citing the hundreds of particulars, we compiled the following "wish list" that reflects people's broad suggestions to the School:

- Follow God's leading
- Decide who you are; state it clearly and widely; and then be it. If necessary, revise the mission.
- Be bold, creative, transformative, even radical
- Establish a new definition and model of Quaker *leadership* ["Be positioned to support and equip a 'new brand' of Quaker leadership unlike any in our recent past."]
- Prepare Quaker pastors (includes continuing education for existing pastors)
- Prepare others within the Religious Society of Friends
  – for unprogrammed Meetings (clerks et al.)
  – "lay" leaders (youth leaders, First Day School teachers, elders, pastoral care, spiritual direction, etc.)
  – Friends organization leaders/administrators
  – followers
  – seekers (individual discernment)
- Specifically, prepare change agents for the Religious Society of Friends
- Reach out to young Friends; identify upcoming leaders
- Help set the Religious Society of Friends' vision; inspire renewal; be a catalyst
- Be Christ-centered
- In the spectrum of Friends, take the middle ground
- Reflect on our heritage; teach it and preserve it
- Articulate and model Quaker life, practice, and identity ["So that here at least is one clear strong identity of Quakerism." / "Teach us to be Quakers."]

- Keep in touch with Friends nationally and internationally—and not just for fund raising
- Partner with international Friends whenever possible
- Be a facilitator of dialogue, a bridge between various Quaker groups, a center of discussion, a gathering place
- Be a place of seeking and questioning
- Be a think tank about Quakerism; a source of creative and critical thinking
- Produce leading Quaker scholarship
- Be a resource for Yearly Meetings
- Help local Meetings learn how to get started, sustain, grow, and raise funds
- Be visible/audible; publish information. Let us know what your graduates are doing. Be a presence.
- Establish and carry out new programs for Quaker education and nurture
- Set and hold standards not only for academics but for leadership
- Cooperate with other Quaker educational centers
- Relate Quakerism to the larger world
- Keep a sense of humor
- **and** Don't try to be everything to everyone!

That's the good news. The bad news—or perhaps just the news that clamors for recognition—is this: Earlham School of Religion has six full-time faculty members and even fewer primary administrators. Ranks of extras are not waiting in the wings. As the first-born child in the Quaker-seminary family, ESR bears a heavy share of the family dreams. The attendant responsibilities—and sometimes, the sheer load of expectation—can create a burden that is difficult to heft, much less carry.

As ESR continues assessing, deliberating, juggling in an effort to construct an academic community and curriculum that can address the needs of Friends, satisfy the accrediting agency, and fit within the budget, we hold up for consideration the words of two Friends, each of whom seeks a revitalized Quaker movement. A focus group yielded one person's earnest questions:

> "Where's the openness in Friends to allow Christ's Holy Spirit to expand us—and not just to renew us so that we can maintain, but to create something entirely new and fresh and different, something that's still in

the balance of remaining authentic and faithful to the scripture, to the tradition of the church, and to one's personal experience of the Christian faith? How can we begin to stop worrying about maintenance and survival and instead open ourselves to whatever good and new can emerge from us in the next hundred years?"

Much later, talking with a Friend individually, we heard this idea:

"Why not offer a course that asks questions of transformation: How do people get changed by God? How does the devotional life develop life-changing vitality? And how do pastors and other leaders and anybody in the unprogrammed tradition as well, how do those people minister out of contact with a living God in ways that change the people around them? If ESR can get its prayerful searching around those issues, I think it would be an amazingly exciting place, for all Quakers but also for people beyond Friends."

Where *is* the openness that the questioning Friend seeks? And when that openness comes, what will it look like? Regardless of whether ESR decides to offer a course on human transformation, the two comments above are worth noting by individual Quakers and by the Society at large, because they broach the twin topics of *experiential spirituality* and *transformed lives*—which, in combination, form perhaps the strongest, most distinctive message that Quakers have to offer. Within that message, ESR and the Society of Friends can work together to realize a new understanding and practice of Quaker leadership.

It's simply a matter of getting a move on.

Many people we met referred to modern Friends as "individualistic," overly influenced by the "me generation" and thus exacerbating the Quaker tendency toward self-styled theology. Looked at in a new way, could individualism again become a strength? Change, after all, takes place one person at a time: listening for a personal leading; standing for one's own *why*; contributing individually and faithfully to the *how*; meeting others halfway; being willing to change. Along the way, evangelizing.

Evangelizing? We can imagine some Friends bristling at the very word. But again, Friends' individualism provides a perfect opportunity to reframe. An *evangel* is simply a bringer of good news. What Quaker does not have good news to share? Friends certainly shared it with us: a deep, personal connection with God; a transformed life; an egalitarian community; a centuries-old heritage of peace and justice, along with ongoing projects that keep the heritage vigorously alive.

If the widely used Protestant phrase "good news" makes some Friends squirm, maybe it's time for new words. Could Quaker evangelizing take the form of *expressing? inviting? making plain?* When Friends share their individual version of good news, are they *letting the Light shine?* If a Friend has experienced and claimed a truth, isn't any conversation a happy occasion for quietly *proclaiming* it? Countless vocal ministry possibilities exist.

In a focus group we learned of a Friends Church that boldly created its own bumper stickers, which read *Ask me about Friends.* That sounds like a step in the right direction—evidence that Friends are willing to emerge from their virtual hiding places and to share their long-hoarded spiritual treasure. But we would advise taking a step further: Instead of waiting passively to be asked, how can Friends carry their faith in an open hand? Birthright Friends, who may tend to accept Quaker reticence as a given, can learn to weave their faith subtly into the texture of a conversation; convinced Friends, especially those still recoiling from too-forceful proselytizing in another religious tradition, can speak their new discoveries in as natural and as nuanced a way as their temperaments allow. One Friend told us his favorite approach: "As a pastor and as a person who feels really called to share the gospel, I try to share it one person at a time, and to love people where they are. I don't try to make anybody a Quaker: I try to make everybody a friend, and those who feel called to be Quakers are certainly welcome."

Quakerly difficulties can be solved in Quakerly ways. When mountains of tradition block the path—whether they represent long habit, theological disagreement, inherent reserve, or simply new ideas— faith can move them. For Friends, faith is a movement: It leads from the One. To each one. To many. And from there, out toward the all. If Quakers are to live their witness, no part of that process is dispensable.

When the School ceases to be self-critical and experimental, it will have ceased to be a living and vital community of teaching and learning.

WILMER COOPER, THE ESR STORY

~

WITH THE HELP OF FRIENDS throughout the United States and even a few Friends abroad, ESR has *listened:* to Quakers' assessment of the Society, to their individual and corporate needs, to their feedback about the School, and to their ideas for ESR's future. The listening, of course, is not over. Quaker voices will continue to influence the School's thinking as its administrators refine and strengthen ESR's ongoing work.

Earlham School of Religion has never claimed to be other than an experiment, a hopeful venture not wholly unlike the "holy experiment" of William Penn centuries before. Its work was new, untried. Its founders and leaders were spiritual pilgrims, academic pioneers, researchers absorbed both in lab work and prayer.

Now, after four decades of theoretic and empirical operation, ESR is still standing. And it's definitely not standing still. As we reviewed the founding of the School and considered its steps forward and backward since that time, we were tempted to shake our heads regretfully: "In 40 years, has ESR come only this far?" Many Friends, we know, believe that the School abandoned or at least shortchanged its original intent of training Quaker pastors. Even people closest to ESR—administrators, board members, faculty—acknowledge that inadvertent deficiency. The overall quality or the thrust of education at the School, some people think, has varied as well. And they are right: cultural trends, shifts in the student population, faculty appointments, size limitations, finances, and other influences have variously marked the School's several decades and even individual years. Earlham School of Religion, well-intentioned but occasionally clumsy, is still learning not only how to be a seminary, but particularly how to be a seminary for the complex body of Friends.

On the other hand, we also can say with enthusiasm—and with many of the Friends we met—"Just look what ESR has accomplished—and in only 40 years." In effecting personal transformation among its students, as we have noted, the School has proved enormously successful. And despite its erratic record in pastoral training, Friends credit ESR with having produced a highly respectable cadre of Quaker pastors and other leaders within the Society:

> "We have a lot of pastors here now who have been trained at ESR. And one of the reasons that North Carolina Yearly Meeting is so strong, so dynamic, is because there are so many really fine young products of ESR down here."

> "ESR is making a difference. Leadership roles across Quakerdom are staffed by a remarkable number of ESR products."

> "Almost everywhere one looks today among unprogrammed Friends, one will find ESR alumni/ae."

> "ESR set out to create Quaker leaders, and it has done a good job. Look across the country at our leaders, and see how many of them went to ESR."

> "ESR graduates are often working very effectively and very quietly, and oddly enough the downside of that is that people don't realize they are ESR graduates."

> "Pastors in Iowa who came from ESR are having a very positive influence. They're good people, well trained."

> "There's a lot of very fine Friends pastors out there that I have met over the years who were trained at ESR and who have gone on to very fruitful ministries as pastors—sometimes shifting out of that into other things as well. And there's quite a number of important leaders here in the East among unprogrammed Friends whose training at ESR was a strong imprint on them."

> "As a group, the folks who graduated from ESR are a beacon of hope. They are sensible, often deeply

reflective and well trained. The School has done,
by and large, a great job in that regard."

A number of Friends commended the ESR "crossroads community"
for enhancing the well-being of Quakerism itself:

> "ESR has been successful in drawing a range of people.
> It doesn't appeal to everyone, but it *has* appealed to
> numbers of people in all the Quaker traditions, not
> just one."

> "The function of ESR should be to assist each branch
> in achieving the clarity it needs. Such things take a long
> time. But in the unprogrammed tradition, ESR has had
> a noticeable influence."

> "The most profound thing for me was encountering
> people from different groups—studying with them,
> knocking each other around on theological points
> in the classroom, eating together, playing together,
> worshiping together. The personal acquaintance that
> is sustained over the years after the ESR experience
> can be pretty powerful."

> "There's less hostility between Friends groups now
> than there was, say, two or three decades ago. There's
> more conversation and people engage better. I think
> ESR has helped with that."

> "The fellowship among ESR graduates has formed
> a good network of shared understanding and visions
> for the future of Quakerism. I think it has been a
> good thing among both pastoral and unprogrammed
> Quakers."

Buoyed by its successes and edified by its failures, ESR continues
the experiment. What worked well? What didn't? What was responsible? What do we need to do now? All of those questions bear
consideration. The School, however, must also remember its *why*—
and not only remember it, but articulate it, publicize it, and work
faithfully by its Light. The *how* of ESR, we believe, encompasses more
than educational methods, well-chosen personnel, and financial
underpinnings. Those are the School's vehicles and enablers. Its deeper

how matches the "leading" process among Friends: from One to one, from one to another, from one to many, and ultimately to many more. As assets for the School of Religion, the practices of individual receptivity, response, and commitment must not be undervalued.

Not all of the School's distinctive *how* happens on the ESR campus. One person told us of ESR-inspired transformation that began well in advance of a student's arrival:

> "A student from our Meeting will be going to ESR this year, and we're very excited about that. ESR has done a superb job recruiting her, with follow-up calls about things like housing, so she's very enthusiastic about going there. And she's been talking to us about the School throughout the whole process. When Jay Marshall comes to ask us for money, we'll remember that student's experience."

In another story, the transformative *how* happened only gradually, some time after the student had completed an ESR degree:

> "I served two years in a strongly evangelical church, but at the beginning the people weren't sure they wanted me. The church was already divided, and to some of them an ESR graduate was suspect. Over time, as love and trust built up between us, people began to say, 'Well, maybe ESR is okay after all.'"

One person at a time, then, can ESR meet the leadership needs of Friends? Obviously the School can't accomplish everything on Quakers' lavish "wish list"—or at least not anytime soon! ESR clearly needs to add some programs, bolster others, and find a formula that keeps students, faculty, curriculum, and funds in salubrious balance. *But the task does not belong to ESR alone.* If every member of Friends takes ministry seriously—acknowledging accountability to God, to the Meeting, and to the Quaker movement in the world, then similar give-and-take relationships are possible between ESR and its extended constituency.

ESR and Friends must meet, in the best sense of the word. ESR must take its stance and make itself known; each would-be beneficiary of the School must be willing to know it in return, and must keep up that end of the conversation. "I don't know much about ESR" is an inappropriate statement from anyone who either seeks to receive from the School or feels free to criticize it. "Where ESR is concerned, we need to do our homework and not just criticize from afar," one Friend acknowledged.

Each interested Friend needs to ask, "What is *my* relationship to this School? If I hope to gain from it, what can I give?" And "give" doesn't necessarily connote financial contributions. Financial gifts matter, and ESR needs them; but without spending a dime, Friends can give encouragement, invitations, responses, referrals, and respect.

Both the time and the conditions, we believe, are right for a meeting between ESR and Friends and for the enlivening movement that can result. "This consultation is very important—wonderful—a huge step forward," we heard from numerous participants. Their appreciation was unmistakable: "I'm overjoyed." / "It's so good to do this." / "I'm encouraged. They're listening!" One Friend said, "I've wished someone would ask me these questions." Others sent messages: "Don't give up on us! We need you." / "Tell the people at ESR that we love them. We're in this together; our futures are tied. They're re-including us, and we want to help heal the wounds." Another Friend ended our interview simply and with great compassion: "God bless them for what they're doing. I hope they can stay the course."

The past 40 years and the feedback from this national consultation suggest that the School can indeed stay the course. But just as ESR must re-include Friends, so Friends must re-include ESR. Earlham School of Religion can exist, serve, and thrive—but only among Friends, and only with their active support.

My sense is that ESR has relied on its own richness of knowledge and creativity but has not been good at making connections and nurturing them.

A FRIEND

~

EARLHAM SCHOOL OF RELIGION, as a perpetually evolving experiment, already understands the beauty of the progressive tense. So do Friends in general, with their reliance on *leadings,* their practice of *meeting,* and their sense of *continuing revelation.* For both ESR and the Society of Friends, the subtle suffix *-ing* is crucial. Within three letters it combines past, present, and future; unobtrusively but plainly, it connotes movement and possibility and hope. It also admits, without apology, "God isn't finished with us yet."

All of those intimations inform the ongoing process of *leading* and *following through* that we recommend for ESR. We realize that the School's national consultation asked us only to deliver a perspective — not to prescribe solutions. But as educational consultants, we couldn't help ourselves. In addition to the countless specific suggestions voiced by participating Friends (and thus included representatively in *Quaker Voices*), we bring to ESR our own list of techniques for the School to consider.

Besides the explicit educational requests we heard among Friends — such as the repeated calls for academic programs that are more accessible, more plentiful, more pointed, more thorough — we emerged from the consultation convinced that Quakers want and need from ESR three broad *whats:*

1) ***an identity:*** a clear, defensible statement of who you are, whom you serve, and what you offer—a statement that underlies and shapes your every institutional move

2) ***a presence:*** an institution and a faculty that is knowable, known, and worth knowing; that both reaches out and responds; that listens and communicates; that initiates, contributes, and keeps learning

3) ***a model:*** of education, of scholarship, of Quakerly thought and practice

These three elements comprise everything else that the School might be expected to deliver: curriculum, methods, programs, people, outreach, participation, community, influence. And we believe that all three are deliverable—provided both ESR and the Society of Friends stay open to leadings and keep following through.

We look forward to watching it all unfold.

Quaker Voices

INTRODUCTION

In this section, unattributed comments from the consultation's three primary sources of information—focus groups, telephone interviews, and essays—are categorized by the topics listed below. Details that might identify the speakers or writers in this representative selection of quotations have been removed.

Message and mission

What inspires me is the stories of Friends who follow their leadings and have taken some risks and been faithful to where God is guiding them. That's what got me involved with the Society of Friends. I could have been a Presbyterian or Methodist or something else, but I didn't see those people stepping out in faith the way I did amongst Friends.

~

The two pieces of the foundation are that we can know God directly and experientially, and that that's available to all people everywhere, no matter what the names, labels, etc. There is no separation between sacred and secular. When you put those together that means that we just totally infuse the world. Every nook and cranny of human experience should be permeated with the love and presence of God. We do that naturally if we take God with us totally and invite God's perceptible presence in everything we do. The church then becomes the gathering place for the training and the educating for ministry that we are all about. For Quakers it's incredibly simple but we make it too complicated.

~

Our mission is to model a holistic and transforming relationship with the living God.

~

I'm reading a book right now by my favorite professor from Fuller and I'm struck by our need to have a theology and a practice of our faith that is community oriented, that is communal and not just individualistic. Early Friends practiced that really well with Meetings for Clearness, with the way they did worship…but the way we have articulated the essence of our faith has been so individualistic…I mean the idea of Christ speaking individually, of unmediated revelation is true. But I'm struck by our need to recognize that a relationship with the God who was involved with all of humanity means we have to be a part of that communal relationship as well. It's not just Jesus and me, or God and me, but it's us together as the body of Christ. I can't articulate it very clearly…but somehow we need to work that into the way we think about our central message and about what it means to be convinced as a Friend, nurtured as a believer.

~

…devout Quaker personalities embodied a vision of the gospel I had not experienced before…

~

The greatest challenge for Friends is knowing who we are and what message and vision we want to offer the world. In my experience with unprogrammed Friends, I find many people uncomfortable with Christianity and Quakerism as an expression of Christianity. With programmed Friends I find many people more connected with general conservative evangelical ideas about the expression of Christianity than anything particularly Quaker. So what do we want leaders to be like? Do we want them to be like the many people in our pews, or to know and work out of a bigger picture?

~

I believe the Society of Friends should be a revealing place for God. The best way to do that is in living out love and in working on justice projects and showing love for that of God in every person.

~

When you ask what is the mission and the message for the Religious Society of Friends, that's a difficult thing to answer because that is such a very broad group. The spectrum that constitutes the Religious Society of Friends is immense and we don't even call ourselves part of the Religious Society of Friends. We are the Friends Church and there are reasons for that. So when we talk about what is it, or maybe what it should be, I'm sure we are voicing things that would probably not be held by an awful lot of folks. We are looking at it, I think, from an evangelical perspective, a Christ perspective. Given that, the mission… or what it should be for the Friends Church, is essentially to take the world for Christ. Jesus gave us the Great Commission and that's our charge. Our mission is to take the world for Christ and to do that by being Light and being salt in the dark and decaying world. Our message is really the basic gospel message.

~

…to be Christian is to love your neighbor as yourself and for me this is the basis for service and for ministry and for mission, because your concern for the other person is to help them catch the vision of Christ who called us to get out of ourselves and to live for others.

~

In our time of religious pluralism the prevailing tendency is a tolerance which would reduce everything essentially to nothing, that is, no foundation. So it is important for Quakers to raise up the message which drew them out in the first place: The unity between Christ Jesus, historically revealed, crucified, and risen, and Christ as the Light which lightens everyone who has come into the world. I think it is timely for us to reinforce that fully and without separation. If we do that, we will survive, if we don't, we will polarize and be lost. Holding together that message about the unity of Christ revealed historically, of Christ revealed inwardly is vital.

In terms of the mission, we have to hold together the things that have continuing value such as our sense of being a covenant people and our sense of gathering, the sense of the meeting and being under the Spirit. We should be open to whatever methods have integrity but work within a given culture.

~

As a Quaker Meeting, this is a Meeting that would stand pretty solidly against war, against violence, and generally believes that all Quakers do that.

~

…one good question which Friends have to really ask themselves, and it's a hard question, is: Why should we continue to be called the Religious Society of Friends when that terminology seems an insult to many people? I know it has become a favorite name in some ways, but it is an 18th century name. I wonder if we wouldn't be stronger for just being the Friends Church around the world. Our mission is always to witness by proclamation, by fellowship, by service. As long as we retain those three pillars of the church, then the methods by which we pro-claim, and the methods by which we have fellowship, and the methods by which we serve, will vary from culture to culture and from time to time. But that balance has to be sustained.

~

[Some aspects] of the Religious Society of Friends: There is God in everyone; there's a direct personal relationship with God....we also seek guidance from the Bible, the holy scriptures. We know there are contra-indications in the Bible, but it is a very significant foundation for our faith. Mission has been mentioned. We need to let our Light shine out to others. Works are important and it is important and this is the evangelical part of it—that we let others know the source of our energy, our actions, and why we are doing these things.

~

I would like to be a mirror of Jesus' Light onto the dark world. If Jesus really loves everybody, how can I personally hate anybody? If Jesus died for everybody, how can I possibly dehumanize anybody?

~

I understand Quakerism to be a religion of direct experience, rather than dogma, doctrine, beliefs, systems, and it seeks to bring people to a realization of the Light or the Inner Christ within themselves and within all people and all beings perhaps. Out of this realization of the Inner Light or the Inner Christ we are empowered to walk cheerfully over the earth answering to that of God in everyone.

~

I'm probably first and primarily a peace and justice fan, and right now in this country I'm particularly concerned about what I regard as the lack of compassion and civility. Somehow it seems to me Friends ought to be able to play quite a major role in helping there be some kind of return, worldwide, to a basic care for one another. That applies from a personal level to the highest level of politics...world peace needs to be based on that kind of level of concern.

~

I would say—in terms of how I would try to explain the theology— I always grew up with a very strong understanding, both in my home, in my Meeting, among Quakers at large, that it was never enough to say that you believed, but your belief had to show in every single thing that you did and in every action, every feeling, every perspective, anything that we projected out had to be reflective of that belief.

The very unique testimony of Friends is that God exists in all people—and I would include animals and other creatures on the earth. When one behaves in a hateful, unkind, insensitive, unthoughtful way, one is personally affronting God and God's creation. That even includes people who do heinous, horrible, terrible things—God is within that person even though we may not be capable of seeing it.

~

I want to add another aspect of Friends that's been very important to me and to others: our peace testimony. This is unique among Christian denominations…the Religious Society of Friends and some of the other peace churches have stood for peace.

We live right now in a world still torn with all kinds of conflict, in the inner cities, suburbs, and internationally, and we have a real mission to help others find ways of bringing peace in this world, and it begins within ourselves. What I learned in the Religious Society of Friends is that we have to first of all find some measure of inner peace, then we have to learn how to deal with conflict in our families, in our Meetings, and in our organizations. In learning those skills we can help others who are struggling to find peace, which is one of the goals in the religious life.

~

Distinctives

The thing that is actually unique among Friends is our relationship with truth, our understanding of how we discern truth together and how that is related to an interior experience of God. I'm not very acquainted with how business is conducted by Evangelical Friends, but certainly liberal unprogrammed Friends, in our Meetings for Business, we gather together and open ourselves up for the experience of God leading us…and confirm our leadings corporately. There is something about knowing this tension, this relationship between my personal leading and the confirmation of the community. I really don't know of any other faith that does anything quite like that.

~

In the wake of Littleton, folks ought to be just streaming to Quaker Meetings and communities who have for 350 years said: There is another way. We teach our children about peace, we talk about conflict resolution, and our children learn another way of relating to others. Look across the United States and see the deep interest in the voluntary simplicity movement; we've had it for 350 years! Look at the deep concern about race and gender and equality; we've been talking about that for 350 years, too. Meditation, silence, reflection—look at the stuff that's popular out there these days. So why aren't people beating a path to our door?

~

We talk about simple living, but very often it turns out to be Volvo simple living. We crank up the peace testimony when there's a war. We talk about integrity, but in our Meetings we're afraid to speak truth to one another for fear of offending one another about theological or lifestyle issues. We could be Unitarians or Unity people or liberal Jews— it's hard to tell.

~

There are distinctive things about Friends...commitment to equality, egalitarianism, the notion that every person is precious in the eyes of God and therefore must be for us, too. The peace testimony is a distinctive expression of that. The determination, and here's a good example of what I'm talking about, not to make gender an issue in service is in everybody's book of faith and practice, and is only moderately practiced in some parts of the world and in this country. Yet, every time Friends are challenged about it, it is something they hold to.

~

One of the things the Society of Friends has to offer is a lack of chauvinism, if you want to put it that way. There is a willingness to work with Mennonites or Catholics or evangelical Protestant denominations or people who don't come from the faith base but still have the same concerns.

~

Use of silence is something that Friends can bring to the world.

~

Quakers could have something really special if we were to truthfully carry through speaking directly to God and listening for continuing revelation...and not just occasionally.

~

Again, [what defines the community of faith in this church] would probably be a bit different than most Friends churches and that is simply the desire to allow Christ to be the center of one's life and together to team, and to explore, and to wrestle with what does that mean in the marketplace? What does that mean in everyday living? And discovering that together.

~

My experience across Friends is that you will find an awful lot of people who believe in the possibility of divine guidance and that you can act on it. It's that combination, with the basis in community, that may be a unique contribution of Friends.

~

Having grown up in one of the other historic peace churches, Church of the Brethren, this is one of the parts of the Society of Friends or Quakerism that was attractive…what I would call *simplicity*, as compared to what I grew up with.

I have become very comfortable with the idea of the sense of the meeting in decision making and that particular process is now working well, to step back and go through a process of seeking clearness about issues. Even though there have been some very difficult times since I've been in this Meeting over one or two issues in particular, at the end of the process I have not felt any kind of strong division within the Meeting. I can clearly remember those kinds of things happening in a business process of decision making…

I find that to be a very unique and very worthwhile way of considering business as a Meeting for Worship for the purpose of Business. The other thing that I don't recall having any particular terminology for before I became involved with the Quakers is the idea of the Inner Light and that of God in everyone, me or every person. I'm not saying that the concept was not there in the previous experience, but it didn't have words that described it or a way of thinking about it, and I found that to be unique.

~

I like what Johan Maurer, who is the General Secretary of FUM, said last year at our Quaker lecture. He said somebody asked him what a Quaker is and he said, "A Quaker is someone who wants the most uncluttered approach to God." To me, that is the start of everything else that we are about as far as Quakers go. We want the most uncluttered approach to God, so we can have a direct experience of God in our daily lives and in our Meetings for Worship. I don't know if that makes us unique, but ordinarily, even though I'm a part of a programmed Meeting, our worship is pretty simple and we don't have the ceremonies or the rites that other denominations have. Our mission is that people, all kinds of people, no matter where you are from or what your status is, can have this direct experience of God.

~

I knew the Society of Friends as a child from a different point of view. That's when the older Friends were still around who were venerable, sometimes wealthy, but simple in their demeanor—humble but often powerful people who were very traditional, who would not have dreamed of showing up in bare feet at a Quaker Meeting.

~

Commonalities

My favorite phrase from George Fox's journal appears early in the journal in which he writes of the hidden unity in the eternal being. I like that on several levels. It's the unity in which we all share but which is hidden from us by our own limitations and our own biases. To know Christ, or to know God, to know the Spirit, is to rediscover or reawaken to that unity that is hidden from us most of the time.

~

How come all those liberal Friends are going to ESR? It's because the aridity of the individualistic liberal tradition was not satisfying them. They are looking for something else. ESR was one of the places they could find it. I think that's important. There have been events that have brought encouragement to people like me who think that all Friends are Friends. I was at the Pendle Hill conference on Vietnam last summer and all the branches of Quakerism in this country were represented there. Now, granted, Evangelical Friends were represented by a person or two who might be regarded by some Evangelical Friends as dangerously liberal, but they were all there. It was productive and it found us able to disagree about a number of things but it really was a more common experience and purpose than many people expected.

~

…just the fact that Friends, however contentious it becomes at times, are most often willing to embrace plurality within the Society of Friends…a liberal Friend is usually still willing to admit that super-programmed evangelical Quakers are still in some sense Friends. I think that's remarkable.

~

[Unity] appears and occurs most powerfully in worship. Friends World Committee holds a week-long triennial every three years and at those Meetings, Friends from all churches come together with all of their suspicions and doubts and hopes and they worship together. Both programmed and unprogrammed worship through five or six days and it is astonishing what happens. They know they are among their brothers and sisters even though their cultural differences are immense. I believe, personally, and I keep saying it every time I get a chance to in a speech, that our most difficult issues of separation from one another are cultural, not religious.

~

Friends and science have always been on good terms because they are both based on observation of experience and learning from experience.

~

Religious experience is different in different personalities. How it works for me is not the same explanation as for an evangelical. The basic belief is *that of God in each person*. If you really believe that—and I don't see how you can't—we're together.

~

As clerk of a Yearly Meeting, I've been traveling and listening a lot... We have all sorts of Friends in Yearly Meeting and I have to listen to all of them and not discount or discredit them and I still have yet to find out what we meet together on, that common thing that we share. In our Yearly Meeting, it's unprogrammed worship, but beyond that I have no idea. I would hope that it would be some of our early testimonies, but I'm not even sure of that—that they hold water with other Friends.

~

I participate in both programmed and unprogrammed; both are very meaningful.

~

I see more and more people out there who are willing to stick their necks out a bit and say it's not really very loving for us to be judgmental and isolationists. Let's go ahead and associate with other Friends and not try to impose our convictions but share them openly. I find that it can be both rewarding and frustrating. Frustrating if you think you're going to convince a lot of people to see things the way you do, but rewarding in that there is generally acceptance and love extended back to you.

~

Across the spectrum, if there's anything that unites us, it's the peace testimony.

~

If I were to try to describe the Society of Friends, I would start by telling people about the similarities between the Society of Friends and other religious denominations: We are very diverse in terms of theology and belief; we go from what we would call our orthodox to our unorthodox; we have liberals, we have evangelicals, and especially for the size of our denomination—if you look at groups of Friends around the world, not just within the United States—we comprise a wide diversity.

That it would be absolutely impossible to describe who and what a Quaker is. For a denomination, we are extraordinarily small in number and we have had an extraordinary impact on the world collectively. I've had the experience of meeting people all over the world who have had a connection with Quakers, or know of Quakers because of a project or a commitment to a program that has really had an impact and changed the way of life for some people. A lot of people may not know about the theology or the belief system of Quakers, but they know what Quakers do.

~

If we could agree on some basic principles that we all espouse or believe in, then we could be more unified. I think there's far more sameness than we think there is of what we really want and what's important to us out of our religion.

~

I'm a war tax resister—since the early 1980s. FWCC set up a committee to study and act on that issue. One qualification I insisted on: The committee must have representatives from all three major groups of Friends. The evangelicals were remarkable—there was no real difference between us. Some practices are different, and their description used different words—but they were the same as mine. *We're all Quakers.*

~

I suppose the most basic glue [in the Religious Society of Friends] is the commitment to religion based on experience and the certainty that any one of us, fragile as we may be, can have a direct experience of God and be turned into a disciple. That runs through all branches of friends. My Evangelical Friends would say [being turned into a disciple] is being born again and having a changed life. My liberal Friends would say it shows you clear places to make your witness. I'm persuaded that at the extremes, the liberal extreme, the evangelical extreme, there are probably irreconcilable differences. Whether on the liberal end one thinks he can be a Quaker and at the same time be an atheist, which is what some people claim. Or on the other end, there are those who are biblical literalists, fundamentalists, who really feel closer to Protestant Right evangelicals than they do to other Quakers.

…those are relatively small fringe groups on the edge. The great body of Friends, over and over and over again, when they get together and work together discover a unity that they were suspicious of.

~

If we can get to know each other, person to person, we can see that we're all together.

~

Differences among branches

There's definitely a truth that transcends any of our individual under-standings. If we can stay in touch with that truth and act out of it, the differences between us fall away. I don't let go of my uniqueness but it falls away in a certain way.

~

New England YM is most consciously trying to hold both pastoral (11) and unprogrammed (six-and-a-half) Meetings. We want to be tender with each other's mode of meeting.

~

The overwhelming number of FUM people are those that want an emphatically Christian emphasis in their presentation of Quakerism.

~

I like to see a variety of Quaker flowers on the root. Some of it I'm not personally comfortable with, but I think it's important that it's lively and vital.

~

The question still is, "What is our collective vision for the Society?" That's a good question and I'd like to hear some discussion on it because we represent different perspectives. We could probably agree with some of the points, like we believe all life is sacramental, but then getting to the specifics is where we run into trouble. You can believe in the broad terms no matter whether you come from the evangelical or the liberal end of things. It's when you get down to the specifics that we run into trouble.

~

My fear is that the different branches of Quakerism will stop trying to seek together and find inspiration. I hear a lot of Quakers from the dif-ferent branches saying, "Well we don't have anything in common with those liberal, new age people"…from the evangelical perspective. Or from the liberal side, "We don't have anything in common with those Methodist Quakers." If we continue down that path, that's going to be a real sign that we have lost touch with our Quaker roots.

~

While we have general agreement on the social missions and positions (except abortion and same gender marriages), we have little common theology. We are hung together by a bland and mediated set of Advices and Queries. Some of us are grounded in Christian faith while others are immersed in wicca, Zen, and a variety of other sects. We at times try to celebrate this as a triumph of our diversity but most of the time we try to ignore it. We certainly do not engage this issue and that weakens us.

~

We go through the stage of thinking *it's just language.* But no, there's a real difference in belief. Among liberal unprogrammed Friends particularly, many people consider themselves Christian, but they're not willing to say it in their Meeting because they don't feel safe. Once they find others like themselves, they can talk about it.

~

Well, to me having been brought up and exposed to the two traditions of Friends, I think that many a time we blind ourselves in only seeing one direction, and the most important thing to me has been that of learning about the two traditions. The way I see it, neither of the two of them has the whole truth.

~

A number of years ago, a camping consultation was hosted by ESR for Quaker camp directors. This was a first-time meeting which was attended by representatives from several camps. The primary purpose was information sharing and it was an eye-opening experience. We learned that camps in the west and mid-west are more evangelical and of shorter duration than east coast camps; they're also staffed more by volunteers. It was intriguing. The story of the gathering was written by Ken Jacobson and published.

Primarily what we discovered is that essentially there aren't that many differences between us. When you put that many Quakers together in one room—we're camp people so we know how to build community—those differences melt away. By the end of the meeting the people from the west left with a greater understanding of why we do what we do in the east, even though they wouldn't choose to fashion their camps that way, and likewise the folks from the east coast listened and were impressed by the spirituality and the commitment of the other folks. There was a good sense of fellowship. One spin-off was the formation of the Quaker Camping Network which sponsors an annual conference.

~

…because I'm a serious Christian I have always been very stimulated by the seriousness and consistency with which evangelical Quakers go about being Christian. I struggle because they've not seen that there's something particularly strongly Christian about Quakerism.

~

Evangelical Friends refuse to take part in dialogues. Some say they have lost faith by talking to other Friends. A lot in Northwest YM don't want to send people to ESR, because "someone told me." They're not talking from their own experience. If ESR was training pastors to be strong leaders and to plant churches, they might be inclined to send people there. But I don't think that *should* be ESR's role. There's a tension: Liberal Friends want to sit around and talk; evangelicals want to proselytize and evangelize the world.

~

I would urge Earlham School of Religion to keep saying *all* branches of Friends, rather than the word *both*. The word both divides us into two groups. The language about *both* divides us into two when we really are multifaceted and we are very different in many different ways and you can't draw a line that puts half of the Friends on one side and half of Friends on the other.

~

...[the absence of people in the 30- to 45-year range is] an issue that's peculiar to unprogrammed Friends. Where you have Quaker churches, programmed Friends, obviously many of the clergy might be in that age range, but in our unprogrammed tradition,...it's just pretty rare to find people who are really active in leadership roles or public service roles.

~

Connecting and finding our common heritage is hard work. Marge Abbott is doing it right. Liberal Friends are way off base; we have a lot to do. I'm led to work with FGC. All of us need to become more intentional in our lives, be open to how God communicates with us. My sense is that when Jesus shows up, that unnerves and surprises liberal Friends. We need to pay more attention to that.

~

The overwhelming numbers of pastoral Meetings are certainly not in FGC and not in FUM combined. They are in EFI.

~

Liberal Friends tend to dismiss the Christian aspect, or people in the evangelical branch sometimes dismiss things like peace and business methods as irrelevant frills that can be dropped by the wayside. We all drop off pieces of what the message has been, and so we have a real challenge if we want to be a whole Society of Friends across the branches to re-look at what does it mean to be a Friend. What does it mean to live out this kind of very radical message; what does it mean both in terms of belief, faith, that kind of thing; what does it mean in terms of living; and what is faithful abidance all about, and can we accept that?

~

The difference between the programmed and the unprogrammed traditions is crucial to understand. In the unprogrammed side, one of the things that is a critical factor is that Quakers want leadership, but they don't want leaders. They want things to be managed, they want things to go forward, they want people to take responsibility, but they are extremely cautious, if not frankly allergic, to people exercising authority. You can't have one without the other and from my point of view, that's the crux of the leadership problem for the unprogrammed tradition of the Religious Society of Friends. It has been, and will probably continue to be, for a long time.

The only antidote that is at all effective, as far as I can see, is that the people who are in leadership roles among unprogrammed Friends, who are very clearly rooted in their own spiritual life and represent a kind of authentic spirituality, tend to be given some credence and some latitude to function in organizational leadership roles. That may not be true for people who don't show that kind of spiritual depth. But even then, leadership in a Quaker organization is just a very hard thing to do.

When we do get good people in those roles, the tendency is for them to burn out or get cut down in what some people would consider a fairly short period of time. I know very few people who have managed to take on those kind of roles and be effective for more than seven or eight years, and if you last three or four you have done well.

~

…I came to a sense of personal meaning and comfort in being a Quaker or being a Christian in a Quaker way, which to me is a serious way of being a Christian but always with a kind of open-endedness that knows that the same Light that I understand as the Light of Christ is shining in people that are not necessarily Christians and they may understand it in a different way. So it has created a situation in which I'm comfortable and stimulated in different ways by different groups of Friends. Evangelical Friends nurture and stimulate me in one aspect of my Quaker life, and more universalist unprogrammed Friends stimulate me in other ways. I'm both satisfied and dissatisfied in both streams.

~

Concerns

The thing that concerns me is our loss of identity. Maybe we are irrelevant because we have allowed those truths to become stale… I mean we are talking about such incredible truths: God is alive; Christ has risen; Christ speaks to people; the kingdom of God…all these things. It seems like we've so balled it up in our organization that it just can't get free sometimes. On the evangelical end, we're way too enamored with models that lead more toward the cultural religion than true Christianity. To me the concern is the loss of identity.

~

When I think about the Religious Society of Friends today, my greatest concern is *irrelevance*. We have been blessed with such a wonderful history and powerful insight into truth, but I'm not sure how successful we have been at times in connecting with the culture around us. We have just told these wonderful stories and they're true, I know they are, but I see—not just among Friends—but lots of others groups too, we are talking to each other and some other group is over there talking to each other and we are not connecting. There is a whole lot of the world around us that we are not communicating with, or in connection with, and we really are irrelevant to them.

~

…a concern in terms of a direct connection with Earlham School of Religion: I wonder what kind of support there is for those who have completed their program and are out in the world. I don't know that we are unique here at First Friends, but we are geographically a long way from Earlham and for our pastor to have a support group of like-minded pastors or other leaders may be difficult because of our particular circumstance and our relationship with other Meetings. That may not be an issue for North Carolina or an issue for Indiana but when you get out to the greater geographic reaches of the country, it could be an issue.

~

I've been concerned about this. I understand the historical momentum or why we stopped having elders and overseers. I understand that, and I understand why liberal Friends don't have recorded Friends. I know the history of the Society, but without a leadership class, so to speak, it's very difficult to communicate values. I'm quite aware as I get older that I'm becoming more conservative, and frankly, on bad days, I think it would be a great thing for Quakers if we rediscovered the hedge and began to look behind the hedge again. There's something very appealing about 19th century Quaker culture, a lot of bad stuff about it too, but I think there's a lot of great stuff there. I don't see how our Society can cohere without a consistent way of telling our story, and I don't think there are any people who are the identified storytellers in the Society of Friends anymore, like the elders and the overseers used to be.

~

We have become too individualistic and probably too economically privileged. We don't give enough of our money to the work of our community, so we may have lost the capacity to speak prophetically to our culture effectively.

~

My immediate response is "burn-out" and the many small Meetings here in Southern California with 25–30 members who struggle to survive and for whom the energy for that witness is very difficult to come up with. The spiritual resources in these small groups can be very thin so that those messages that we need to hear, we are not always hearing them. If you go to Quarterly Meetings you have a better chance, but while we have a lot of participation in Quarterly Meetings, everybody doesn't come.

~

That's one concern, our willingness to both understand and to say who we are.

~

I was greatly disappointed when I found that intellectual innocence is a virtue among some Friends.

~

Outreach is critical in a variety of ways. It's sometimes easy to identify with international issues right in front of your face, for example, Kosovo, but seeing what's right under your nose is a little difficult. As Friends, we sometimes become so involved with taking care of others, we forget to take care of our own. For example, I wonder how tolerant we are of each other. Do we perhaps expect too much of each other?

~

I am quite intrigued with how common our concerns are. I thought I was one of very few people that had this concern. Wow!

~

The concern I have is that we have a tendency to get very comfortable, and I don't think faith is always meant to be comfortable. One of the reasons we don't communicate with others among our branches is that it makes us uncomfortable, and one of the reasons unprogrammed Friends have difficulty with people they don't agree with is that messages that come with a lot of passion make people uncomfortable in Meeting. My sister became a Catholic. She joined the Catholic Worker Movement because she felt they were *doing* what we were *saying*. If we get too comfortable, we lose the transformation experience that faith really does have power.

~

What would be my greatest concern for the Friends Church? I don't have much exposure to the Religious Society of Friends, but I have a pretty good exposure to Evangelical Friends International (EFI), which consists of six Yearly Meetings. Just recently I got the statistics for all those. Now you would think after hearing the stories that we just told that we would be spreading like wildfire. These are great stories. The fact of the matter is, out of those six Yearly Meetings, only two of them are growing at all. The two that are growing are growing because of only two or three churches in their Yearly Meeting. Southwest Yearly Meeting is growing a little bit because of two churches. Eastern Region is growing because of three or four churches.

The fact of the matter is if you were to drop about 12 select churches out of the hundreds of churches in EFI, you would see substantial decline. So being irrelevant or not really carrying out our mission of engaging the world in a way that is effective is my major concern.

~

My greatest concern is that we will say and will believe all the right things and it won't make a hill of beans difference in how we live, either corporately or personally. My biggest personal fear is that I will die before I see genuine renewal among Friends.

~

I would say the greatest concern is that we would forget the basic foundation that George Fox said that there is one Christ Jesus who can speak to thy condition…all conditions, unity, diversity, homosexuals, whatever the condition, it is Jesus Christ. That would be my concern.

~

I'm concerned with the fact that many Friends will be settling for so little from God. I think God's power is infinite. If we can connect with that energy we have more than enough to do everything that needs to get done, but often Friends get bogged down in procedures, traditions, old battles that they have been fighting with one another, and they find themselves exhausted and burned out because they are not living in the moment in the Spirit of Christ and in the Spirit of God. So my big concern is how do we lead people to Christ? Lead people to God? So that they don't burn out. So that every moment they are filled with that energy. I guess that's what I struggle with because I feel blessed, I feel that God has been so empowering for me. I wish that power could be shared with everybody.

~

My concern is twofold, that we will miss seeing the signs of renewal that are among us, and, secondly, that if we do see the signs of renewal we won't devote convergent energy to consolidate the renewal into a stronger structure. Because all movements have to take on structure. I think of our system of colleges, for example. Quakers are starting a whole bunch of colleges…they have done a lot but some of it is divergent energy, in respect to Friends that is. Maybe we need to have some convergent energy, for example, with ESR and the other Quaker schools—Houston, Azusa, George Fox.

~

My greatest concern is that we have the courage to hold on to our traditional beliefs in a world that is changing and not feel that we have to throw out the old to embrace the new, but to respect what we have and to find how that works in the world today. [Our traditional beliefs include] the respect without a thought for every individual, the Light within, the traditional corporate worship, and seeking God's leading in our lives.

~

…the graying of Quakers. There are many long-time Friends who are really practiced in practice, and it makes a real difference to have them in Meetings because as we lose them for reasons of moving or whatever, that really makes a difference to the quality of what goes on in Meeting and the quality of the Meeting. That's probably my deepest concern.

~

My greatest concern is—let me be specific with respect to different kinds of Friends—liberal Friends becoming desiccated and dry and out of the Light, and loss of charisma and loss of energy. For Evangelical Friends the dangers are different, perhaps. I can't speak as well about those. Perhaps a danger would be dogma and exclusion. So it's a concern that growing so far apart that we lose the center.

~

My greatest concern is that I'm not sure that if you gathered 10 Friends from across the country, all of them could clearly state what the Religious Society of Friends stands for that would make sense to someone who is seeking.

~

We often want to be nice over being truthful. As a Society, and maybe this applies more to liberal Friends, we actually avoid conflict within our community. We may be very good at going out and being peacekeepers in other environments, but in our own home in a way we want a kind of peace or unity when there isn't and we bury our differences and say we'll make nice. That's a very dangerous attitude for us to have and it doesn't create a healthy culture.

~

Our most serious deficiency is a glaring scarcity of trained and active Quaker thinkers and scholars. By this I do not mean Friends of intellectual achievement; we have plenty such. Rather, I mean scholars and thinkers whose main subject is Quakerism, in its various aspects.

~

My greatest concern is that diversity is pulling us further apart. Some Friends are becoming more fundamentalist and some Friends see no relevance of the Bible and the teachings of Jesus. Those would be the extremes that I see.

~

Strengths and hopes
I'm optimistic. It's an exciting time to be a Friend. The Quaker message is important to the spectrum. I hope it's still us holding up that color.

~

I'm a member of an unprogrammed Meeting in Pacific Yearly Meeting. I see the following strengths in my particular part of Quakerism:

1) We have a strong sense of social mission (peace, justice, caring) grounded in the belief that we are all the creation of the Lord and therefore sacred.
2) We are aggressively seeking to fulfill those missions.
3) We have a gifted and deeply spiritual core group. I would not describe them so much as leaders as I would moral examples and mystics. Many are older women who possess great knowledge of families, community, and personal relationships.

4) We seem to project an image in the community greater than our
   numbers would warrant. The Quaker *brand* on everything from
   long-term care institutions to positions on the death penalty carries
   a connotation (justified or not) of integrity.

~

The greatest strength of the Religious Society of Friends now is the
people. There is just something special about people who are Friends
or who join Friends.

~

At the recent Annual Meeting of Friends World Committee, I spent
a good bit of time talking with the people that are spinning off Right
Sharing of World Resources from Friends World Committee. They're
in a difficult situation. They're a tiny, tiny group of people, of Friends,
with small resources, but what they're doing, I expect Friends will look
at this and give it as much weight as some big, well-known, successful,
well-funded operation, because what they're doing is trying very hard
and very sincerely to get at the spiritual root of that work. They're talking now about quietly and gently trying to labor with Friends all over
North America about what is it about the material wealth that we live
with that gets in the way of their relationship with God. Friends will
look at that and listen and respect it…first of all respect it, and that's
I think a real strength that we have.

~

One of the strengths that I have always experienced in being among
Quakers is the continual tension between individuality and community,
between local and national/international. Quakers seem to have a very
unique concern to balance diverse priorities, which is very difficult to
do. As I attend the Evanston Meeting for Worship each Sunday morning
and share in the community life, I'm constantly impressed with the
process of search. Not that we are achieving great achievements, but
we are making small steps.

   I don't think there's anything the matter with working behind the
scenes. It's a very important way to be true to our values. This is not to
say that we should lapse into self-righteousness just because we're taking
small steps, but the balance of the large scene and the small scene, the
balancing of the individual and the group is a very, very difficult one,
and we are living in an age of such rapid change and high technology.
There's no way we can keep from being caught up in the fragmentation
of stimuli that come into our lives, from our children, our grandchildren,

our friends, our community, our mechanical devices. It's a challenge to keep focused on our true values. I just feel that Quakers are doing a very good job, the ones I know, of balancing all these pressures and keeping on working, not giving up.

~

One of our greatest strengths is that we are concerned about our weaknesses. There are cycles, if we can be philosophical about this or Arnold Toynbee or whatever about this. I guess you can't expect us to be at the forefront at all times. There are quiet periods and then there are very active periods. I would be very concerned if all of a sudden Quakers decided that they had to go and market themselves. I think that we are concerned about what we are doing and where we are, and queries are a very important part of Quakerism.

~

Humility would be very valuable in the coming years.

~

a) Its willingness to be unconventional as one of the results of a belief in continuing revelation;
b) as an advocate for justice and empathetic understanding of oppressed peoples;
c) its daring to witness, in a humble spirit, to persons wielding power (political and ecclesiastic).

~

[Our strengths]: Heritage, regarding social problems; bringing a fresh perspective of the Christ Spirit. Also, women's issues, freedom of religion, abolition of slavery, prison reform. And women in ministry, peace testimony, corporate discernment, integrity in decision making. Our theology is also a strength—how we look at the Word. It's the Bible, Christ's living Word. The Holy Spirit is an acting agent, fresh.

~

…we are strongest when we don't fall into that, when we form coalitions and work with other groups, and it's a strength and a challenge of unprogrammed Friends that we have a lot of people who come from other traditions to unprogrammed Friends because it's welcoming to a variety of viewpoints. It is one of our strengths but it is also a potential challenge, or very definitely a challenge, of finding that balance between working with other people and being clear about your own vision.

~

I would postulate that the main strength of Quakerism lies in our testimonies and processes providing the tools to address the major issues of our day. What are these major issues? Though every individual has his or her own take on this, there is perhaps some agreement that the issues stem from causes such as the lack of caring and supportive community for much of society, social and economic inequality worldwide, ignorance about the means and value of peaceful conflict resolution, and the complexity of modern life which neither makes time for nor holds as a priority a mindful relationship with God and creation. This formulation of the issues and others such as Social Security reform, the war on drugs, the crisis in public education, and Serbian belligerence, all can be addressed by our Quaker emphasis on community, equality, peace, simplicity, and integrity.

~

There's a lot of yearning for us to be much more than we are now, and ESR is a key to that. I hope we can recover some of that energy for vision and change.

~

Over the years I have been impressed with the fact that wherever I have gone in Quakerism I have always found some sense of community. Not among the whole group of a different church or Meeting, but there have always been some who felt, as my mother used to say, like a Quaker. And one could find that in Northwest Yearly Meeting, Indiana Yearly Meeting or our own Evangelical Friends Church of the Eastern Region from which we separated here in Ohio long ago. Usually there is a sense of awareness of the tradition that reaches far back, but it's also a feeling that you can sense with these people…

~

It continues to excite me that whether we are talking to a programmed or unprogrammed Friend, there are those who recognize that it's not the form but the inward reality that counts. And it's not the words, although words are important, there is something beneath and beyond words. That's why I have always considered myself a translator. So that's where I'm hopeful.

~

I believe that the focal strength of our Religious Society is the character of its people. Specifically, I cite tenacity, integrity, and the pursuit of truth. Another strength is our work in social issues—peace and pacifism, justice issues, civil rights, equality, and working for the right to life of unborn children. Spiritual issues are another strength—we have a contemplative orientation and a Christocentric theology. Finally we have strength in our heritage, 350 years of progressive achievement.

~

Consensus is *not* our method—*unity* is!! The difference between individuals and corporations: We are trying to have a *corporate* sense of the Spirit.

~

Widespread understanding that our challenges are *spiritual* challenges at root.

~

There's a growing group of what John Punshon called "centrists" who are willing to do the work it takes to bring people together. ESR has the potential for doing more.

~

Can we through Quakerism, create the means to let go of our fears by replacing them with the security of love?

~

I guess I'm pretty optimistic generally. It has seemed to me, perhaps because I have spent most of my time in my own Meetings among liberal Friends, that the individualistic aridity is being challenged by a real spiritual hunger that is being met in ways that are consistent with Quaker tradition. There are things that have contributed to bringing Friends some strength. When we—no matter what part of the traditions we come from—work together, we always do better and come closer to being comfortable with one another. For example, the sanctuary movement was a good illustration of that. Friends across the country, from various traditions, were helping with that. I don't expect that the problems that I described, that I see, are going to be easily resolved, but there is movement and so I'm optimistic. I think that we still have a valuable witness for the world.

~

Quaker higher education introduces a lot of people to Quakerism who later on become convinced Friends and become some of our most valuable members. My wife is a case in point. She went off to Earlham a good American Baptist and came out a good Quaker. That just happens over and over again because Friends, in spite of all our foibles and short-coming and failures, still have a tremendous amount to offer the world.

~

It's vital that we keep our connection with the roots of Quakerism as Christian.

~

Let's hope that as we go on we all get clearer on what God's will is for us and we are all willing to change.

~

I wouldn't call it a renewal yet but I see things happening in our own [Northwest] Yearly Meeting, I see things happening across the country. I see things happening that are very encouraging.

~

I treasure the experience of how the Holy Spirit can be released in a group of people; theological vents don't matter next to that.

~

Our strength is our weakness: The sense of individual responsibility to be obedient to God's will. We take on personal responsibility for peace-making and social justice, care for the poor, etc. We're not many people, but we do an amazing amount. People are drawn to us because of that; they want to join with it.

~

Open to the Holy Spirit, not bound by rituals, most Friends churches are solid theologically.

~

I'm a history teacher and so I studied a number of American history text books used by high schools and colleges. My methodology was simply to find out how many mentions there were of various denominations. The Quakers come out very, very high on that scale in terms of positive mentions. On the other hand, if the study were made at the time or just before certain events occurred, it would be very low. In other words, we were very unpopular in society at the time that these things occurred. Yet we do reap a good reputation after the fact.

~

Challenges and fears

The challenge of the Religious Society of Friends, as always, is to live a life grounded in God's love, mercy, and forgiveness. Our strengths shine when we take the time to wait upon the Lord using our skills and gifts to discern and implement God's will.

~

One of the challenges facing Friends today is to recognize that we cannot duplicate the original Quaker story. New occasions do teach new duties. We can, however, seek to better understand the process by which our forebears became an incendiary fellowship. Before they sought to transform the world, they were themselves transformed. That was their strength and today it is our challenge. The Yearly Meeting, the local Meeting, ESR and its faculty together must address the issue of transformation, assessing the extent to which the lives of those involved at these levels are themselves transformed. Leadership identification, encouragement, and equipping for ministry involves more than an academic exercise. Even as Cambridge and Oxford cannot make a minister, neither can ESR. Nevertheless, the local Meeting, the Yearly Meeting and ESR are all essential components in the process of calling forth and nurturing leaders who are indeed new creatures in Christ Jesus.

~

It doesn't matter about what we know about Christ. It doesn't matter about hearing the Lord ourselves. It doesn't matter about the power to transform or to be transformed, we're not connecting. I guess that's a fear, and at the same time I feel a sense of wanting to listen more closely to the Lord to see if there is something He is trying to tell me, to tell us, about how we connect better, how we get out there.

That's a story that could be repeated over and over again, about six churches sitting around Skid Row, and it not having dawned on anybody how to connect with those people and somebody coming from Kansas to do it.

~

Planting new churches, attracting new attenders and members, remaining scripturally sound in all Friends Meetings.

~

1) resisting imitating popular religiosity which often confuses current cultural values with the Christian gospel and minimizes the distinctives of Quakerism;
2) excessive individualism that is wary of accepting responsibility toward the corporate body's (Meeting's) spiritual maturity and experience;
3) the fading hope to be an effective movement for change.

~

Weakness: Our vision of what Christ asks of us is too limited. We have settled for individualistic religion. We should bring more in and we should show what it really means to be followers of Christ, hurting with the hurting of the world.

~

The way I like to express it is that in being committed to conflict resolution, we often find ourselves avoiding conflict.

~

I spent 31 years serving five different Meetings and in each one I was privileged to work with wonderful people who were deeply committed and gave loyal service in various leadership roles. What impresses me however, as I reflect on those years, is to realize how much of the energy of a local congregation is expended on keeping the organizational machinery running.

The focus is largely introvert and that defines, in many cases, the unacknowledged reasons for Meeting existence: self-perpetuation and survival. This has been an underlying theme for the last half-century. Yet, the need for the Quaker testimonies is as great today as it was in the seventeenth century. The world is impoverished, and is in a sense dying, for lack of community, quality, harmony, integrity, and compassion, those qualities of social relations which Friends perceived as avenues for both being faithful to the gospel and for transforming society.

Likewise, the broad spectrum of Christian traditions needs the witness of the Friends' emphasis on simplicity in worship, on the ultimate value of the individual, and on peace and reconciliation. In our diverse and fragmented condition, however, contemporary Quakerism hardly makes a credible witness to these testimonies. Thus their power and influence, both within the Quaker family and in society, is largely dissipated.

~

ESR did consultations in connection with Quaker Hill Conference Center on worship and membership and service. That was quite fruitful though it did not directly engage current students very much. Frankly, I despair of the effort among Friends to think that we are all somehow going to be a big happy family and draw closer to each other.

~

The Quaker label needs some thought. It is sometimes put on institutions with little connection to our faith or practice. How can we nourish the worship groups?

~

What I notice in the Meeting that I pastor is that Friends sometimes have a sense of low self-esteem because we used to be this great movement and we're now just limping along and trying to keep ourselves afloat. The death of the movement will be sectarianism that says unless you know our jargon, we'll let you be here but we won't let you be fully involved and have influence in who we are as a movement. Sometimes faith and practice get elevated above Christ.

~

We live a bit more on our heritage without trying to go on and do more about it as a Society in general.

~

A challenge that has plagued us since George Fox is the temptation to be who we are not. In so many ways we have bent to be like the church and culture around us. We want to accommodate everyone and at times this rings as shallow or untrue. Another challenge is ingrownness. In many areas where Quakers have been for generations, our Meetings are known more for the families who attend there than for the ministry they generate. Finally, I believe a principal challenge facing Friends is an old one—the Hicksite Separation of 1828. To my mind, that breach has never healed and has marked the beginning of a slow decline in the Society of Friends.

~

I believe the most significant challenge is essentially to revitalize our own religious community and to grow again. We have been shrinking in numbers and influence for a long time and I believe that's a direct function of the loss of our spiritual center. We've been, like most religious groups, co-opted by our surrounding culture and absent a real commitment to that spiritual center and to living out of that center. I think we are not a real vital religious community.

~

We've lost the balance of *accepting* other people's journeys compared to *challenging* their journeys.

~

ESR has done pretty well, frankly, at being Christ-centered. One of the ways that Quakers would get along together at these conferences is that they kind of agree to lie to each other and accept fuzz words, so courtesy is well served but the Quaker integrity sometimes is not.

~

There are so many things that Friends are reticent to speak to, but need to speak to, because we don't know who we are anymore; we don't know what we all think about because we can't openly talk.

~

A lost generation of elders. Many of our elders never took on the role of "eldering" in this current crop, so younger ones have taken over.

~

It goes deeper than an identity issue; I think we have failed to provide the kind of process for decision making as a whole that people need in order to conduct their lives. We go to default positions so often that the real issues in our daily lives are not addressed in the meetinghouse.

~

Driving to a recent conference at Earlham, I saw on highway 40 a sign to ESR. But there was no sign at all for ESR as I came into Richmond— though there was a big sign for Bethany. That's so Quaker-like. The Quaker tradition seems one of diffidence, unwillingness to promote ourselves. I tease about our being the *Secret Society of Friends.* We'd love to have more people—but we don't understand that they need to know where we are. Sometimes you can't even find a Meeting's address in the phone book.

~

Well, it may be because I'm feeling under the weather or it may be just that I'm acrimonious by nature but I think truth to tell—at least the truth I have to tell—is that there are precious few strengths in the Society of Friends these days, that the pastoral branch has become very mainline Protestant, hard to distinguish, and liberal Friends are all over the map. Inasmuch as we do have strengths, it has to do with the fact that we have a vital, maybe unique, way of experiencing the divine. But even that, as a theological liberal you can read any number of liberal theologians, some of whom are Quakers, so I'm not sure right this minute that we have very many strengths, and quite frankly I'm pessimistic about the future of the Society of Friends.

~

…there is a way to be true to historic Quakerism and to have a strong Christian theology and service emphasis and evangelism emphasis. There is a vision awaiting our action that we need to discuss and grapple with and move toward, and not be defeated by smallness or discouragement.

~

I see one of the strengths of the Religious Society of Friends as being a conscience. As issues arise, as conflicts arise, the Religious Society of Friends steps in saying, "Excuse me, but that is not an appropriate thing to do to the human world." One of our challenges is in fact to continue doing that and being a strong voice as social justice issues arise and, in particular, in the corporate world where corporations are concerned about doing what they can to make the most profits.

~

My biggest corporate fear is that just at the time when our culture needs Friends' message about our core spirituality the most, we'll abandon it for some other more attractive way of being. That scares me. Maybe I'm an alarmist but it seems to me that most of what I hold so dear as God's call to us is just slowly eroding out between my fingers and there is nothing I can do about it. It gets sometimes overwhelmingly discouraging to me because I believe so strongly that that is how God has called us to live and to worship, and that there are so many other churches that do those other things. Why can't we just be ourselves and be obedient? My fear is God will abandon us because God has called us to something and we are reneging on the deal in favor of some popular movement. So that scares me.

~

The main challenges are three-fold:

1) The first is to articulate a Quaker response to the major issues of our day. Though we have paid ample lip service to testimonies, our active reply to these as a faith community has often been minimal. We may speak of community, and have strong mutual feelings of support and friendship within our Meetings and churches, but we have few examples of deep community as exhibited by the early Christian church or the first couple of generations of Friends. We talk about peace, but very few of us withhold our war taxes. We speak of simplicity, but few of us do not feel the stress of consumerism during Christmas holidays. We have many important and ongoing conversations about the implications of our testimonies on our lives, and we have individual Friends here and there who have stepped forward to implement aspects of their beliefs on a day-to-day basis, but we do not know where our "movement" is going, and we even have very little dialogue about a relationship to God in the fullness (that is, all sides) of our lives which, ostensibly, is the point of our faith—as it is with every religion…

2) The second challenge facing Quakers springs from the first. Once we're able to express more clearly where we'd like to be and articulate what the most troubling inconsistencies in our lives are, we must work on developing the bridges Friends will need in order to cross from where they are to where they would like to be…

3) The third challenge facing Quakerism is awakening among us both courage to challenge the *status quo* and faith in the understanding that the Kingdom/ Commonwealth of God truly is at hand. This will not be easy, as we have bought into the *status quo* for so long. We need some catalyst to rouse us into action. That catalyst could be a new vision of leadership.

~

What's good about Friends is what's bad about Friends.

~

There are often things that Friends pat themselves on the back about, and these things are strengths like our commitment to social justice, equality, and integrity and historically how that was witnessed to in many ways in the history of the United States and Europe and elsewhere in the world. One of our challenges is continuing to live in that Light in the face of times when there seems to be less agreement about where that Light needs to shine.

I see disunity as a challenge as well. Our religious society is very diverse and it's a fairly popular thing these days to say that diversity is a good thing, that there's unity in diversity, but I'm not exactly sure what that means for the Society of Friends. I think that can be really debilitating and divisive. Far too often we find ourselves divided when we need to continue to be engaged with that challenge, which is not an easy thing. It's a spiritual issue. It's part of the Lamb's War, to use a good old Quaker chestnut.

~

The challenge is continuing to be viable; we're losing ground. The Lutherans keep telling us: We *need* you! Stay!

~

In an effort to counter the erosion of the Quaker vision, Quaker historians produced a steady flow of books setting forth the essentials of the Quaker message and I was enamored with the ideals of the movement. Within a few years working within the context of a local Meeting, I began to discover the discrepancy between the ideal and the real, and to see the vast distance between what I, as a convert, understood the Quaker vision to be and how it was acted out in grassroots Quaker communities.

This bit of biography is by way of my commenting on the strengths and challenges of the Religious Society of Friends. On the one hand, the Quaker vision and the way that vision has been embodied by the giants of the movement through the centuries relates a powerful story. On the other hand, the way we transmit that story and the way we embody it in the local Meeting leave a great deal to be desired. We need to acquire new skills in communication and nurture.

~

Quaker *culture* precludes us from doing some of the most important things, like evangelism or outreach, which the culture says we don't do but the *faith* says you definitely do.

~

I think of the Great Commission. I really do believe that is our mission, and our particular understanding of that Great Commission is that the baptizing that we're to do is to immerse people in the knowledge of God…But I don't think we have hope of doing that unless we are immersed in God ourselves and I'm aware of the tension. I see it in my own life. I see it in this congregation. I see it in Friends in other places. Some of us do a good job of trying to immerse ourselves in God, and some of us think we do a good job of trying to tell other people how to be immersed in God. It's probably important to try to hold those two together.

It is a challenge for the movement to be called Friends or Quakers to try to do both of those things: To really, ourselves know God, but also to engage the culture, to get out there and try to point people to Christ.

~

We have to begin to learn to use words. We're frightened of it. We *like* our smallness. It's a psychological desire *not* to grow for fear of getting impersonal.

~

I believe our conventional Friends churches will wither because they're not differentiated enough. We can't out-Meth the Methodists. Our genius is prophetic genius.

~

Any living faith is going to have a part of it that scares people. Getting too comfortable is a danger that I see in a lot of our Meetings.

~

When I was in the Midwest I did lots of preaching and pastoring small churches all over the Midwest. Most of these churches to the outward eye were deader then a doornail. They were small. I discovered an incredible secret in almost every one of those, and it wasn't their sin—they all knew their sins, small towns all know their sins. It's all their secrets about what God had done. They would tell me as an outsider. They would tell me that their marriage had been healed, or that their son had been healed, or that at this job they had this answer to prayer but they refused to tell God's story to one another. They didn't have any forum for being authentic with one another. Consequently it feels like we are the most selfish people on the face of the earth because it's like having the cure for cancer and refusing to tell anybody about it.

~

Growth

One important thing is not just church growth—how we make ends meet and that kind of thing—but the spiritual core of Quaker experience, the conviction that God changes people's lives. My belief against church growth "experts," is that the most significant factor in a Meeting's health and growth is its spiritual tone: Are people being *changed* by God in the Meeting for Worship and during the week? That's the most pressing question for Quakers in the world. And that has always been Quakers' strength.

~

When I hear about an unprogrammed Meeting growing because people come into that Meeting and experience a sense of a living Christ in their midst, that is very encouraging to me. I know some of the very hard decisions that leadership in the Friends United Meeting is taking both domestically and internationally. They've had some very hard things to do and to face, and I see them acting with integrity and with vision, and compassion, and that encourages me. I see some things that are happening at ESR that encourage me. While I agree with what has been said about some of us letting things slip through our fingers, I also see another trend, the opposite trend of people discovering in fresh ways what our people have known.

~

When it comes to unprogrammed Quakerism in the United States, I am an optimist. I believe this group is vital and growing, both spiritually and materially. Not everywhere and always, of course, and not unambiguously, but overall.

~

There are a lot of small Meetings that would be economically challenged to sustain pastors, no doubt. Many of those Meetings, if they had effective leadership, could grow. Some are in situations where everybody is struggling. There are places I know in Western Kansas where Methodists and all other kinds of folks are struggling with small Meetings, where towns are getting emptied out...

So I have kind of a double perception. One is that the small Meetings need strong leadership and folks ought to be thinking about how we prepare people to serve in those places and perhaps even how to envision a life of ministry in which people can serve in places like that. I don't think that any of us have done a very good job with this yet, frankly, among Friends. Our initial notion of free gospel ministry... wasn't really a commitment to poverty...but I discover now and again there are some folks who still believe in the free gospel ministry.

Anyway, people don't go into ministry so that it would be lucrative but, of course, they have to be able to support their families. Maybe there are models of ministry that need to be explored, and I would like ESR to be a place where some good, creative think-tanking could be done, drawing people together to think about those issues, because theologically we have the resources to think creatively about that in ways that maybe some other groups don't.

~

1) We seem to be holding our own (and even growing a bit) in numbers after years of decline. This is clearer if one adds regular attenders to active members of Meetings.
2) In the west, many new worship groups have emerged.

~

Speaking from an institutional perspective, all the Quaker schools have a 51% requirement for Quaker membership on their boards. There are 45 Quaker schools in the Philadelphia region and they can't find Quakers adequately thoughtful and trained and prepared to served on their boards. Many of them are talking about giving up the 51% requirement. They can't survive. So there are a lot of institutions depending on the thriving of the Society of Friends.

~

…[there are] people who tell us what is Quaker and what is not. For example, it's not Quaker to advertise the Society of Friends and recruit members. Who told them that? It's false.

~

If we're ever going to address the decline in membership or the decline in attendance, the fact is we're losing people right and left to the more— for want of a better term—sexy churches, and my home Meeting is a case in point.

There were 150 in average attendance when I was growing up and about 35 now. Part of that is the sociology of small rural Meetings but one of the major reasons is that folk now have their satellite TVs, their radios, they travel more, and they are seeing other forms of Christianity on TV or visiting other churches. There see these folk with all this joyous worship and off-the-wall music, all this spontaneous spirituality, and thousands of members and they watch this on TV and see First Church Atlanta or Coral Gables, Kennedy, Falwell, Robertson, Stanley, and then come back to their Meetings and say: What are we missing?

Quakers, without a deep appreciation of their distinctives and what they have to offer, are never going to compete with the Baptists down the road at the music game, or the sacraments game, or the programs game. Yet I think there is a crying need out there for exactly what Friends do have to offer.

~

In the early days of Quakerism, 652 leaders were not made, they were CALLED OF GOD and for the first period in our history there were "added to the Church daily such as should be saved"…

~

Each group has to listen, to hear the other group. That's the future. If so, we have potential for revival. Now, we have a church that's aging— except among liberal Friends, who have no basis for what they believe. Revival would mean the Religious Society of Friends [would become] active, alive, doing things, so people won't say, "I thought they were all dead." Some people do ask if Quakers still exist.

~

History *could* be an incredible strength if we'd let it energize us! Continuing revelation is so powerful. We *could* be dynamic and growing.

~

We are losing members because they are not being nurtured. And we are attracting people who have a singular vision of things. They may be there just because they want to have same sex rights or just because they want a feminist interest, or just because of the peace testimony, and they seem not interested in the broader understanding of the Society of Friends as a religious society.

~

Membership

I suspect most Quaker Meetings and churches have the problem of people who remain members but are not active, even if they are half a world away or half a continent away. We need to discover much better ways of keeping in touch with people and making sure that they really are committed to what the Meeting generally stands for…we need to develop an administrative query that will get each Meeting to answer every year what they are doing to nurture children who are associate members up to the age of 25, then what they are doing to help them reach a decision by the age of 25 whether or not they want to remain members.

~

I had reckoned without friends who were Quakers—friends who thought I should be part of the church. These mentors changed the direction of my life's course. When I voiced my intellectual doubts about some events recorded in the Bible, I learned that many modern men and women had traveled this road ahead of me and had arrived at a faith in God which did not include an idolatrous attachment to a book which recorded mankind's checkered response to God. I learned that one need not take leave of one's critical faculties to be a Christian. My mentor Friends convinced me the Quaker faith has everything to do with fashioning one's life according to the precepts of Jesus—not in believing impossible things about his birth, death, and resurrection.

~

One of the strengths of the Society, one of its testimonies is *community*. The readiness with which that community gets fragmented by geography, by culture, by language, by articles of belief, is a serious weakness in my view. I don't mind disagreeing with other Friends as long as we recognize that we are in the same community and that if we fully understood what God's purposes were, we would be God.

So we are limited. We human beings have a very minor understanding of what the purposes of the divine are, but one of them has been for us to be in community. Among liberal Friends the emphasis in recent decades has been on an individuality that I think is extreme. Friends have always wished to affirm other people's experiences, but within the context of the community the extreme discipline of the 19th century taught us the danger of the narrowness. There was a woman who applied for a liberal Friends Meeting who said that she wanted to join Friends because they didn't have to believe anything. I hope she misspoke, but there are those who, damaged in other churches, still want a religious home and come opposed to anything that smacks of authority. The community must have some authority. There has to be accountability to the community and mutual nourishment within the community. I regard that as one of the present dangers and weaknesses.

~

So many people come to us who have limited backgrounds in spiritual life. They are seekers, they are tourists, pilgrims perhaps. We need to find ways to draw them into the community so that they actually become owners of it rather than just drop-in visitors.

~

I have a concern that there is a wide variety of types of Quakers, but I think this stems from the fact that our individual Meetings have different requirements that we ask people to go through before they become Friends. Some people bring them in just when they say they would like to join the Meeting, and they say, "Great, you're a member." Our Meeting has new members go through a Quakerism 101 course, and we have clearness committee for sometimes several months, and yet we're not as strict as some other Meetings are. So we get all these people into Quaker organizations making our Quaker decisions at Business Meetings.

This is something that is a challenge because we have people coming from different degrees of Quakerness or even knowledge of Quaker history and priorities making decisions that are for the whole group. Not that I would want any big outline…I know FUM tried to get a Quaker creed one time and it went flat, but I think we need some guidelines.

~

I think in part leadership has to do with developing Friends who are really good at Quaker practice. A part of what makes for the distinctive history of Friends was how the social activities were rooted in faith and practice, and with the growth of people coming into the Meeting, I'm concerned that we're not doing a good enough job of teaching and modeling for them good practice.

That's as important for the adults, the new members, the continuing members, and the children. That's part of the issue about who's participating in the decision making in the name of Friends. I have lots of faith in Quaker practice, and when decisions rise out of that, then we can say that this was done by Friends in a way that we can't when it's not rising out of that kind of practice.

So, part of the way this relates to leadership is we really need to identify people who have gifts for practice and to really nurture and develop that so that we are really good at worship and conducting business and clerking and discernment and all the other things. That made for a distinctive Quaker history, and probably my deepest concern is that we are losing that. That's the greatest weakness that we have.

~

Diversity

In the east coast among liberal Friends, there are Meetings that seem to be more lively and growing and risk-taking than others, for example within Baltimore Yearly Meeting there's growth and new Meetings are being developed. Some city Meetings are becoming more racially diverse but not enough. In some areas, I think we're lazy and excuse ourselves by saying that our kind of worship doesn't appeal to African Americans, for example. We reflect the comfortable middle class society of which we are a part and it's easier to find reasons why it's awkward or difficult to change than to think carefully about how we can change. This is an area where the Quaker colleges and schools have done better than the Society of Friends.

~

While we have stabilized our numbers, we have not managed to grow. In California, where this year European Americans now are a minority group like the rest, the Religious Society of Friends continues to fail in attracting those of other races and ethnicities. We also seem to be a haven for intellectuals and the upper classes. Are our Meetings becoming as elitist as many of our schools and colleges? Is our faith welcoming to those who work with their hands, who don't have college degrees or who work in business?

~

We have a number of people who really feel that the Quaker voice or the voice that they believe is Quaker, the Quaker distinctive, needs to be emphasized in the broader world, in the political world. Not in the same way as the Christian Coalition or in terms of that kind of politics, but in terms of talking for peace, talking for justice, standing up and saying this is what we believe.

People from the fringe…this tends to be their issue rather than how many Christians are we making in the Third World? How is our government using the money? What are the policies that can change people's lives in a positive way? On the other hand, our Meeting also has had a number of people, in a kind of odd way, become connected with native peoples in different parts of the world, and have begun making connections and talking about native issues. As a result, the minority in this area is Native Americans, and so we have had some Native Americans come in and begin to talk about the issues for Native Americans and the broader country.

~

Basically in the last 50 years, unprogrammed Friends, due to the influence of historical factors as much as anything else, have bought in lock, stock, and barrel to a white, liberal, educated, middle-class culture, that has never reexamined itself and never adjusted to the realities of life—and they love preserving it. For example, there's no mistake why we don't have black members. It has absolutely nothing to do with anything but that protective white middle-class culture…It reflects the narrowness of our culture and our constituency.

~

Quakers aren't really racially diverse, but theologically we're all over the map.

~

Everett Catell said that the church always grows at the Cambrian layer, which means that you have to have the steady trunk to hold the thing up, but the growth occurs at the Cambrian layer. The Cambrian layer is in Guatemala or in Kenya or in Rwanda, wherever there have been more Quaker martyrs. There have been more Quaker martyrs in this century in Africa then there ever were in England in the 17th century.

How do we get [convergent energy for growth]? We may have to be willing to be the recipients of some of the energy from elsewhere because the Friends Church is now south of the equator and is no longer predominately Anglo European. It's Latino and African. I have been present at world conferences, Friends World Conferences, where the impact of a Guatemalan Friends pastor upon the skeptical European Quaker was profound.

Here was this woman coming with the radiance of Christ and speaking of the ministry that she was engaged in, and here were these hundred Quakers struggling to preserve Quaker identity without being Christian. My concern is that we will miss what God's already doing among us and won't harness that energy in some convergent way so that we feel a sense of being a people around the world. I would think ESR would want to serve as the focal point for providing that convergence.

~

One of the best signs of hope that I know of is what's happened down at the Cape Junction. A Friends Meeting was started in an area of 70% unemployment with people who have been on drugs and discouraged and all the symptoms that go along with unemployment. Jesus said the poor have the gospel preached to them, and maybe we have to counter the upward social mobility that always occurs in any religious movement by going again to the poor. It may be that our institutions have to do what they did when they were poor.

They sent out gospel teams to down-and-outers and poor people, to little school buildings to gather in Sunday School kids who were poor. I mean, who am I to say, when we live in an upscale community, where my lock's worth more than my house is…We've raised up a number of professors and educators but we have not raised up evangelists, who tend to have less timidity than professors and aren't afraid to tackle somebody in an evangelistic way and preach the gospel to them and reach across. If we're going to be content with the top of the pyramid of the educated people, then our schools will fail and up will start again some Bible training centers which will minister to the down-and-outers or the poor.

So how to do that with people who have gradually made the upward spiral is not easy. But our institutions have to face that and I think they can.

~

At the 1977 conference in the round table in Wichita, it was very revealing that some Friends from Latin America said, "We have never heard about Quaker testimony. We have never been told about the peace testimony." Many of these groups in Latin America say they want to hear more about it.

But I also feel that we need to learn more from the Latin American groups. My concern in all of this, and I have expressed this to FWCC and other Quaker organizations, is that we come to these places—and I say we, because some of us feel that we in the North are seen as not so evangelical perhaps, but in the pastoral tradition and with a little bit of reserve—we need to learn a lot about what is happening in these countries. It is very important that we come to these places with an open mind and learn from another kind of Quakerism that has developed in these countries. It is very important. So we don't come only as the teachers. We come to learn also from them. That is terribly important.

The thing that unites more…it's our exponential faith more than those things that we have learned in theory. What it is there and in which ways Friends in Latin America and in any country live our faith on a daily basis and what can we share with each other. We have to learn a lot in that sense.

~

The pluralism and individualism of American society is now reflected in nearly every Friends Meeting. Diversity of experience and view-point tends to create conflict and Friends pastors and Meetings are ill-equipped to constructively resolve differences. Consequently, controversial and substantive issues tend to be avoided and each person is left to think as he or she chooses without benefit of shared insights and understandings. The homogeneity which prevailed when most existing Friends Meetings were established has vanished, and neither the Meetings nor their pastors usually have the skills to work through the tensions created by serious disagreements to the point of enabling a *beloved community* to emerge.

~

…accepting racial and theological diversity in recognition that different persons may be a potential source of spiritual insight and strength.

~

All of us need more openness…to emphasize more the pluralism and the pluralistic world that we live in and not worry about diversity as something to overcome rather than something to enrich our life. The difference is some people can be inclusive but on their own terms—if I can agree with you and you're okay, I include you, but it doesn't mean that I think you are equal.

~

Youth

Trust or the glue that holds this group together [Mid-America Yearly Meeting] would be our experience in Christ. Probably with other Friends, Christ is not the center or the glue that holds it together. It's other experiences. Some would be the work of Christ in the world, social action. It might be how to help people accomplish their own dreams, their goals, their aspirations. I'm reflecting on a group of youth that went from our church to a national conference of Friends, and the diversity that existed among that group of youth in terms of who Christ was, was really eye-opening to this local group of young people who attended the conference. I think we really struggle on who the person of Christ is.

~

I think that [the 17 to 25 or 30-year-olds are] the hardest group to put a handle on, just because the traditional pattern—and this is not particular to Quakers—across the scene of American religion is that's the stage at which people tend, even if they were comfortable with their upbringing, to walk away from their roots and explore. They are starting careers and they are starting families and they are doing all that stuff that often takes them out of active participation in religious life, at least in community religious life. They may have a very active spiritual search going but they are not being part of the community in that process.

Certainly, we have a number of younger people who are involved in our Young Friends program, including some college-age folks. I see some of those people in our Meetings, and I think they are more often than not in the spiritual search mode, which is to say that they are often not terribly active in the life of the Meeting in terms of service. They are just there on Sunday morning and looking to be part of worship and maybe making some connections with people they think can help them sort things out.

But it is fairly rare to find people in that age group who are active in service work, committee work, certainly in any kind of leadership role. The far greater concern from my point of view, both as an individual Friend and one running one of the largest Quaker organizations of this sort in the country, is the absence of people in the 30 to 45 age range from our ranks. They are often very active in the local Meetings, but because of life choices and constraints of time simply tend not to be active at all at the organizational level beyond the local congregation. That's a very serious challenge for us because we skew the choice of clergy…we have few persons in leadership roles who are in the age range where they are good models for people who are similar age.

~

At our high school camp in the summer, we have classes during the day where our teaching takes place. Then we set aside our evening for full group time that is used to have an evening speaker. We set that aside to be experiential worship with space for unprogrammed worship, but also space for worship elements that we do corporately that help create a sense of receptivity to the presence of Christ. So, in a way, it is kind of a semi-programmed Meeting because we program some things, but they are all geared towards helping us as a group become quiet and aware and sensitive to the presence of God. Those have been really moving experiences as the kids live together in community for a week but then have this major emphasis each day on coming before the presence of God as a community and listening and speaking out of that.

~

Quaker Life is a good forum and YouthQuake is an excellent forum. We have been involved here with some of the regional FWCC gatherings and that has been good. There has been some talk of trying to do a young adult age YouthQuake type experience and I think that would be great, but I don't know who's got the energy at this point, or time, to initiate something like that. Probably the best thing really is going to be personal relationships rather than trying to do some huge conference where everybody comes with their agenda and their preconceived ideas and defenses.

~

Parents, not just Quaker parents, are so involved in trying to pay the bills and meet the responsibilities that they don't have the time to spend with young people to teach them the basics—manners, ethics, values. To a certain extent, there can be a trend on the part of some parents to care more about what goes *into* their children than what comes out. They're very concerned with environmental issues, the clothes and fabrics they're wearing, the books they're reading, movies they're seeing, and not paying attention to listening to what is coming out of the child: What are the child's opinions? Is the child being considerate and thoughtful? Does the child have a sense of compassion? A sense of ethics? That seems to be lacking.

~

The way we have tried to train leadership in the past is through classroom experiences. The way I learned best, and perhaps the way we experience it here in this particular church, is to emphasize more the mentoring concept of leadership training where the academic aspect is part of it. Being on the front with someone else, or wrestling with life with someone else and having the opportunity to sit one with another, to me really is a leadership experience.

We have what we call the mentoring experience here in the local church with our youth. Last night they were together—we have four or five youths with one of our key leaders—and they spend at least one Sunday evening together, just talking about life and then trying to do something together. That to me, in today's culture and society, is a critical way of training leaders. In a way, that was part of our history as Friends. We had a *weighty* Quaker that we would be mentored by, but in some ways we've taken the CEO concept and have designed training events around top-down leadership.

~

…most of us grew up with Baby Boomer parents who rebelled against authorities, structures, and dogmas that were handed down. I think most of us then had the opposite experience because our parents would say, "Well, you have to find things out for yourself." My generation would say, "Well, tell me something about what you believe in" or "Tell me about this, tell me about that." Our parents would say, "You need to find that out for yourselves." So we didn't know what Quakerism was. We didn't get anything that we could relate to. I think our parents were afraid of indoctrinating us, and our sense was more that we're quite capable of making our own decisions, but we'd like to have something to start us off, to bounce our ideas off.

~

I think it's a difficult time in your life to be doing anything religious in general. There aren't very many people who are in my age group (18 to 25) who are active in some sort of spiritual community, and the few who are, are often fighting for identity enough that they're sort of reluctant to take on responsibility. Once you put all that aside, then I think it becomes a question of having the deep understanding of how one carries out being a Friend at an early age, because it's such a multiplicity of things that on some level it just takes a little bit of time to get used to what you do as a Quaker. Some people start that earlier. I was doing stuff in Junior Friends in a leadership capacity very early on. So I don't have a clear answer from a Young Friends perspective on leadership concerns. I think patience and willingness from elders to elder and to be a resource is very useful, and being persistent in reaching out to younger generations and telling them, "Yes, you do have a lot to offer. Here's what you have to offer. We would appreciate you participating." I have been reached out to in that manner.

~

YouthQuake has done more to cross that divide for the coming generation.

~

My impression of those Western Young Friends is that they do not drop in attendance and commitment as they enter their 20s. I'm amazed at that, but it seems that they have that solidarity, that peer group identification. I'm awed by that. I don't think it was true in Philadelphia in the Meeting. Maybe [they have] a little more concrete mission statement.

~

I think that most Junior Friends and Young Friends are leery of Christianity and of the label "Christianity." It takes quite a while to get past the label to get to the concepts and the beliefs, and to see that as being Christian instead of seeing Christianity as evangelism, and destroying cultures, and all of the bad things that Christianity often has associated with it. I think it just takes patience and the availability of the resources to think about that and to have people willing to talk openly with young Friends and junior Friends. It's an interesting puzzle.

~

The issues that kids are dealing with are issues of identity and meaning. Is there meaning to life, and how do we discover that and be a part of it, and who am I as person? I think those are pretty basic issues for youth anywhere. We have really chosen to tackle both of those issues by finding both identity and meaning in our relationship with Christ. And it is not a historical, creedal belief system but it's an active present reality that kids can encounter Christ in a very alive, active way today. That, therefore, then provides them with a sense of meaning, and a sense of personal identity, as they discover how Christ sees them and who Christ is in their life. That for me is one of the most exciting things. I get really excited when I see our kids experiencing Christ in an authentic way and when I hear them talking about encounters they have had with God, and ways that they have seen God in their everyday life, and ways that has given them direction.

~

I'm involved with the YouthQuake planning committee, which is a national triennial gathering of high school youths, and the committee is comprised of 16 people representing different Yearly Meetings from FUM, EFI, and FGC. We have some really dynamic conversations... in some ways that's our whole focus for YouthQuake, to try to bring those two poles together and help the kids experience the kind of unity of the early Quaker message. We're getting really positive kinds of energy from that and from kids who've experienced that over the last few years.

Northwest Yearly Meeting has a real unique relationship with New England Yearly Meeting because of YouthQuake...There has just been a real dynamic relationship there and an interplay between who we are (Christ-centered Quakers) and who they are as unprogrammed Friends and how we can share our faith experiences and really learn from one another. So that's been a really dynamic experience as well.

~

...that same child we were looking for a school for years ago went on the Quaker Youth Program five years ago. I have said to people this week from FWCC that was a pivotal experience for her in really solidifying her Quaker beliefs and her inclusion of all different brands of Friends and that's been a really lovely thing for us, that her connections with Friends have kept us involved. She has written for some information about ESR and the committee called us, so I visit with folks from ESR on occasion.

~

It's really feeling God moving in our lives in a significant way through spiritual formation and through an immediate experience of the presence of Christ. We wanted to make sure that we were expressing that to our kids and creating opportunities for them to encounter Christ in a similar way. So we have worked really hard to make sure that all of our programming contains training about how to experience God in your own life, but then it also contains experiential opportunities and time for the kids to really experience the presence of Christ and for them to be able to leave our events with an experience of that, but also with some tools for how they can continue to do that in their own lives.

~

In relation to Evanston Meeting, where I think we've had great success with children, young children, the concern from my perspective and I think other people at Evanston Meeting is what happens when the children become high school age? We have many children pre-high school but what happens at high school age? We're grappling with this problem right now.

~

As a former high school teacher and parent and grandparent of a whole bunch of teenagers, I do think this is a place where trained leadership, people who are very gifted at working with this age group is the key. I grew up in a church on the south side of Chicago where we were lucky to have just extremely good leadership for the high school group, and trips were planned—visits to the jail, visits to the inner city, visits here and there. There was always something. We took hosteling trips. I think this is a place where, if the Earlham School of Religion wants to have a sub-category of projects, Friends Meetings can really use some help.

~

High school to young adulthood is historically the time of the demographic drop in terms of attendance and commitment. It's also the critical answer to where the leaders come from. I know this is true personally because I probably wouldn't be an active member of the Religious Society of Friends today if I hadn't gotten involved with the Young Friends group of Baltimore Yearly Meeting where somehow, someone recognized that I might do a good job as clerk, which got me hooked.

It's of course flattering personally, but the chance to have had the leadership in that relatively non-threatening, friendly environment of a Young Friends group made me believe that the process of trying to come to a sense of the meeting works, and that when we quiet our hearts listening for God's spirit to try to come together in unity that miracle will happen. The opportunities for young people to have those kinds of leadership roles in small groups locally, in a relatively non-threatening environment, is very important. That's how we get people to believe that there is a future for the Society of Friends.

~

When I look around at a Meeting, I see a lot of gray-haired people, and I want to know, "What are we doing to attract the younger people into becoming Quakers?"

~

In the first 300 years, the Society of Friends attracted people who'd been through considerable Bible study (George Fox knew the Bible almost by heart). Now, in the past 50 years, youngsters don't have that kind of background. For Quakers to get the leadership it must have, we need to get leaders with a good background in what the Religious Society of Friends is all about, plus actual experience of spiritual life in one's own self.

~

I have been working with teenagers, watching them evolve, and watching myself evolve with them. One of my initial concerns about Quaker youth in unprogrammed Meetings was how deprived they were of basic knowledge about the Bible, about Quaker traditions.

When they hit puberty, they stopped getting any training whatever and all this kind of stuff that I think is really important. I was disturbed about this and frustrated. Because of working and doing a new service program, there wasn't much I could do other than occasionally mention that Barclay is a good person to read. I read the Bible and it's a good book, but there was no systematic training. It was just haphazard.

Now I'm watching some of those same teenagers go on to college and three of them have gone to Guilford. They are in a Quaker leadership program and I'm feeling really, really good about that. Another one of the teenagers has just started at Whittier and she is working with me on a book project. I'm feeling really good that she is finally getting some opportunities to learn about her Quaker faith. I have a feeling that there is a great untapped potential here among Western unprogrammed young people and a chance to set up some kind of program that won't be threatening. I don't think they would jump at the opportunity of taking a whole full-fledged program of theology or something. But maybe summer programs or something that eases them into it, to get them to have an opportunity to really read seriously when they are ready at the college level. I would love to see that.

~

We need to work together. George Fox has just had an association with Western Evangelical Seminary, so technically now with George Fox and Friends Center and Earlham there are three seminaries and I say we ought to work together.

One of the big things that has happened at Friends Center, is the Field Ed Program where students have to work 12 to 14 hours a week in a local church to get experience. Then they come back to the seminary and they dialogue about things that they learn, about the problems that they encounter. So when they go to ministry, they are somewhat prepared, more than if they are just students for three years and just centered upon book learning.

At Southwest Yearly Meeting, we are trying to challenge churches to be alert to young people who they feel are called to ministry. We just recently had a conference inviting young people of any age. They were hoping to have 30 or 40 people of all ages. It turned out they had over 120 and it was really very exciting. I wanted to come because the people that I admire within the Friends denomination are those who can speak across the lines, whether you come from programmed and unprogrammed or you are liberal or you are evangelical. We need to dialogue across the lines.

~

We have a lot of young people coming to us also seeking, and it's a fairly new experience for us…I mean new in that it's been just a couple years or so that there have been sizeable numbers. So it's too soon to tell what the long-term effect is going to be. At the moment what I sense is that the leadership is very much needed because the people who are coming, looking for something have energy, but energy and leadership are not the same.

~

We have a Junior High Samuel School and a Senior High Samuel School. They are weekend retreats where the elders of each local Meeting select one to two kids who they feel are spiritually sensitive and ready for the kind of experience that Samuel School offers and they send the kids to the retreat.

It's based on the story of Samuel in the Old Testament who heard the voice of God as a kid and built a lifestyle of listening for and hearing God and became a prophet for his nation. So we talk with these kids, both male and female, about how they can begin to hear God in their lives and we talk about hearing the voice of God through scripture and through the faith community of their local Meeting and through journaling and through solo experiences of being alone through meditation.

We take a whole weekend to talk about different ways to hear God and then give them some time to experience those things. We also ask the local Meeting for an adult who will serve as a mentor for six months after the retreat experience to follow up and help the kids bring that back into their daily life when they return home. So it's not just a mountain-high retreat experience that doesn't have any connection to their home.

~

Quakers today

Quakers are experiential—not theologizing—therefore it's hard to get clarity about these deep theological issues.

~

Question: What's your sense of where the Quakers are going?
Answer: I read our history and it makes my palms sweat. It makes such sense how those dear people had such a gift to interpret culture and to interpret Christ in culture. I long for that as a Quaker today. I want to know culture and I long for the revelation of how to allow the person of Christ to so radiate through my life, through our life as a community, that the kingdom of God is felt and we make a difference.

We've hit on a key thing here. In our Meetings, a lot of these things tend to happen—maybe it's true in other bodies—in waves and we just happen to have people who can work with young people, who are dedicated to working with young people in the Meeting and it clicks. Then when those people fade or lose energy, it falls off again.

…one thing that I've noticed with Quaker communities in this area, it seems we need to figure out a way to help each other out, to figure out how to connect these people [with interests in the same issues] among Meetings to channel that energy and to keep that energy going. As Meetings, we don't have that consistency and continual energy that we can give each other collectively. How do we do that and how do we nurture that in each other? How do we come together? I don't feel us filling these real strong connections. How can we feed off each other's energy…how can we help each other out?

~

Many of our most gifted spiritual models are older women. They often lack the resources for any type of extended training even if it is available. Can we do better by them and therefore for our Society? *(male Friend)*

~

I think Quakerism itself is facing a crisis as it goes into the 21st Century. Who is it? What is it? Where is it going? Why is it?

~

One of the things that happens all too often is that we see some of these great men in the Society of Friends and don't realize that the women are equally great. We have Douglas Steere but I would have rather studied under Dorothy…we have Kenneth Boulding, the economist, but I would have much rather studied sociology under Elise… *(male Friend)*

~

I'm personally really excited about what Christ-centered Quakerism can offer. I feel our society is at a point where people are looking for an authentic Christian witness that's not just about whether you get into heaven or not. It's about really impacting our society and our world with the message of Christ that involves non-violence, and efforts with poverty, and with systems that are evil because they are oppressive.

Quakers are one group that has struggled both with the inward and the outward journey, with the tension between social concern and transformation of a society, along with spiritual concern and transformation of the individual spiritually through Christ. One of the keys to the power and authority and impact of early Quakers on their society was that they held those two poles in balance. Here in the States we have each grabbed a pole and run to our extremes. So we have lost some of that vitality because we are holding on so strongly either to social action without Christ, or Christ without social action.

I feel that our society is just ripe for a real authentic and powerful mixing of those two poles again and Quakers offer the framework and history and language that can speak to that. There's definitely a hunger in our society for experiential spirituality that's not just about joining a club, but about really experiencing the movement of the Spirit. Again, that's a strength of Quakerism [that] comes through with our emphasis on programmed worship and Meetings for Business and experiential Christianity. Who we are historically has poised us uniquely to really speak to the needs of our world and our society, if we can only begin to come back to the balance of those two poles and be authentic in our expression of relationship with the living Christ.

~

I'm spending focused amounts of time really in the presence of God and trying to let that be my foundation. I have a friendship with somebody with a similar goal and we hold one another accountable to check in with each other and actually take an hour a week together for meditative prayer, just to make sure that we both have that accountability.

~

…as someone said we'd better not sit on our laurels or we're in danger of squashing them.

~

Our Meetings are inexperienced and reticent in outreach activities, seeming to fear looking like we are *selling* our faith in the manner of Jimmy Swaggert. How should our Meetings communicate to the outside world that our beliefs extend beyond good works and can provide spiritual fulfillment to more than a select few? I have spoken to many who think that we are extinct like the Shakers or insular like the Amish and Hutterites.

~

Do you ever wonder if we are not living up to what other people perceive Quakers as doing? I mean, for example, we've had a hate crime situation in Morgan Park, a high incidence of racial hate crimes, and it's interesting that although Friends are very small in number, other churches seem to expect that we will take the leadership in terms of standing up and saying this cannot happen. We have taken the leadership—the community seems to expect that, respect that, and turn to us. I'm just wondering if we are failing to live up to people's expectations.

~

What can the Friends peace testimony mean in the current world situation, in which the Cold War has ended, and dozens of smaller, hotter wars are breaking out, along with calls for the U.S. to intervene militarily to stop outbreaks of genocide?

~

We have a strong peace message—350 years—yet we can't work together.

~

We don't understand how well thought of we are.

~

There are lots of individual Friends who have made differences in ways they may never have been aware of with other individuals. They were completely anonymous in daily kinds of situations. That is part of Friends history, and that's still an important role that we have.

~

What's happened to us as Quakers is that we've let the organization do more than the organization was really designed ever to do: To put the emphasis on the organization's rather than on the individual's relationship with God and being led by God, which is driven by a need to fit in. It's part of our societal need for everybody to look the same, sound the same. I think it is driven by fear. Nobody wants to be out of the Christian center, for goodness sake, because then you might not actually be one…There is a lot of pressure on organizations to look the same, sound the same, to be appropriate, to be proper. I personally think that what it leads to is organizational stagnation.

Then we build efficient organizations with great committees and a kind of inner-focused family where we are okay, and there's something wrong with the rest of them. But the point is "the rest of them" are our sisters and brothers. As differently as they seem from us, we really need to be showing them how we love them. Whether that's Milosevic or other Meetings or non-Christians or whatever. As a pastor and as a person who feels really called to share the gospel, I try and share it one person at a time, and to love people where they are.

I don't try to make anybody a Quaker. I try to make everybody a friend, and those who feel called to be Quakers are certainly welcome.

~

We want to *speak* Truth, not to *hear* it.

~

…we should just try to walk our talk. That's all.

~

The people I work with are not Quakers, not pacifists, and what they know about Quakers is the way I do my job. It can be a small thing, not expressing theology, but expressing things like work ethics and being responsible to other people you work with, caring that way…If you are not working in a leadership role in the Society of Friends, it's in those day-to-day things that you have the real opportunity to express what it means to be a person of faith, acting your faith in your life.

~

…in the Meeting, a number of the Friends that I talked to when I was working on the project for spiritual growth and development said to me, "Well, the reason I'm a Quaker is because Quakers can believe anything they want to believe."

~

Dare we think of entering a new century assuming that what has been will always be?

~

In all those places where there is real engagement and real conscious moving into a lively and rooted Quakerism that takes on the issues and the concerns of the culture in which it is embedded, it's very exciting. Quakerism is not dead.

~

The ordinary Quaker in the pew often has very little knowledge of the other branches.

~

Quakers have a reputation as being open to seekers and so we get seekers all the time—people who don't want anything to do with the traditional for some reason or other and they're looking.

~

I read our history and it makes my palm sweat. It makes such sense how those dear people had such a gift to interpret culture and to interpret Christ in culture. I long for that as a Quaker today. I want to know culture and I long for the revelation of how to allow the person of Christ to so radiate through my life, through our life as a community, that the kingdom of God is felt and we make a difference.

In a way I have to say to you, our church is not a Quaker church. But I can't leave that sense of our history until I find some answer to it for today's living. I think some would really not grasp how we can have a band in worship. We have a lively kind of worship experience. I feel it's Quaker, though to me as I interpret culture in what my brothers and sisters did in 1650 to 1690, they ministered to culture, I think, as I have ascertained what culture is.

The ingredients we have in worship now are a part of helping to touch that culture, yet it would not be readily accepted…I would be a bit embarrassed for an eastern Quaker to come and worship with us. Some would have great difficulty with what we do. We serve communion here with bread and the wine. I baptize people if that's important in their pilgrimage of faith. Those are just some of the for instances. An important part of our weekly worship is the aspect of silence. It's a very powerful way to understand who God is and what God is doing in our own lives. We use that wonderful gift on a weekly basis here and it's a very powerful experience.

~

To me, grasping and studying and being a part of the culture, and understanding how I bridge the wonderful dynamic love of God through Christ—I hold that in one hand and I hold the culture in society that I find myself in here…that to me is what a Quaker is. That's what I felt my brothers and sisters did in 1650 to 1690 when we grew like never before.

~

I really feel that George Fox said it the best: There is even one Christ Jesus who can speak to thy condition. I continue to believe that having a relationship with Jesus Christ and growing in that relationship is how individuals change, and change radiates outward.

~

There are many within the Religious Society of Friends who are open to continuing revelation that there is the possibility that within the context of a particular time and place that which is written may bring to light a different way of thinking about society and the relationship with God, indications of what it means to be a Christian Quaker.

~

What's needed isn't Quaker culture (the unwritten stuff like no biblical foundation and simple dress) but Quaker *faith* (the biblically based testimonies).

~

I'm very interested in this discussion and in the situation that we as Friends have and the interplay of the specific and the universal, because we live life in very specific ways and we have beliefs in very specific ways, and every human being has that specificity. When you think about who we are as Friends and what we teach or how we equip people, how we train people, we have this specific history and content and experience to relate to.

The religious communities that are the most resilient, that have the most to say, also somehow have a continuity, have a connection between the specific and the universal so that someone, for example, can say, "I'm a Christian." Whatever that means beyond words and concepts, there's something there that can connect with somebody else who might not use that word at all, that history, and this comes around to whatever particular testimony or thing we're focusing on at the moment. Whether it's pacifism or issues around sexual identity and relationships, whatever it is, those specifics are very important, but having those specifics function in contact with the universal is a theme that I keep coming back to.

~

Quakers [have been described] as *people who chain themselves to a submarine.*

~

I'm odd. I hold to evangelical tenets like the resurrection and the scripture, but I also strongly believe in the Quaker testimonies.

Universalists want to deny Christ; some evangelicals want to deny Quaker heritage and the testimonies. But without those, a person might as well become a Nazarene.

~

The *released* Friend was the mechanism that nurtured Quakerism. How do we *release* Friends today?

~

I'm wondering whether we have morale/authority at this point to take on any witness of that kind…I'm talking especially about liberal Friends where it seems to me that we've forgotten how to love our enemies. We love the people who agree with us. We reach out to groups of society that are marginalized by other groups. For instance, we're very open towards gays. At the same time we condemn those who condemn gays, and so our tolerance and our openness is more towards the people we agree with than those we disagree with. So I think we're kind of at a stuck point.

~

Most of the pastors that I have seen are gray.

~

We (here I mean especially unprogrammed Friends, but I suspect this applies to most pastoral groups as well) are still attempting to subsist on the stores of intellectual capital built up by previous thinkers in this century. But their renewal value is largely used up, and what remains is little more than a series of platitudinous slogans. Or we borrow gimcrack and mostly third-rate theology from other groups.

~

…it's real hard to get a very wide group of Quakers to talk to each other in a very honest, open way and to develop the kind of trust where people are willing to interact.

~

When George Fox was talking about hireling priests, he was talking about people who were hired by the state to minister to the religious needs of people, whether those people wanted those hirelings to do it or not. That was a totally different situation from Friends today who frequently need to be reimbursed for services that they are performing on behalf of the Society of Friends, like teaching or pastoral work, and various kinds of administrative work. I don't think a lot of Friends are clear about that. They have this prejudice against paid staff. They don't call them hireling priests any more but use the words "paid staff." It's not quite the same.

~

When I think about Quakers today, my greatest concern is that we learn to get along together.

~

Leadership

What are the qualities of a good Quaker leader?

    Gift to understand.

    Quietly lead.

    Fertilize.

    Servant leadership.

~

We have to come to terms with who we are as Quakers…getting back to the concerns about losing Christ as the center of our experience with God. This may pertain more to the programmed Friends but there is also the question of how we define leadership. As a pastor I find that Quaker Meetings don't know how to handle pastoral leadership because they are afraid of it becoming too dominant. Yet, they want leadership from the pastor. But how do you define that leadership? What kind of leadership is appropriate to a Quaker Meeting? Maybe that pertains to unprogrammed Meetings too. Obviously unprogrammed Meetings need leadership too.

~

What I'm really wrestling with in my own life is that I look at a lot of the people around this table, and at people in our church I really respect who are older than me, who largely have given me a great amount of freedom to lead, and realizing my own self that I don't know what to do with that.

~

I just am not sure I can really articulate an answer to [the definition of leadership qualities] very well. I don't mean to be difficult, I just think it's kind of—how do you know when you are in love? I mean, the real thing is the real thing. Some of the indicators of that, I guess, are people who take on those kinds of leadership roles and do it from a place of true spiritual calling. They tend to be relatively ego-less in their leadership style, which, particularly in our culture, is very rare. That's usually a real good sign.

They may—and I say this with some caution because it is certainly one of the things that I wrestle with all the time—for better and for worse at different points keep a better sense of balance in their life and that may be visible. That is to say they are not willing, on any kind of regular basis, to work 70 or 80 hours a week and to try to be the hero that makes an organization work even when it's not functional otherwise. They tend to be in some way—and I say this cautiously because there are different ways in which people do this—it may not be a matter of being a great public speaker or writer, but they tend to be more articulate about how their faith connects to their work and what they are doing.

The phrase from scripture that often comes back to me is a wonderful line from First Peter where he talks about always being ready to give a reason for the hope that you have. People who are genuinely engaged in leadership as a matter of religious calling, are able in some way or shape to articulate so that others can understand how the work they do is an expression of their faith and a response to God's work in their life. People recognize that when they see it.

~

…to train leadership the way I learned best is to emphasize more the mentoring concept of leadership training.

~

I spent my time coming from Seattle actually thinking about this leadership issue among Friends, because to have leaders you have to have people that are willing to follow. Now it doesn't have to be a permanent investment—you are our leader, we shall forever follow, because we think leadership is Jesus and we all take our place through the giftedness of the Spirit.

But Quakers refuse to follow. We refuse to trust. I love that word "convergence." We refuse to let ourselves converge. It is this refusal to follow that means that we are going to be having leadership problems for ever and ever and ever. Even the jokes that we made around this table today are anti-leadership jokes. Fascinating. We've got to stop that; we have to stop it in our humor, we have to stop it in our side comments, to stop it in our suspicions. We have to stop it in a hundred little subtle ways in which we say to one another that we're not going to trust anybody to lead us.

~

One of the things we keep saying is that we are all ministers. But for any vocation in the world you have to be prepared. It's good to have this democratic understanding of everyone participating and making decisions and so on. But you also need to prepare people to serve and act and make things happen.

~

ESR reflects the ambivalence in Society of Friends regarding leadership: They say, "We train leaders," but there are no leadership classes! When I was there, I took a Quaker leadership class at the college from Henry Freeman. I know that Friends who went to other seminaries received a lot of training in management. In 1994, that wasn't a part of ESR. Freeman's class was good; it was on general leadership and management. Our classes with John Punshon helped, because his style involved a lot of back-and-forth dialogue, a lot of sharing from people in the class— a diversity of opinions.

~

…it's not a connotation where people have powers or authority over others, but that they have been empowered to do some work. This is what my definition of leader is. There are people who are able to do certain things because of their different abilities. But the preparation is essential.

Informed thinking, careful study, and serious discussion, these are the forms of Quaker leadership in shortest supply today. This verdict applies across the branches, as far as I can tell, and its impact grows more weighty with each passing year. Further, when I look around to see who is preparing Friends for such work, the landscape seems all but barren.

Thus, the reproach of this vacancy falls on practically all Quaker institutions. And, regrettably, if ESR is an exception, the fact has escaped me. I have seen very few scholarly publications on topics like those listed above from your faculty, and I have met few Quaker thinkers among your graduates.

If I am overlooking such work and such persons, by all means correct me, but I doubt this estimate is far wrong. And hence my second recommendation to Jay Marshall as he takes the helm [as dean of ESR]: Seek out and nurture some thinkers and scholars who will devote major attention to Quaker issues and studies. We need them. We need them very much.

~

What gets you in a position of leadership is promoting the party line.

~

It seems to me that the pastors I encounter in these pastor short courses and so forth, don't know what to do. They don't know what it means to lead a congregation outside the building. Some do, and there are some bright spots, but many just don't. They just don't know what to do except the latest technique of who to attract into the building. That concerns me and I think that it eventually shows up in the strength of leadership.

~

To me the presence or absence of a pastor or the presence of absence of some structure to worship is not nearly as important as whether there's spiritual life and health there that characterizes worship.

~

God calls every Christian to ministry. That broad definition of ministry needs to be constantly reaffirmed among Friends. It is the task of the pastor, for example, to facilitate the ministry of his Meeting. It says in this statement that Earlham School of Religion prepares men and women of all branches of Friends for leadership that empowers and equips the ministry of others. That's very true. The best Quaker pastors that I've known, many of them graduates of ESR, have been quite clear about that. The title *pastor* doesn't give them any greater status than other Friends, but they had a particular ministry to help other Friends be empowered to facilitate the spiritual life of their Meeting.

~

Based upon my research and some understanding of the literature about Quaker spirituality and worship, I have found the following themes to emerge in connection with issues of leadership in the Society. We do hide whatever modest light we possess under a large bushel basket. Or to put it differently, I found vital, spirit-directed, God-centered practices within the silent Meetings and discovered that Quakers felt real frustration because they could not or did not share their measure of the Light. What's going on, I wondered? Could programs at places such as Earlham address these matters?

~

I would like to respond on maybe a more practical level that anytime we have a leadership problem it would pay us to look at the cultural shifts that have occurred. For example, a simple fact is that when the elders said, "You may have a gift at ministry. Have you thought about this?" I was 16 and so they sent me out with an older man to go and preach at some little school house and I read the scripture and gave a few mumbling thoughts and was encouraged with this.

[Fifty years ago] the church's sociological model was the family and the church was an extended family. Our culture supported communities as neighborhoods of families. But now our culture has taken on a corporate image and the church has to be a corporation that follows the business model, which means that more professional training is expected because our culture expects better music, better preaching. So we are kind of caught between the early Quaker understanding of gathered people as the families gathered together and the church model which is of a corporate structure that puts on a good religious performance…

There are probably leaders available and maybe one task is to find them and anoint them again. It may be difficult for elders to come up to somebody who is 50 years of age and say, "Well I think maybe you have a gift in the ministry. Have you thought of being a pastor?" But maybe it would work. The cultural shift is very severe in our times and we either have to accommodate to a new paradigm in which the church is viewed as a corporation or business, or we have to try to recover a family-centered, extended family community and build around that and be Christ against culture instead of Christ with culture. Maybe we have to do both.

~

The community keeps coming up and I'm realizing that the unit of community that I'm most concerned about is my Monthly Meeting. What it takes for that to thrive is of course leadership and a sense that everyone is a minister. That's not well understood or well practiced in this Meeting. I'm quite bemused by my sense that not only my Meeting but other Meetings are not thriving, and it probably is for want of vision and leadership.

~

…we're used to thinking about leadership in terms of power dimensions as opposed to reciprocity effectiveness.

~

When George Fox was talking about hireling priests, he was talking about people who were hired by the state to minister to the religious needs of people, whether those people wanted those hirelings to do it or not. That was a totally different situation from Friends today who frequently need to be reimbursed for services that they are performing on behalf of the Society of Friends, like teaching or pastoral work, and various kinds of administrative work. I don't think a lot of Friends are clear about that. They have this prejudice against paid staff. They don't call them hireling priests any more but use the words "paid staff." It's not quite the same.

~

We used to think it was a wonderful thing to give a pastor a parsonage. Economically that is a disastrous thing to do; they never develop equity in a home and they never have anything to move on with it. You're here and that's fine and then there is nothing when you leave. There's a lot of those kinds of economic issues we haven't caught up with.

~

I think the leadership very much is in the culture of Friends and in the role models. I had some very good role models growing up just from the Meetings I belonged to, from the Friends that I knew, and so on. I think that's a very important element of leadership in the Society of Friends, the modeling of life rather than the teaching of theology.

~

Friends being reluctant to let people lead…that is a broader cultural trend as well.…you hear corporation people talking about the lack of good leadership and you hear it in other denominations and you certainly hear it in the political realm. We have our distinctive theological slant to that and I really do agree with you. But there is something culturally too, more broad. Anarchy is abroad in the land.

~

Here's a definition of leadership that I have been thinking about for a few years. It comes from a man by the name of Joseph Rost. He says leadership is an influence relationship among leaders and followers who intend real changes that reflect their mutual purposes. When you add in the dynamic of the Spirit as being part of that influence relationship, that is a good understanding of leadership among Quakers at their best. To me, this eliminates the situation in which this person is always the leader because of his or her role. That's not what we believe, but we also need this freedom to say this is the time for this person to lead. Let him or her lead. And it is our time to follow.

~

...the leaders that are being raised may not fit the roles that we have and we won't see it as leadership.

~

We don't do well as employers, and that has something to do with our relationship with leadership. We don't always think through the economics of the lives of our leaders. Many of our leaders are not employed but this is something that we haven't worked out as a Society of Friends. Maybe we just assume that because you are a Quaker employee, you will work 80 hours and you'll accept half the pay because it's God's work. We have this tradition that all they got before was travel and you would pay their transportation and give them a meal, but we haven't worked through that.

~

Not just training leadership, but *sustaining* leadership is the challenge.

~

The best spiritual leadership points us to Christ. There's a Quaker author years ago who wrote the book called *Servant Leadership* and I think that characterizes a Friends view of leadership. We don't think of leadership in our own way. But leadership does a lot of things, like evoking from other people their sense of what God is saying, and gathering in ideas, and helping to articulate in a way that others are able then to connect with the vision. It's not a position; leadership isn't vested in one person but there are different times when God uses different people, but God does use people.

~

...if you look beneath the surface, for the most part Quaker leaders staffing local and Yearly Meetings are lonely and isolated workers trapped in a system no one knows how to remedy.

~

Friends never really corporately approved of the pastoral arrangement; it oozed in Meeting by Meeting. So a standard discipline was never developed or a standard understanding of the pastor's role. Consequently, each Meeting does its own thing and develops its own image or its own pattern according to the vision of the local Meeting constituency as to what the pastor should do. Some of them just become very dependent on what the pastor says goes, but not only that, not only is he the authority, he also may be the errand boy and he spends a lot of his time just doing things that the people themselves can do.

Here we are living in a time when the people are recognizing the congregation can do a lot of ministry. That's what the church ought to be involved in, the ministry. Groups, in another Protestant tradition—even in the Catholic tradition now—are moving more and more toward involving the laity in ministry. Many of the things that the pastor is doing in Friends could be done by the people of the congregation. They would feel much more involved than they do now.

~

I tend to view religious leadership in general from the age-old perspective of a necessary duality consisting of priests and prophets. We need to have spiritual leaders who help us all know, respect, and understand the origins, traditions, and interpretations of our belief structure—the *priests.* Equally important is our need for spiritual leaders who point out the inadequacies of the existing structures while also providing the vision that can take us nearer to the Commonwealth of God—the *prophets.*

~

…our church longs to see a creative leadership developed somewhere.

~

To be a pastor among Friends doesn't require a seminary education, but people are very well served by getting better training and better education.

~

All of us have different gifts and these gifts should be encouraged and empowered and used for building communities.

~

It seems to me that the trend in Quakerism today is to build tiers of leadership, which is patently contrary to the work of Friends in the past. We have had pastors for about 100 years now, and now we have paid staff in Meetings and churches, too. On top of that, there are superintendents and general secretaries who assume leadership by government. I submit that they are *de facto* governments of our Yearly and Monthly Meetings. In addition to this corps of hireling ministers are the academes and Quaker celebrities who create leadership from the top. As I see it, this abdicates a founding principle of Friends—that leadership and ministry belong to Christ, and we are witnesses of what He does in our midst. It is not our job to *find leadership.* That is God's job.

~

To me, it is more than semantics to say, "God selects the leadership and we record the fact" (hence the term *recording*). Leadership in the Religious Society of Friends can only be as well prepared as the Society as a whole is prepared.

~

Local Meetings cannot grow unless they are willing to change the way they relate to the world around them, and to do that, they need leadership with skills in conflict resolution, community development, and bridge building.

~

In 1965 [our] Meeting had 336 members and a pastor. The Meeting had been a programmed Meeting for many years. Slowly the programmed Friends were dying out, and a group was forming that wanted an unprogrammed Meeting. As the group got smaller, we started two groups, one group met at 9:00 a.m. and one at 11:00 a.m. In 1988 we had 150 members.

In those days, we were a community, a loving spiritual community and most of the membership lived very close to the meetinghouse. Quoting dear Tom Mullen, "a group which worships together, works together, and has fun together stays together, don't overlook the importance of having fun together." In 1999, the picture has changed. We are now down to 65 members, many living out of state, some never attend and other are not well enough to be active, which brings the active number down to 22 and only eight members living in the city.

We have people who *do things* but we don't have leadership. It is my idea that we, as possibly many other Meetings, would benefit from a *released Friend*, a spiritual leader and energizer. This person would not have to preach, but guide the group.

A Baptist minister asked me for my denomination, and when I told him he said, "I pass your meetinghouse when I take my child to school, but we don't hear much about you Quakers." I think this says it all.

~

Not only do we have a difficult time with leadership in general, but there is also the sense that we don't respond well to leadership as Friends. We're nervous about it in general, which is too bad, because we need good leadership, desperately.

~

We seem to have lost our sense of respect for the gathered group and individuals just keep pushing their own way. That's why we need to find some way within our Yearly Meeting of discerning leadership. Potentially, ESR would be a wonderful place to send people. But, there's a step missing for us, and it's not ESR that's missing a step, it's us who are missing a step. I hear this in various parts of the Society of Friends. In the more Gurneyite Yearly Meetings, the more traditionally Christian Yearly Meetings, that still seems to be a lot more structured, but in the Hicksite-type Yearly Meeting there's a lot of Quaker ranterism.

~

We evangelicals don't know what to do beyond the Great Commission. We need to ask the question, "To what? Are we just trying to get everyone into heaven and then we are all happy that everybody goes to heaven? Or is there a reason to become a Christian and be a disciple? Will it make a difference here on earth?" Our leaders don't seem to ever grasp the concept of the present kingdom, that our faith in Christ is to change us so that we redeem our culture, not just get into heaven. Sometimes we have no goals beyond evangelism.

~

Friends have this strong commitment to the belief that you have immediate access to the Spirit. This Catholic ex-bishop said that it looked to him that what I was encouraging was the development of technocrats. Well, I can see why he would feel that way when I talked about specializing in conflict resolution or community development, that kind of thing. He was resisting this idea of always feeling like you have to bring in some specialist from the outside. My experience is that pastors are not equipped to do that kind of work. I feel that supplemented with a deep spiritual concern, which most of them have and should have more of, they need those kinds of skills to bring the leadership that's needed to start moving a congregation ahead. But it can't be done simply by ESR by itself. It has to be done in relation to Yearly Meeting executives so that changes begin to occur at the Yearly Meeting and local Meeting level, where Meetings recognize what their need is. Most of them don't, in my judgement. They just want to do more of the same of what's always been done, because their vision has never been raised beyond just parroting what has happened before.

~

ESR has to maintain an awareness of Quaker distinctives that the Quaker pastor is not a leader of First Baptist Church Atlanta. It always has to maintain that kind of understanding. I think it needs to address the fact that we have pastors in the Society of Friends now, and will continue to have, and if they are going to pastor, they are going to have to know how to speak and organize sermons, how to counsel, but they always have to do that within the context of deep appreciation for Quaker distinctives.

~

I think on a personal level, it's coming to grips with what it means to be a pastor. When I first came into the pastorate I was in my 40s. I had had this spiritual experience. I had been nurtured as a Christian by a local Friends Meeting, and really became a Quaker through my interaction with individuals at the Yearly Meeting level and reading. Then when I felt the call to the ministry, I really believed that I was going to enter the traditional pastorate once I was recorded. I moved from Meeting to Meeting doing what pastors do, which I had not a clue what that meant. Generally it was administer and organization, I thought, and preach the Word. But what has occurred is that I have gone through this process of following the leadings. I've come to understand that being a pastor is serving a people, nurturing a spiritual family, living with them, helping them marry, have fears, and I'm still here. And I never thought that this is what was going to happen.

~

We have always tried to see ministry more as function than status.

~

Whether or not ESR is and should be and can be a valuable part of this Yearly Meeting would rest on how they define ministry. Some 20 or 30 years ago when I was speaking to a group (and needed simultaneous translation) I said something about ministry and my translator said, "In our language we don't have any word for that." So I had to come up with a definition of what I meant by *ministry*.

What I ultimately used, and have used subsequently, (and this proscribes me as a process theologian) is that ministry is the process whereby we help both ourselves and others to remove the obstacles that prevent us from having that experiential relationship with God, with the Creator. To me, if ESR can train and devise and design and implement something like that, I'd say there's a real need for that in this Meeting. But not if ministry is going to be defined in a much narrower context of providing pastoral services for programmed Meetings or whatever… I was involved with ESR before they became official and listened to hundreds of hours of reports regarding their establishment. This question as to whether ESR can be and is a viable part of this Yearly Meeting ultimately comes down to how ESR is going to define ministry.

~

Leadership could be developed through a common experience, for example, the experience of participants in the conscientious objector camps during World War I; there was a war, they had something to stand for, they knew each other, and they thought a lot—this had a major effect. The Quaker Leadership Studies Program at Guildford will have a similar effect. The people who participate in this program will know each other and become part of a club. Leadership can be defined as getting a large enough group to have a commonness and to move forward together. Or, it could be recognized as something completely different, that leaders are very, very quiet people who we're trying to support in any way that we can. ESR could play a role in helping to find those people and in supporting them.

~

Leonard Sweet, Dean of the Theological School and Vice President of Drew University, suggests that "the patron saint for the postmodern era" in which we live might be "Leonardo da Vinci, who sketched with his right hand while he wrote with his left simultaneously." In a sense, that is the challenge of leadership for our time. The pluralism and complexity of modern culture requires multi-talented and skilled leaders who have the capacity to work on at least two levels at the same time, engaging the Meetings they serve in multiple ministries that target different needs and different groups.

~

Even if Friends could agree on a vision of pastoral leadership, I am inclined to think that the pastor's role as defined historically is not the kind of leadership that is really needed for the century now dawning. Much of a pastor's time is consumed in pastoral and priestly functions which could be shared by members of the Meeting. In many Meetings, ministry to families, to the sick and elderly, counseling, administration, and leadership in worship, could all be shared, if not delegated to persons with special skills and/or gifts.

~

That would release the employed minister to devote his/her efforts to serve as a specialist in community development, investing much time during the first six months of a new assignment studying the demographics and institutions of the community where the Meeting is located, specifically identifying those areas where there is need for community, equality, conflict resolution, integrity, and compassion. Such a designated leader could then report to the Meeting, and challenge it to see the surrounding community as its field of mission. Much of his/her time could be devoted to equipping the membership through creative biblical studies and the application of Quaker testimonies. Much of the leader's time could also be invested in motivating members of the Meeting, assisting them in identifying their gifts and engaging them to appropriate ministries.

~

I think, in part, leadership has to do with developing Friends who are really good at Quaker practice.

~

Leadership needs

If Earlham School of Religion has had some difficulty over the years in defining itself and in understanding what its role in the Society of Friends ought to be, I would imagine that a good bit of that difficulty comes not from the fact that Earlham School of Religion is doing anything wrong, but from this entrenched confusion among Friends themselves about how they are going to relate to leadership in their midst. The School of Religion is about cultivating leadership in the Society of Friends. If Friends themselves are ambivalent about leadership, then that automatically creates difficulty for the school. I don't know quite how to solve that problem from the point of view of the School of Religion that wants to keep trying to survive. But it needs to be brought out in the open clearly and addressed.

~

I'm pleased to see ESR working on developing whole new qualities of leadership. Both programmed and unprogrammed need a reservoir of people who are thoughtful and informed about the history of Friends, and the testimonies and social activities—people articulate and persuasive, and engaged in the broader work of Friends (government, business, science).

~

In my new position working with leadership development for the Yearly Meeting, I'm going to be looking specifically for resources to help us train our clerks and our people more about consensus and getting the sense of the meeting because that's an area where we are really weak and need to recapture some good skills. I was planning on connecting with FUM to see what they have done and if they have resources. I don't know if ESR has anything to offer or not.

~

We really could see a revival of what we like to think of as traveling ministry of the old style; it would have to be a new style, of course, to be appropriate to the time and culture but the old style would be a person who simply feels a deep concern to travel and to visit and to spend unhurried time with people—if that's possible in our era—and to hold opportunities with them.

Quakerism is not just a matter of ideas and talk, but it's a reality that has to be felt as well as talked about. It's people who bring that reality into people's homes; it's what I call bringing the sacrament. It's the Quaker way of bringing the sacrament into the home. It just lifts up a whole new dimension of what life can be in the home and the family. Not so much the talk as the experience of this presence that is available in ordinary homes. I wish we had scores of people traveling around like that.

There's an openness and a readiness and even maybe an urgency of need for this. So it takes very special, gifted people, people who are gifted and gentle and perceptive and whose real reliance is not in a formula but in being. But they also for the most part have to be pretty articulate when it's called for.

~

We need less leaders and more Quakers.

~

Our church longs to see a creative leadership developed somewhere.

~

I know the history of the Society, but without a leadership class, so to speak, it's very difficult to communicate values. I don't see how our Society can cohere without a consistent way of telling our story, and I don't think there are any people who are the identified storytellers in Society of Friends anymore, like the elders and the overseers use to be.

~

We have the structures and momentum, with occasional bright flashes of renewed energy, to keep Quakerism going as it has been for the past 40 or 50 years. We only require the lowest level of priesthood functions for maintenance anyway, thanks to our do-it-yourself organizational structure. Though we have some wonderfully inspired writers and thinkers amongst us, I do not yet sense a vitality of focused and engaged prophet-leadership that can take us through a sustained renewal and that can address our, or the world's, current needs in a substantial way.

~

I certainly don't mean to be nostalgic, but one of the geniuses of the original ways of operating in the Society of the Friends that developed was an interesting balance between what we then thought of as *ministers* and *elders*. Ministers were people in public leadership positions. In essence, they were the people who spoke, the people who were active in public service kinds of roles. Elders tended to be the people in their Meetings who were responsible for discerning people's gifts and encouraging them to use them, helping them, and providing support and guidance to them.

What has tended to happen, in the last 50 to 100 years, is that the elders have disappeared…because in some ways they connected to being more disciplinary than supportive. A lot of this has to do with our peculiar history as a religious people. But the absence of elders was certainly something that I felt keenly, the absence of a network of people whom I knew I could turn to for guidance and support and who would hold me accountable, in a good way, if I wasn't living up to the ideals that I professed. That's a critical issue.

I don't think we can have leadership without having a support network—not in a namby-pamby way, but supportive in a sense of really being there for folks, providing guidance, holding people accountable. This doesn't exist. I've run into individual people who I think of as elders these days and who one-on-one can do that with me, but there are no networks of those people, and those people don't think of themselves as consciously connected in a network.

~

We have lost the Quaker tradition of elders, at least elders who nurture, encourage, discern gifts.

~

…the perception was that people were not being prepared well to do pastoral service. They didn't have good administrative skills, didn't have good preaching skills, and even though the language and commitment was of equipping ministry, they didn't really know how to equip people and draw people into service.

~

Conflicting attitudes towards leadership

We are often ambiguous about the role and value of leadership. For too many Friends pastors this is evidenced by their sense of financial insecurity. Too many Friends Meetings have come to rely on non-Quaker trained pastoral leadership whose preparation for, and experience in, ministry are at variance with Quaker faith and practice. The emotional abuse and financial insecurity suffered by many pastors and other leaders immediately stifles any inclinations our young people may feel toward considering ministry among Friends.

~

We are very tough on our leaders. We're very critical, and we're not as nice to our Quaker leaders as we seem to be when we're trying to be a peacemaker among other people. I don't know why that is, but it seems that there are two niches: Either we're really critical or we have some Quakers—the people I have in mind happen to be Quaker ministers, but it could be Quaker leaders—who over the years have been just agreed with automatically, with whatever they say.

~

I am an 82-year-old convinced Friend, coming to the Society about 1953 after six years of Air Force service which spanned World War II. As a result of my long-time attendance at Quaker gatherings, including Yearly Meetings, I have had the good fortune of becoming acquainted with leaders across the spectrum of Friends. Due to my liberal bent, I have sometimes been in contention with leaders of the evangelical persuasion. I have learned much from them—and about them. I have learned that *things are not always what they seem.* The adherence to a monolithic orthodoxy by evangelical leaders is a myth. On more than one occasion when the battle seemed lost and my spirit flagged, some-one who I thought to be solidly in the evangelical camp, encouraged me to pursue my goals. Some of my best friends are Friends ministers to whom I shall forever be grateful.

It was in this context I became aware that Friends ministry is in a real *Catch-22.* Theologically literate ministers, in cautious, private conversations, freely admit their deviation from the conservative—even fundamentalist—views of their Monthly or Yearly Meetings. Meetings subjected to the ministry of poorly educated ministers often will not accept new ideas from seminary-trained pastors when pastoral changes are made.

One seminary-trained pastor told me that if he presents ideas in his sermons, at variance with the conservative views of the congregation, he spends the rest of the week answering questioning letters from the congregation. Another seminary-trained pastor lamented that he learned in seminary that the doctrines considered orthodox were questionable, but that he had to preach them to keep a job.

~

We are experiencing a leadership drought, perhaps due to some of the following reasons: As to pastors—why spend years in training to earn less than $15,000 a year when many careers are paying substantially more? Why enter a field that requires great personal input with massive stress in return? Families are often damaged by the high social/emotional/mental demands of pastoring. Pastoring, once a respected career, is now often mocked and maligned by society. As to lay leaders—with membership dwindling, most Friends are spread too thinly. Burn-out is common among lay leadership. This is not exclusive to Friends either.

~

Equipping ministry has always been the ESR mantra. But the graduates get out there and the congregations say, "Don't equip *me. You* do it!"

~

We use a sense of the meeting as a check and balance on people, as opposed to standing behind them and saying: Yes! It is a very interesting kind of twist that we are still controlling, even though our theology would lead us to a great deal of trust of leadership.

~

We're not trusting; we give responsibility but not authority. We harp on blunders and on learning curve problems.

~

We are very hard on our leaders, critical and unforgiving, they have to spend so much time and energy coping with divisions, they cannot strengthen their own Quaker spirituality or knowledge.

~

Within the Religious Society of Friends, it can appear that we are reluctant to promote leadership because we rely in great measure on our individual consciences to act as the priests for our spiritual community, and we demand our prophets undergo the rigorous scrutiny of our clearness committees.

Yet, Quakerism is having a leadership crisis. I would surmise that this lack of leadership has become more notable in recent decades as many Meetings lost, and did not replace, the elders who in the past helped our consciences by overtly assuming the role of the priesthood. At the same time, would-be prophets (who, as biblical scholars will note, are often reluctant to enter their professions in the first place) have been discouraged by most Friends' lack of dedication and seriousness in pursuing our testimonies. In addition, the would-be prophets have perhaps backed off in the face of the seemingly unbreachable wall that separates modern American political/cultural/economic life from radical Christianity/Quakerism.

~

New models of leadership

We have always tried to see ministry more as function than status. We've also thought the ministry belongs to the whole congregation, to all of the people. There are people who are gifted in public ministry; we are very grateful for that and want to release them for that kind of service, but at the same time, it's not a dishonor in terms of status for a person not to be full-time.

I know people talk about bi-vocational ministry and sometimes that's not very effective. I could even imagine sometimes multiple persons serving a congregation in one place, each of whom might be bi-vocational in some sense. There might be a team of people that could be in a congregation or find ways of raising up local folks that are going to be there over the long haul, to call on folks and find ways to liberate and engage them in the life of ministry, even though they'll continue to live in the community and maybe hold jobs.

We have the prejudice in a lot of our churches now that the only person who can preach on a Sunday is a paid pastor. It seems to me that doesn't need to be a given. There are a bunch of other things people think: If the pastor doesn't come, or do this, or do that, then it hasn't been done. So we have fallen prey to some other models of ministry than Friends models. Maybe we need to explore that.

One of the things that intrigued me about ESR early on and over the years is the potential that we might find models for ministry that serve our heritage and serve our modern situation creatively. There have been attempts at it but I don't think we've got it down yet. Maybe we haven't really worked at it creatively enough.

~

We develop elders and clerks through apprenticeship and alchemy. Can we provide better training methods?

~

I am not clear in my own mind that the pastoral arrangement as it has evolved over the last century provides the model Friends should emulate in the next 100 years. While the adoption of the pastoral arrangement may have saved many Meetings from extinction, corporate efforts to hammer out a vision of Quaker pastoral leadership has never succeeded. In much of Protestant tradition, the congregation and the appointed pastor know clearly what his or her role is and s/he is not captive to the congregation. Among Friends the pastor's role is much more vague and ill-defined. Meetings want pastors but are leery of leadership, and the prophetic function tends to become buried under a mountain of pastoral duties. Consequently, Meetings suffer for lack of purpose and direction, except to do more and better what has been done in the past. As we enter the 21st century, to just do more of the same and to persist in this ambivalence about the Quaker pastor will not do. I would hope that under the leadership of ESR, Friends might begin to shape a vision of leadership within a Friends Meeting which is both consistent with our tradition as well as appropriate to the challenges of our time.

~

There might be another version of [leadership] collaboration. When I engaged in my research about Quaker spiritual practices in the silence of worship, I placed my research process under the care and guidance of my Monthly Meeting. In an official Quaker manner, my Monthly Meeting appointed a Research Oversight Committee. We met on a regular basis. The main point was simple: I wanted my research project to be connected to the needs of the community. In the process itself, many other issues emerged, not the least the education of the researcher. Earlham College's School of Religion might explore how to propose such a committee or process for potential leaders.

~

I would like to see them gather together people who have a growing sense of what it means to be a Quaker Christian pastor and talk about that and work some models out because the reason that so many of us are copying the Baptists or the Methodists or somebody else is because they are putting a model in front of us. We need ESR to help us develop some Quaker models of what it needs to be.

~

…I have been engaged in a qualitative research project about the meanings of Quaker worship in the tradition as practiced by silent Meeting Friends…I would like to see Quakers develop a pedagogy which emphasizes and promotes active listening, as well as a different sort of conversation and analysis. It's a little difficult for me to articulate this, but I do have some questions:

Is there a Quaker pedagogy in connection with listening and silence? Would it be possible to think about aspects of being centered, relying upon periods of silence, responding in a spiritually embodied manner, as ways of thinking differently about academic reflection and analysis? For example, I think that Mike Heller has offered some interesting ideas about what he has termed the curriculum of silence. But, in connection with a program of leadership development for Quakers, would it be possible to explore the possibilities of a different sort of analytical and pedagogical framework as part of the program? What would this mean? Parker Palmer's work comes to my mind, as does Mary Rose O'Reilley's *The Peaceable Classroom.*

~

A collaborative model [of leadership], a pedagogy informed by collaboration would be useful. Drawing from the disability community, it might be a version of circles of support, in which key family and community members get together—and stay together—as a team or network of support and connection for the person with disabilities. Now, of course, I don't mean to suggest that these potential Quaker leaders have any sort of disability! Even so, I think that there are real barriers to leadership for Quakers out of the silent Meeting tradition. In part, these barriers to leadership happen to be connected to the dominant culture of individualism, ego, therapy, all of that sort of thing. Hence, a support group, a circle of support, with say an Earlham College faculty person, the potential leader, maybe a peer in the program, one person from the Monthly Meeting, this could be constituted as a planning group. Also I would recommend that such a group be active and try to provide ongoing support and connection.

~

…isn't there at least an implicit Quaker approach to doing scholarship, analysis, and social action? In part, we might promote or develop alternative ways of knowing, approaches that reflect our commitment to be centered, to the leavening process of the silence, to community as well as individual leadings. We might explore what it means to engage in an embodied Quaker leadership, reflecting the Quaker version of *lectio divina*. In some ways, this way of listening and knowing might take advantage of our uses of silence and community, promoting alternative ways to engage the world and ourselves.

~

What's being done to identify and track potential leaders, potential students for ESR, for Friends' positions around the country in Meetings and organizations? For example, we need something like a talent pool, a resource of knowledgeable and capable people to attract to positions of teaching, administering, working for organizations, guiding the work of others.

~

We haven't really grappled with the pastoral system in the context of Quaker practice. Pastoral system puts pastors in *opposition* to the Monthly Meeting. Which one is responsible and accountable for care? Make creative ways to do this! How should we do it? ESR could describe a *new pattern*.

~

I would love to see Friends in our Meetings on the lookout for other Friends who have the gifts of leadership—priestly and prophetic, for Friends who have the gift of discernment, for Friends who have skills that complement and complete those of the people with gifts and discernment, to travel next to them. I would love to see Meetings challenge and nurture such individuals to use their gifts. And I would love to see the concept of released Friends regain prominence, support, and commitment within our Meetings. Too often the obverse is visible. Friends are reluctant to single out others as having special gifts, and our emphasis on equality even is occasionally used to stymie those who obviously have talents to share. Nevertheless, the time is right. At least in New York Yearly Meeting there seems to be a quiet expectancy. With the right catalyst, much could soon happen.

~

Where it's currently working
One last thought on leaders and leadership training: My experience in New York Yearly Meeting with the Alternatives to Violence Project (AVP) over the past couple of years has led me to believe that we have inadvertently stumbled upon an approach to missions, evangelization, and outreach that is exceptionally true to Quaker testimonies while

avoiding the inconsistencies and cultural/ religious baggage of traditional mission work.

AVP presents all the best elements of Quakerism (community, integrity, simplicity, commitment to non-violence...) as mission work. In many ways it is pastoral care, spiritual motivation, searching for the truth, learning the skills to live in the Commonwealth of God, all bundled together. It is respectful of each individual's spiritual path, but demands a high degree of faithfulness. It embraces and serves the poor and the rich, prisoners and school children, the uneducated and the highly intellectual. And with respect to leadership, it teaches the importance of serving others to bring out the good (and the God) within. It demonstrates how groups or communities best move forward after time has been taken to uncover and address the real issues, concerns, and aspirations of the members.

ESR would do well to encourage in Quaker leaders the courage, initiative, commitment, forthrightness, and insight I have experienced among AVP facilitators.

~

I wrote down Reedwood Friends Church as an example of the sort of thing that I think ESR can help programmed Friends to do. I've never been there but I understand it's a Friends church which considers itself a "community of ministers" and it may be that there are some members of the church who would be glad to go back to a strong pastor but others still favor the community of ministers theory of that Meeting. That seems very close to Elton [Trueblood]'s original idea of the equipping ministry. I see it as a real practice ground for cross-cultural Quakerism. And a recognition of a cross-cultural Quakerism which neither shouts nor puts down, but listens with respect and encourages a vibrant, ongoing, not shy faith.

~

In the course of conversations, I heard one Quaker say that as he waited upon the Spirit listening in the worship silence—what he embraced (when it worked) was another, different *voice* which emerged, a voice which originated from the creative movement of the Spirit in worship. This different, emerging voice felt like a gift, like a different way of knowing.

I'd like to see a version of Quaker leadership which paid some particular attention to the possibilities of such emerging voices out of the communal worship silence. How can we encourage such spiritual discipline and practice? What could it mean for a way of leadership propelled by the Spirit, by God, but that originated from the silent Meeting Quakers?

~

One of the reasons I enjoy attending North Valley Friends is that they share some of the same philosophy and right now are going through some real philosophy transitions in two major areas—one, trying to figure out how best to express their commitment to one another, and revamping the whole membership idea so that it isn't just a once in your lifetime life-long commitment that is made, and then you don't really think about it again. But it is perhaps an annually renewed commitment to the faith community, where there are some things that you commit to the group and that the group commits to you, and that relationship is renewed and affirmed annually.

The other thing that they are looking at that I'm real excited about is how to really equip everybody who is there as a member, to be ministers and to hear God's call in their life, and then be supported and encouraged to pursue that. It is a pastoral Meeting but they are talking about ways to de-emphasize the responsibility of the pastoral role and release and equip the individuals in the Meeting, if they feel called to minister within the Meeting, but also outside the Meeting as well. So, those are two things that are really exciting to me.

~

I'm not paid as a pastor which certainly might be one reason why I have lasted 15 years. Well, they love me a great deal but I'm affordable. The way the Meeting has grown, to some degree has had to do with the fact that I'm in an unpaid position so that the kind of people who would be attracted to a highly organized or traditional church avoid us.

~

Five or six years ago, after talking with several Friends, I had the idea of starting a Quaker Leadership Institute in which we'd bring in 50 or so people who were emerging in understanding their use of ministry and leadership within their own Monthly Meetings. I found out that using *Quaker* and *leadership* together is an oxymoron. Leadership is something that Quakers are very hesitant—at least in this Yearly Meeting—to talk about. We had three of those institutes that had a profound impact on the life of many individuals and yes, we're talking about leadership in a different way than ESR would talk about leadership.

What we were doing is talking about how to be a clerk of a Monthly Meeting, how to develop a religious education program, and how to prepare oneself to take on the role of being a clerk. What are the spiritual disciplines one needs to take on that role? It was I think very profound.

~

It appears to me that the last gathering of the Friends Association for Higher Education was on the campus of Friends University in Kansas last June and the theme of that conference was leadership in the Society of Friends. It seems to me the conference proceedings ought to be grist for the mill for this study.

~

A teacher at Earlham School of Religion said the other day to me that she thinks the most significant thing that has ever happened in Philadelphia Yearly Meeting is that members of various Meetings pledge a consistent regular worshiping with each other once a week for a long time, for months. She is convinced that in terms of real bonding and trusting and so forth, and beginning to work together on various levels, that kind of a commitment for the worship part of our lives is essential.

~

Guilford's Quaker Leadership Scholars Program has proved to be a dynamic program of incubating future Quaker leaders in the culture on campus and then exposing them to diversity. It's just become a marvelous laboratory for Quaker leadership.

~

THEOLOGICAL EDUCATION AND SPIRITUAL NEEDS

Rex Ambler is a Quaker and a theologian at the University of Birmingham who has researched into how Friends centered down. He has discovered through his own piecing together of pieces from Fox and other early Friends the process that they used, and has put together tapes and readings and instructional manuals. Now these Experiments with Light groups are emerging around the U.K. which use this process to center down and hold their concerns in the Light and they are finding some pretty powerful response to that. It's called the Experiment with Light. The tapes and manuscripts and anthologies are available through Rex Ambler in Birmingham.

~

There was an excellent article in a recent *Christian Century* on theological education and the denomination, pointing out many of the dilemmas about leadership and theological education that Friends also experience. I appreciate that ESR was committed to confronting me with the Christian roots and trust of Friends and with the testimonies/distinctives that came out of that Christianity. What it did for me as a person of faith is as important to me as what it did for leadership in the Society of Friends through me. Where I would like to have had more help is in what *Christian Century* called "contextual education." I valued my field education experience and reflection. I would like to know more about how to present what I know/learned in an environment that is not asking for what I know. You can become a hired pastor, but will the Meeting let you be minister? You can be one more person in an unprogrammed Meeting, but will the others there let you be a leader? How can you teach New Testament or theology in that context, that is, translate what you learned at ESR for your fellow worshipers?

~

I think there's a place for not only one but several Friends seminaries.

~

I've been reading minutes of Quaker Meetings and studying Quaker history this past year. I've been really moved to own the testimony of the early Friends against hireling ministers. I love that phrase, but I now feel so connected with that ministry and feel it's such an important part of our heritage. I'm not suggesting for a minute that we need to impose that, or even suggest that every Friend should take up that testimony, but I sure would love to see an educational program put its students through those historical roots for an awareness of it. Around the splits in the Religious Society of Friends, I think it's valuable to get people in touch with all sides of those debates. I'm not familiar with John Punshon's work but it seems that what was said is so incredibly valuable, to bring discernment to understanding that movement, and how non-evangelicals can relate to that and feel community with them would be invaluable.

~

I really think that theological education is extremely important for Friends. Many of our Meetings are very small, and virtually no theological education takes place—in that formal way of Sunday School. A lot of Quaker young people aren't getting that kind of theological education.

~

There are a lot of people in this Yearly Meeting having some sense of a call to develop skills, talents, or to respond to *nudgings* about their own ministry who are looking for other schools of religion in the area.

~

On the West Coast, the lively Quaker programs at Azusa Pacific, the liveliness at present at George Fox University and the merging of a theological college and a Quaker college add to the approach that ESR offers. In some ways they compete, but it's helpful to have different choices and different expressions of Quaker theological education going at the same time. In the long run, that strengthens an effort such as that of ESR.

~

I've seen thoughtful, carefully constructed and implemented programs of adult religious education, or even spiritual formation, the kind of program that really tries to help people get in touch with, better understand, and grow in their own spiritual tradition and their own roots. This has been a revitalizing force in several Yearly Meetings. That's probably the single most important influence I've seen where there is good stuff happening.

Certainly one of the reasons those programs have done well in many places is because there is, I believe, a real spiritual hunger among many of our members to be more in touch with the spiritual center, to understand better the religious tradition that they are a part of, and to find ways to reshape their lives around living that out. That, however, is a tough piece of work to do, both individually and corporately.

The other influence which is most hopeful, when it is there, but hard to find is when there is a true *community*, a true *spiritual community*, growing up around that. Many of our Meetings are places where people come for rest and shelter, but not often places where people are challenged and supported to grow spiritually, and often not places where there are other kinds of support mechanisms that are needed to help people change their lives to live out their faith more fully.

~

I have been so glad that Earlham School of Religion has had a spirituality track.

~

It would be wonderful if there could be a staff person, funded both by ESR and by some other Quaker organization, or some grant to free that person from being under a Quaker organization. Somebody who is funded for five years to work both at ESR, and within a reasonable distance, in developing spiritual growth groups in local Meetings, where people can learn how to talk and keep on growing without being shut up by people who tell you you've got to believe it this way or that way.

~

There's a hunger among unprogrammed Friends for a deeper study of Bible, Quakerism, spiritual life. There is a need out there.

~

If the spiritual life of the Meetings are shallow, those who don't have the experience of being moved by and living in the Spirit are much more likely to do their own thing. The spiritual life in our Yearly Meeting is not deep and rich at the moment. And that's partly because we don't have good leadership. It's like a circular thing.

~

I will start with the place where my strongest intersection is, with the spiritual—the movement toward spiritual direction in the Society of Friends. You ought to know about [the School of the Spirit] as a significant phenomenon. [The School attracts] people with more or less of a Christ orientation in their Quakerism, though they vary widely in the points of the spectrum where they are. They tend to be people who just find themselves drawn to finding out nurturing. They tend to be people who have some experience—as Quakers use the term experience—of some mystical kind of experience.

Most of them tend to be unprogrammed but there have been some from programmed Meetings. They represent all ages. They normally tend to be older, and each time they have had a few more men. It's still a predominance of women, but it has always been true that men—I guess it's true generally in religion—are slower to become involved. It's very significant that there are men involved in this each time. There have been about 19 or 20 people in the last two two-year sessions in the School of the Spirit.

~

A study said that in the future, a congregation will need 200 people to be able to afford a pastor. So we have to learn to look at pastoring in different ways, unless we're going back to circuit riders. For me, in unprogrammed Meetings, that means that pastoral training should involve less preaching, more spiritual direction—that is, wider varieties of people who can do spiritual nurture and pastoral care.

~

Others of us have been involved from our Pendle Hill days in actual one-on-one spiritual direction…and a group of us in the Philadelphia area spent part of a day a month, for several years just talking through how we could find our own spiritual direction in a Quaker way, without simply becoming Catholic spiritual directives or Episcopal spiritual directives. So that's an area that has been very important to me. That's related to the growing awareness of the spiritual dimension of Quakerism. I suppose it's a cultural awareness at this time in history, not just within Quakerism, of a spiritual dimension that is absolutely necessary for classic Quakerism.

~

We've diminished form and everything else to emphasize the human/divine relationship and the fact that God can change people's lives. Yet theological education generally doesn't deal with that; it leaves God out of the picture. It would be very easy for ESR to follow that pattern of dispensed education as opposed to spiritually engaged education. ESR could be a leader in the world in that vein—the belief that God is at work even in the academic venture; that the academic venture is a spiritual quest.

~

One of the things I really applaud is ESR's commitment to spiritual growth and spiritual development of each student. They have done that well and I hope they continue to. Preparing for ministry is not a textbook calling but a development of the human spirit.

~

We're starving because the traveling ministry among unprogrammed Friends is not there anymore. People are yearning for spiritual direction, but have to go outside Quakerism to get it.

~

I found Friends spirituality an incredibly workable way to understand faith.

~

The point of such a collaborative [mode of working together, faculty, prospective "students" and others]...a pedagogy informed by collaboration...would be to promote and encourage Quakers to develop an intentional direction, a spiritual direction, open to the gifts of the Spirit. Indeed, I have wondered: Shouldn't Quakers be clearer, more direct and systematic about offering guidance in spiritual direction? Why not? What would it take? Is there a Quaker version of spiritual guidance? If not fully articulated, could we develop one?

~

I came among Friends and knew I had found a spiritual home.

~

With the Quaker tradition, the ministry is a spiritual gift, not something you get by learning. The fact that we do have a seminary stretches some Friends' understanding of the whole thing. That doesn't bother me, but I want to go back to that presupposition. My sense is that there is need for the opportunity or some academic training in spirituality for people—either at ESR or somewhere else. I know that with accreditation, and with ESR's goal to provide leadership, there may not be the room to have these other people along as well.

I would have felt very happy if I could have gone to ESR and said, "Look there is no way I can do a degree here but I'm sincerely interested and I do have the qualifications of being part of the community for the limited time I'm here." I think if there are too many people around like that it becomes a problem. But I don't know if there could be sort of a dual track available so that ESR could provide an internal certificate for people, but not a degree.

~

The people who are attracted to the Society of Friends in Canada at the moment tend to be Hicksite-type Friends—people who come in because of their involvement in social justice and things. And some of us are very concerned about that. There's more interest in the fruits of the spirit in terms of social activities than there is in nurturing the feeding of the spirit and that well runs dry if it isn't nurtured.

~

WE NEED COURAGEOUS LEADERSHIP IN SPIRITUAL MATTERS…folks who are willing to speak truth about lack of depth in worship and what may be the causes and the results.

~

The fact is that in the last 20 years while ESR has not changed a lot, the landscape of Quaker theological education has changed an awful lot. You now have at least three other institutions that do somewhat similar things. They all happen to be affiliated on the evangelical side of the spectrum.

~

George Fox University has its own seminary now and offers not only master's degrees but they're implementing a D.Min. program so it's substantial and growing—a pretty impressive institution. Houston Graduate School of Theology, I don't know what their numbers are, but they are viable and healthy and serving more of a regional or local area. And then Friends Center, at Azusa Pacific University, has had a following mostly within that Yearly Meeting.

~

I believe one of ESR's most important contributions to Quaker leadership in the coming years will be to help create some competitors to itself. I am under no illusion that our Society can support two or more seminary-type institutions, with all their overhead of staff and plant and so forth. This concern appears to call for some institutional creativity. One thinks, perhaps facilely, of the Internet and other technological tools as providing potential surrogates and substitutes; then again, decentralized institutions are very much part of the ethos of unprogrammed Quakerism, so perhaps this is the area to explore. Unprogrammed Friends are big on workshops and short courses. (There are typically [hundreds] at each FGC gathering, with room for more; indeed, one could, if so inclined, practically run a whole mini-seminary there…).

~

ESR should look at other seminaries and graduate schools with good models of distance learning. The potpourri for graduate education is now so vast—pick up on it! What about programs for Friends schools *teachers*?

~

Some of the folks in George Fox University, Houston Graduate School of Theology, Azusa Pacific University, and ESR have been trying to get people from those four schools to sit down at the table and say let's get to know each other, let's talk about our different missions. Is it true that we four are all in some way doing similar things? Can we understand each other and accept each other, and then say it most likely would occur that we will each do slightly different things. Then we will try not to disrespect one another or speak ill of one another and especially not to say that we are the only ones doing what we are doing.

It would behoove the folks at ESR to say: Why don't we take the initiative and call the meeting and contact persons at each of the other places and say, wouldn't it be a good thing to talk? Then see where the conversation went. The very least that would come from it would be an awareness that would cause people to speak with some accuracy about the different missions of those other schools.

~

[I'm attending] a Presbyterian seminary and everybody there is really quite high church and then there are five of us Quakers. What's interesting is that their religious experience is completely different from ours, but what they are pursuing is trying to teach all these high church folks how to step back from ritual and really step into an experience of Christ, and they are using a lot of Quaker materials. In fact, they do one whole week of group spiritual direction where their emphasis is talking about Quaker clearness committees and how Quakers have clerks and how they listen for the sense of the meeting and all those sorts of things. So they were really excited to have us come and join them. From the reading that they have done of Quakers, they think we have got it all figured out. The reality of our life is that we really don't. So we are learning as well.

~

Mission

Choose a position; be clear about what it means, and then stick to it.
Make sure that the curriculum and goals fit it so it becomes a reality.
ESR needs to create a picture for people: If I go to this School, this is
what I'll find, and these are the options I'll have after graduation.

~

I see ESR as a key player in shaping American Quakerism in the next
100 years. It is imperative therefore, that ESR resist the temptation to
function within its own comfort zone as an institution, without reference
to its larger calling as a mover and shaker within the Society of Friends.

~

One of the surprises in ESR's history is that it has drawn people like me,
unprogrammed Quakers, and many others followed me. I was part of a
minority there at that time, a very small minority. It has drawn a lot of
unprogrammed Quakers and may have—I think in the eyes of some—
moved aside from its primary role of what I would call (and this is my
language) saving the pastoral system and keeping it within the real
Quaker tradition. I have great sympathy with that original vision at
ESR to save the pastoral system which does need some shoring up.
I have great sympathy with the original ideal that if we are going to
have Quaker pastors, they need to be trained by Quakers and have an
understanding of the original genius of Quakerism that can be adapted,
particularly as people like Elton Trueblood and Wilmer Cooper
articulated it.

~

What I have been very concerned about as someone who has watched
people come and go for 23 years, I've been serving a Friends pastorate
for almost 20 years but I've watched a lot of people leave ministry
totally. I wonder how ESR can help people better prepare for the reality,
the hardships, the temptations, the struggle with personal choices that

can lead them into, can I dare say, sin, that will allow their authentic calling to ministry to fail.

~

People who just need nurturing on their spiritual quest can get it in other places: Pendle Hill, Woodbrooke. They shouldn't be allowed to dilute the original vision of what ESR was for. There could be better discernment of people who are coming into the School.

~

There is a tendency at the seminary to be caught between that professional guild which right now in biblical studies and in religion is caught in the culture of unbelief. I would hope that Earlham School of Religion would be forthrightly, strongly, apologetically Christian in a scholarly way and would reinforce the local churches. Otherwise the gap will increase. Every seminary faces that tension between the guild which is the professional religion, and the church. I think that the seminary has to identify with the believing community. If scholars are not comfortable there, let them go to the university.

~

I would start with phrasing that mission somewhat less arrogantly. They can't claim to be the only graduate school of theology among Friends.

~

ESR has been trying desperately to hold on to non-pastoral Friends and I think that's great. But the difficulty comes with those Friends who have simply abandoned Christian faith altogether and their members are leaving and joining the Mennonites, or whatever the Christians are. This is happening in some of the Yearly Meetings. ESR a few years ago got its mission statement stated clearly, where they were. I think that we would urge ESR to stay with that mission statement and whatever the implications of that are. The effort to draw all groups of Friends together can tear ESR apart.

~

In the Christian tradition, Christ himself embodies contradiction: the Lion and the Lamb, the Alpha and the Omega, the first and the last. In addition, however, He is also the *logos* and as learners in His school, we are called to work with Him in bringing the ends, the opposites, together. I am persuaded that ESR can be the *logos*, the Presence of Christ within the Quaker family not only to bring the ends together and to create harmony but also to equip leaders to be the *logos* in local situations, skilled in building bridges, and committed to building community. Being transformed themselves, they aspire to engage in a ministry that makes a difference, that of transforming the world.

~

I really need to know better what ESR is. I really don't know that much about it. I just have a very generic sense what its mission is.

~

I really don't think that there's a core understanding of where they want to be going. The old prophecy says without a dream the people perish. Without that vision, and unless you know where you want to go, you can't figure out how you're going to get there.

~

…no other seminary that I have been a part of has the history of our movement and the difference we have made. The next step is saying, "How do we enculturate? How do we allow our history to speak to culture today?" I don't see anybody else doing that.

~

All ESR classes are potentially classes in training leaders. I see two roles for ESR: to train leaders, and to be centrist. It would help ESR to be clear and to state it. The mission statement is fine, but people aren't convinced of it because of the Quaker feeling about leadership. Some principles of pastoral leadership are the same for pastoral or unprogrammed Quakers. Our Quaker organizations need leadership, too.

~

ESR is about changing people's lives, not changing institutions.

~

…late '70s into the '80s, ESR started emphasizing more academic preparation for Ph.D. work and began servicing more and more unprogrammed Friends and pre-Ph.D. sorts of programs. I think they began to lose their way a little bit about who they were. That's when I think more and more Evangelical Friends at ESR began feeling uncomfortable. They were having some struggles maintaining their connections to the pastoral and evangelical branches. I don't think they ever fully lost that. I think there always was a commitment there but I think much like Earlham was always keeping an eye over its shoulder at Haverford and Bryn Mawr and Swarthmore and wanting to be thought of in those circles. ESR, I think, was always looking at University of Chicago and Yale Divinity School and other seminaries saying we want to be thought of in those circles as well.

~

I would say if we could come to grips with that aspect of our history, come to understand culture in society today, if the seminary could help us do that, that would be a delight.

~

I know there's a lot of concern about in some circles wanting ESR to focus on turning out pastors. I hope ESR resists the temptation to go too far down that road.

~

There has been a very checkered relationship between ESR and evangelical/pastoral Friends, who have the possibility of offering employment to the School's graduates. ESR needs to be clear whether it wants to serve that group or not, and then to *act* like it.

~

The role of ESR is to help Friends know, to have a place to stand against all the fads and trends and religious excitements that pass us by. It must nurture what is authentic in the Society of Friends so that we have a place to stand.

Now that's pretty general but let me be a little more specific. One of its original purposes was to train pastors. In my travels among Friends of all sorts, I still see that as a primary need. The influx of liberal Friends to ESR has frightened some would-be students away from the evangelical Yearly Meetings or even some of the Midwestern Yearly Meetings. I think that is too bad. It is something that's got to be addressed, and I wish I had wisdom enough to say how.

I visited in North Carolina Yearly Meeting and in Mid-America Yearly Meeting that were being pastored by guys who were graduates from two-year Bible colleges and who were not Friends. I don't think we can anticipate that they are going to strengthen Quakerism. They may be wonderful people and good preachers, but I remember a service I attended where there was a special program and it was a very valuable program, I thought, and I said to the person who was running it, "In your mind, how does this particular program relate to your Quakerism?" The leader looked at me and said: "It has nothing to do with it." He looked at me as if I had asked a foolish question.

Maybe it was foolish but, at any rate I do think pastoral education is a major task. Getting those people from the Yearly Meetings who are suspicious of ESR to come there and to send their people there will be harder.

~

ESR can extend the olive branch to the extremes, but be clear about the vision of the School. And then quit worrying about it. A school can't be everything to everyone.

~

ESR should keep its door open to all branches of Quakers, but its *original* reason for being was for churches in Indiana and Western YM (FUM). That was a worthy thought.

~

Vision statement: Earlham School of Religion shall be a global influence in the formation of religious leadership trained to penetrate and to transform society and its structures toward greater equality, community, integrity, harmony, and compassion.

Mission statement: The Earlham School of Religion, an expression of the Religious Society of Friends, affirms the universal ministry, believing that God calls every Christian to ministry. Earlham School of Religion seeks to prepare women and men for leadership among Friends and other faith communities with the goal of empowering and equipping others for ministry. In addition, the Earlham School of Religion addresses the need for specialized leadership toward enabling local Meetings and churches to define their mission and to carry out a transforming ministry to persons, groups, and society.

~

...maybe that's the role of the Earlham School of Religion, to see the happy medium that can join us all together and prepare leadership to meet the needs of all the groups and also across the board. Not just the Society of Friends. Join hands and form networks of like-minded people across other churches too, as well, that can strengthen us and strengthen them as well.

~

If I were to read from that experience [of taking a course at ESR], what I thought the goals of ESR would be, it would be firstly, as portrayed through that learning experience, quality of relationships, development of one's own spiritual journey, and equipping for pastoral situations and all of those. If those were the goals they were well lived up to.

~

ESR actually serves several roles. One that is useful is because of the variety of folks that come there, it does help the larger conversation among diverse Friends groups. I think that's an important thing to continue to happen. So maybe that's another way of saying they do still need to serve a broad population. That's also one of the things that makes it very difficult. Because if that becomes overriding, then sometimes certain elements of service might get neglected or under-emphasized. The largest number of Friends in the United States these days, of course, is still a pastoral persuasion and many of these Friends Meetings are looking for strong pastoral leaders. ESR needs to be tuned into that and have the kinds of studies that serve that need as part of what they do. Over the years that's been kind of uneven.

~

What we need, and what we need from places like ESR, is the equipping and the enabling of people, whether in their pastoral or unprogrammed traditions, who can excite people about the deep treasures and deep resources within our tradition, excite people about that and help them to access the best of our own tradition.

~

I thought its primary function was originally to keep the programmed tradition alive and close to the genius of Quakerism. But I would be sorry if it leaned too far in that direction and weren't still serving the unprogrammed tradition. Actually, what it feels to me, of course, about ESR is that it continues to be a training ground for Quakers listening to Quakers across different traditions.

~

One of the major problems, which is not just characteristic of ESR, of this denomination, is narrowing your vision and your objectives. One of the problems with education in this country is that we're trying to do way too many things in schools. Networking is fine, building a bridge is fine, but I really don't think it's ESR's role. That role is the Society of Friends' role as a whole and many other institutions need to work on that. But to simply say that ESR builds a bridge, no. ESR has a very defined role, it needs to figure out exactly what that role is and work very hard at doing it; to narrow rather than broaden what the vision is.

The [narrower] mission should be academic excellence; philosophical and theological excellence would be really good. If ESR started a debate among Friends about who we really are, they would probably do something which would be of value to us 50 to 60 years from now. If the people who are coming out of ESR came back to our Monthly Meetings aflame with the notion of what Friends really stand for, that would be of real value to me.

~

ESR's vision shouldn't be defined by whoever is on campus at the time. The administration and faculty and board should define the vision, rather than the vision being defined by whoever is on campus at the time. They shouldn't become a cozy, quaint place of let's all get together as Quakers and talk about our experiences.

~

Impact

What I liked about ESR for unprogrammed Friends is that we went out there and were changed rather dramatically. We were challenged; our liberal theology and politics were competently challenged. We got into the Bible and into disciplined theological reflection and we ended up, many of us, revising and deepening our understanding.

…in the circles where ESR has had influence, it has maintained a vital Quaker culture where there are places that Quakerism can be maintained and revitalized. That's probably been its major contribution.

~

This web [of connections] is a testament to the School's success in fulfilling its mission. With but few exceptions, these functionaries are capable, serious and dedicated, a credit to their alma mater.

~

In the 1980s, some students from my Friends university went to ESR and I had encouraged them to go and frankly they got beat up pretty bad by other students mostly, but it was a climate which was tolerated by the administration and the faculty, and I chewed on them about that. It made me real reluctant to send students or to encourage students to go there in that period. Students trusted me to give them an idea about whether that would be a good place for them or not. When it turned out not to be, it was really troublesome. Now I think that things are better. I have students that have gone from George Fox or who are currently there, or have just finished and returned who have had good experiences and been accepted and respected and liked in the community.

~

Why aren't people beating a path to our door? I think in large part it's because we have forgotten who we are. And one of the things that I have appreciated so much about ESR was that it reclaimed that tradition for me. I think at its best ESR equips people to go out and share that message that Friends have a distinctive message, and that when we are true to that message, we have a great deal to offer others.

~

My sense is that ESR has worked very hard to serve people who have come from unprogrammed Meetings. I think that is good and important to continue. I would like to think that they are working equally hard to do a really good job of preparing Quaker pastors and I don't honestly know. I know what it was like 30 years ago.

~

ESR has a better shot, actually, of creating understanding than conferences do. Because you are with people over an extended time and it probably does more good than a lot of the other conferences do to tell you the truth.

~

Our perspective is definitely committed to Christ-centered Quakerism and that's what we are pursuing here and the people that have been to ESR have not felt like that's been undermined at all.

~

Certainly ESR is a place that I've taken hope in because it is a meeting place for people of the different stances within Quakerism to meet and learn together, to learn from each other.

~

There is no disciplined ministry in our Meetings, except that which is provided oftentimes by graduates of ESR who actually know something about the Bible, about Quaker history, about theology, and can give some content; not that ministry can't be inspiring from the heart without any content, but there's a relationship between having enough people in a Meeting who know what they're talking about and are trained, and the quality of the ministry.

~

I will have to say from being up close and personal with ESR, that it is amazing how many unprogrammed, vaguely formed folks have come to the ESR community and have found Jesus. I would say the movement from the ambiguous to Jesus is far more persuasive and influential. I can't think of any Christ-centered Quaker that went away ambiguous. But I know I can count on my hand folks whose lives have been transformed who've come from just been led blindly by the Spirit to the community and found the living Jesus.

~

Almost everywhere one looks today, among Yearly Meeting staff and other paid functionaries, one will find ESR alumni/ae.

~

As a group, the folks who graduated from ESR are a beacon of hope. They are sensible, often deeply reflective, and well trained. The school has done, I think, by and large, a great job in that regard. The problem is there's no place for them in the unprogrammed tradition; they're working as volunteers, most of them, and on committees, and trying their best to be influential in a situation where they really have no power.

~

I'm very glad [ESR] exists. I remember when ESR was formed, and there was a crying need—and still is—for what I thought was its primary purpose at that point of training pastors for pastoral Meetings. The Meeting that I grew up in had a good many pastors who were not Friends. For people to have a really good sense of Quaker history and good Bible study is, I think, tremendously important across the board. Talking to various people before coming here, my daughter mentioned things that she thought people who had gone to ESR had brought to us that were useful: Bible study, Quaker history, spiritual friends, and spiritual direction.

~

…how can ESR assist in preparing leadership among Quakers from both traditions? I think it is already equipped to do that. The flood of unprogrammed Friends at ESR have frightened away some of the others from the pastoral tradition but ESR is equipped to do it now and has been doing it pretty well. It has not satisfied those Friends who don't want any obscurity about truth. But I think it does that pretty well.

The simple problem of ESR is they've produced a lot of people who are well trained and have no jobs. It's as simple as that as far as the unprogrammed tradition goes.

~

I haven't followed ESR all that closely over these years. But I would say in the early years that was primarily its role. I think of pastors in various parts of the Quaker world who would come through ESR and I think of others in various parts of the country who have come through ESR. I don't have in my mind statistics about how many of those have reached positions of leadership like superintendents or in comparable terms in the programmed Meetings. I do know that quite a bit of the leadership in the eastern unprogrammed Friends has come from ESR. In fact, for example, I was teaching at Pendle Hill for 13 years; that could never have happened if I hadn't gone back to a school like ESR. I don't think Pendle Hill or Woodbrooke would have prepared me in the same way.

~

…our graduates are very often working very effectively and very quietly, and, oddly enough, the downside of that is that people don't realize that they are ESR graduates.

~

[ESR contributions to the Religious Society of Friends] would be going back to what Elton Trueblood and Tom Jones, Landrum Bolling and Wil Cooper, Alexander Purdy and those folk envisioned in the late 1950s. That was 100 years after the beginning of the pastoral movement in the Society of Friends, when the vast majority of American Quaker Meetings had pastors and they were not being trained. There were no Quaker seminaries, and if they were being trained they were being trained at other denominations, or were coming ill-equipped out of Bible colleges. There had to be some institution to address the fact that we've got to train those leaders in our programmed Meetings.

I think ESR has had partial success in doing that. ESR was the first seminary. There are now two or three. [These other seminaries'] track record is very mixed, but ESR has certainly been successful. If you look at the Yearly Meetings, a lot of the pastors have come out of ESR; others have gone off to colleges and started campus ministry programs, counseling, you name it, they've made vital contributions. But ESR has not revitalized Quakerism as a whole. Quakerism itself is facing a crisis as it goes into the 21st century. Who is it? What is it? Where is it going? Why is it?

~

Perceptions of ESR

There was a period of time, particularly in the middle '80s and beyond, when they had a lot of folks hanging around that weren't really headed toward leadership. They were doing personal exploration. There has been some tightening in recent years. If people don't perceive that ESR is doing a good job of [pastoral training], then students don't come from those traditions and now they are really competing with institutions regionally that do that work.

~

There hasn't been a good working relationship between the Yearly Meetings and ESR. They have to have leadership that can comes to the various Mcctings and tells the story. They should have ways to involve meeting people that could light a fire under them to turning out something worthwhile. Meetings would be responsive to this. If you don't tell your story, nobody knows about you and that takes a consistent effort. You can't appear once every five years and expect results.

~

ESR is not too narrow. It's too wide.

~

I have known numbers of people who grew up in evangelical circles and went to ESR and went on to get a doctorate and felt fine about it. But I've also known other people who were well prepared to teach at a place like ESR but who felt like they, as a person of evangelical background, wouldn't have been accepted there.

~

I don't have any real specific images [of ESR] that come to mind. It seems like the thing that I've heard that I really appreciate is that they have a real strong sense on ministry and equipping people for ministry. That doesn't necessarily have to be paid pastoral ministry. It sounds like they're doing a good job of trying to investigate and balance both branches of Quakerism: Christ-centered and non-Christ-centered.

~

The School at ESR may be wonderful, but we don't ever see any of it.

~

I have a sense that ESR's isolated, not in touch with the real world of what the Society of Friends needs and wants.

~

We've known ESR's fund raisers but not their products.

~

ESR is all campus-based. Why?

~

It's a place most Friends do have a feeling about, even if it's to reject it…in love and hatred, all kinds of wonderful things can happen.

~

I heard from evangelical people that they felt unwelcome at ESR, as if made to feel out of place.

~

The most common misperception about ESR is that it's liberal.

~

ESR could stand for something, even though it may be hard to pull this off institutionally.

~

Earlham is disadvantaged in the larger community of Friends and this probably extends to the School of Religion, in part, because it is perceived as a hot bed of political correctness and the controversy about wicca and witchcraft has been decisive in the Indiana Yearly Meeting. I'm not surprised to hear it said that Guilford is a more comfortable home for folks from this particular congregation than Earlham is. That's clearly a difficulty (to use a crass term) in *marketing* ESR to the greater community. This is a bit of an albatross around their neck. Whether it's fair or not is another question in terms of people's perception of what it is like to be a part of this community.

~

…down here in North Carolina there is both an unawareness of ESR because they haven't done a lot down here. There hasn't been much outreach to North Carolina because they have had to work so hard at what's going on up there, the relationship with Bethany, putting out the brush fires of Indiana Yearly Meeting, all that kind of stuff. On the one hand there is just not a lot of awareness. But on the other hand, we have a lot of pastors here now who have been trained at ESR. One of the reasons that North Carolina Yearly Meeting is so strong, so dynamic, is because there are so many really fine young products of ESR down here.

~

Earlham is very open as a university but the setting of the state, it is a little bit more parochial.

~

ESR has a lot to offer Earlham College students but this relationship isn't being developed.

~

Earlham does have a very unique position, because they are in FUM-land. This positions them very interestingly in the Religious Society of Friends, because FUM is an organization that's affiliated with Yearly Meetings that are reunited. It's like a bridging kind of an organization in and of itself. Earlham School of Religion is about training pastors which is essentially—I mean, in some obvious ways— interesting to pastoral Friends, but seems to have an identity that is interesting and exciting to unprogrammed Friends. It seems to me it has the capacity to gather together a diverse group, which is a very hard thing to do.

~

I see ESR as Christocentric rather than universal. I don't like that way of dividing it; it accentuates differences that lead to alienation, rather than looking for commonalities behind those labels. I would like new words, without all the baggage that the old ones have.

~

[Earlham is] very well known as a *liberal* liberal arts academic institution. I think that it's not real well known that ESR is separate from Earlham. I think ESR is not particularly well known.

~

The beginning of the ESR was a wonderful thing. I think it has made a real difference. But I see it now slipping into a pattern that doesn't encourage me, a pattern of just doing the same thing over and over and over without either having the resources or else the vision to cut some new territory. I think that it's essential, not only for Friends, but for the whole church to be doing this.

~

ESR is where sick people go to get well.

~

I felt conspicuously uninvited to ESR as a resource…

~

There would be a sense of respect [for ESR]. I think probably the major expression would be, "We don't know anything about it."

~

One perception I have of ESR is that they got overrun by liberal Quakers and started making adjustments they never should have made. They should have been changing these people and instead they got changed by them, and in some respects, for the worse.

~

There's more of an acceptance of women at ESR, at least there is the perception because of our history of women being equal in ministry. The reason I went to ESR was because I felt the calling. Women were nurtured and encouraged in a way that I couldn't imagine happening in the early '80s at other seminaries. *[male Friend]*

~

At ESR, people get *embroiled* and self-involved. Too inwardly focused.

~

ESR can serve leadership needs of a wide number of Friends and I'm glad for the ways in which it has done that.

~

ESR seems to be doing pretty well at keeping connected; you also have different alumni keeping in touch with each other which works out pretty well.

~

Alumni perspectives on ESR

My experience of ESR 20 years ago was that ESR was a very different model of a seminary from the conventional model, which is to say it felt to me that its focus was as much about being a community of faith that lived and learned together as it was about being an academic institution.

Which doesn't mean that academics weren't taken very seriously. I worked very hard and was pushed very hard by some very fine teachers and still certainly draw regularly on my training in scripture and church history and theology and all those things. They prepared me well to go on and do other graduate work, even though I didn't do it until 10 years later. And I stayed relatively well connected to the institution for the first five or six years I was out, then began to lose touch and, frankly, they did a lousy job of staying in touch with me. So there is a kind of 10-year gap in here where I don't really have much of a feel for the institution. I often did not hear very good things about it from people who had graduated in the later '80s and early '90s.

~

They're just not devoting the resources necessary [to alumni relations]. They're way under-funded. They should have a full-time alumni secretary who does nothing but maintain contact with the alumni groups.

In the old days, Tom [Mullen] and the others circulated and had regional meetings on a very frequent basis. They were much better about keeping in touch. I've dealt with a number of alumni over the years and my favorite alumni are those who are just broken-hearted over the institution. If you give them the time of the day, they'll tell you what's on their hearts and then they'll work relentlessly for you and those are the ones you want to listen to. [ESR is] just not listening.

They should staff that [development] function and they shouldn't have a shared fund raiser. They should have their own fund raiser who is on the road constantly. They need to put money into that institution.

Money drives a lot of this. And if they're going to raise money, you have to spend money to raise it.

~

I love ESR and want to contribute in every way that I can.

~

When you have interested, concerned alumni with some serious concerns about the institution, it is incomprehensible that ESR is not on the case and responding immediately and is not even seeking them out and meeting with them to the extent possible. If Thom Jeavons is on your list, listen hard, because ESR has ignored him. He's one of the most influential and prominent Quakers around and they haven't given him the time of day for 15 to 20 years.

~

I have heard not a rotten thing from ESR for ages. They're completely out of touch with their most prominent graduates.

~

The School was doing some very interesting and active things to recruit students that drew on their alumni network in good ways. Since a few of us had immediately ended up in leadership positions, we were important people for them to be in touch with. They were making some direct effort to do that. Then later on, certainly when I moved off into the academic world, that didn't seem to be an important connection.

~

Where's a *list* of what ESR graduates are doing? Why can I not get that?

~

My work at Pendle Hill I regarded as a kind of being a translator. Always translating between one type of Quakerism or another. I got that background at ESR.

~

ESR is a really important mixing place for Quakers. There's really no place like it in the world where people come together from different groups of Quakers and bring both their background and strengths, but also their questions and contribute to the larger community. For instance, someone said to me the first couple of weeks I was there, "So you're an evangelical. What's it like? I've never met one." And that was my opportunity to say, "Here are what things are like and this has been my experience." The person asking that question has become a lifelong friend. It's such experiences that can be very jarring in the sense that there's a huge amount of diversity within the Quaker movement, especially in America. Yet, that becomes one of the riches of the community.

~

If you're not into the culture wars, ESR is one of the few places to be with people who are theologically different.

~

It might be a hugely valuable thing to get some of the "old guard," as I would refer to some of us, together again, graduates who have been out serving the Society of Friends, many of whom have left their service in the last 10 years, with varying degrees of disillusionment. It might be very productive to get those people together to talk about their experiences, what served them well in their training, what they weren't prepared for, and so on.

~

It was incredibly valuable for me to be with people [at ESR] who came from different backgrounds. I was with a group in constructive theology where there were four of us who met at the local diner: one from Iowa, one from EFI, and an unprogrammed Friend from California, and me. And it was so funny to see the four of us come to a more central place and even switch places. It was just a microcosm of what took place at ESR.

~

Another thing about my Quaker development and what was really significant for me about my ESR experience, where also feeds into the work I'm doing now, is the exposure to the wider world. I'd basically been an east coast unprogrammed Friend and I got to ESR when a bunch of unprogrammed Friends were showing up and we were thrown into this basket together. It was a really rich environment for the evangelicals to see people like me who didn't think the same, but we were all Quakers, and for me to see what was important in the different experiences that people had had.

~

I would say that ESR is not for everyone. I would not recommend it for someone from my own [evangelical] tradition who doesn't have a strong understanding of what they believe. So, if a person graduating from George Fox, for instance, is a new Christian or a new Friend, I would want that person to have majored in religion before going to ESR, or to have a pretty strong background...at ESR they will be stretched beyond that. But I would recommend ESR for more courageous and resilient folks.

~

…the two main things that happened for me were, one, a deep appreciation for learning distinctive Quakerism through Hugh Barbour, Wil Cooper…those academic courses, a real, real good introduction to the history of Friends, and secondly, outstanding biblical studies, especially through Gene Roop and the real awakening of interest in Bible, and understanding that you didn't have to be a fundamentalist to appreciate the Bible, that you could have your brain fully engaged and be able to read the Bible as well.

~

I have a real fondness for the place [ESR] and a vision for what it actually could effect and it's a big job. Something has got to happen in the Religious Society of Friends.

~

I would be willing to help ESR get some kind of satellite operation opened in North Carolina so people could legitimately get class credits, degrees, without having to move to Indiana full-time.

~

ESR needs a top-notch development officer who's going to put the energy into it and knows how to do it. Their annual fund hasn't grown much at all, as far as I can recall, and I've actually gotten away without giving a gift for a number of years. They should be coming after me. Of course, I'd be inclined to give.

~

There is a wide diversity of students there. When I was there, I think, the majority were probably unprogrammed Friends who went into various kinds of ministry—from retreat centers to chaplaincy to campus ministry, and did a lot of work in different kinds of ministries, not just pastoral ministries. You mentioned things that continue and I think that dialogue that ESR has between the unprogrammed and programmed is a start because I came out of an Evangelical Friends church in Southwest Yearly Meeting and my roommate was from Pacific Yearly Meeting, and he had a different background than I did even though we came from the same state. He had books on Eastern Spirituality and I had my books on the defense of the Virgin Birth kind of thing. But we became great friends, and he gave me a new appreciation for the Bible and spirituality and I became a little less doctrinaire, and so it was a great benefit to me. That's the kind of thing that can happen at ESR, at its best anyway.

~

At the time I thought ESR was doing a very respectable job of straddling the two major traditions of Friends, the programmed and unprogrammed, or pastoral and non-pastoral. ESR was able to speak pretty effectively to both and they've lost, in some ways, both camps. If you were to talk to pastoral Friends, the criticisms are of a much different sort—not evangelical enough, not Christocentric, not Bibliocentric, the politics are too liberal, and the list goes on. On the unprogrammed side, it's that we needed you to change us and provide us with leaders who are going to make a difference, and some of your faculty sold out to the unprogrammed tradition too much.

~

I'd like to give testimony to the positive contribution that ESR gave to me. It gave me a good grounding for pastoral leadership. But by the same token, I don't think ESR has done its job in attracting potential pastoral leaders. It's a major problem still as it was when Wilmer Cooper came and said we need to prepare men and women to go out into the local Meeting and give leadership.

~

Would I encourage someone to move from North Carolina to go to ESR? I'm not sure I've come up with an answer as yet, or that I can say that what you will gain from that experience is profound enough to warrant the sacrifices you will have to make. And that concerns me, particularly since I'm from the pastoral tradition and I'm dealing with people interested in pastoral leadership.

~

There's a problem with volunteer service, even within Yearly Meetings. People are too stretched for time to serve on committees. If there are so many groups needing volunteers, perhaps if ESR had service as part of the curriculum, then ESR students could be of help, for example, to the Meetings, to youth camps, the Quaker volunteer witness program, etc. There are lots of areas and places that need such help.

~

There was a disunified vision of the Board at ESR at the time, and there were those who have gone to ESR who experienced that ambiguity of purpose from the professors at ESR. I have always wondered if ESR from its very beginning was setting itself up for one of its main purposes, but not the only one, to help equip and better prepare men and women for Christian ministry in pastoral settings and did everything they could to secure funds from the pastoral and semi-programmed Meetings and

Yearly Meetings. Why has there yet to this very day been no installation of excellent coursework for Christian education, youth ministry, children's ministry, creative ideas programming? There has been this ambiguity of purpose within the very structure of ESR which has created an unsettled sense of camaraderie, purpose, plan, trust, amongst the whole ESR community. There are those who have felt strongly the call to move into pastoral work and at the end of working hard to prepare themselves, didn't feel that ESR celebrated that.

~

I have picked up from some other ex-students that there seemed to be some frustration with ESR. I don't know what that is. I'm too far out of it to know what that is so I'm going to assume that you will be contacting alumni. But if I would have any concern, it would be that if it is attached to particular periods of history, some healing needs to be done because they need to be freed from that.

~

I'd be open to being one of those people who met at ESR, if invited. But I hope they pay our way and wine us and dine us. Don't be cheap.

~

I really can't think of any one piece that could have been removed and the ESR experience would have been as valuable. The community was very important. The conversations we had, the diversity of theologies and histories, and just sitting around the library or sitting at Common Meal, or playing ping pong, and just talking. It's very important, I think, for ESR to continue to have a good mix from across the spectrum of Quakerism. The faculty at the time were all absolutely committed to both Quakerism and to the academic enterprise. So they had the whole matter of the heart and matter of the brain sorted out. There was no bifurcation between critical and clear thinking and hard academic work and being a person of faith. They all modeled that and they all showed that you don't have to check your brain at the hat rack in order to be a Christian or be a person of faith.

~

I haven't heard an awful lot in recent years from folks at ESR.

~

There are misperceptions, especially coming from the more liberal and conservative extremes, that people won't be served well at ESR because they are members of the community that are from another side of the spectrum. While this is true that there are people from other sides of the spectrum, what isn't true is that therefore people won't be served well.

~

One of the things I picked up from some of the older women was a real sense of anger. They had been in a class right before the one we were having and that seemed not to be going well at all. And there seemed to be some sense of gender inequality going on, some sense of ageism that they had taken the risk of giving up careers to come here but they weren't sure that they were being treated seriously and they weren't sure that there would be opportunities for them when they left. I picked up on that because I was of that age. The younger students seemed to have a much more optimistic view of their future. Not a lot of them were defining themselves, say, as entering Quaker leadership positions. Some were looking at social work and seemed to be worrying that they would find places to go to.

~

The academic part of ESR was great but that's not the reason I was there. In my search, the education for me was being a part of Miriam Burke's classes on personal and spiritual prep for ministry. In describing myself here, I put *mystical* first and developing some of those mystical aspects of myself were important to me, developing the mystical understandings, and trying to understand what was going on as I was having some of these experiences. So being a part of her classes, being a part of a small group that got together around issues of healing, that for me was one of the main reasons for being at ESR; as I said earlier, to sit down at a meal with an alum from eastern region and on the other side an alum who's now on staff at ESR from Pacific Yearly Meeting and have those very divergent views and being able to talk and talk and come to a common understanding, being able to really listen to one another and hear what they're saying.

~

ESR was a transformational experience for me. What it taught me— and I don't always live it out—is the difference between defining myself and defending myself. The invitation to be involved in our own learning built confidence in me to say who I am.

~

What a lot of seminaries emphasize and ESR does not is that mentoring relationship between a seasoned Christian pastor and a young person who may be sure of the call or maybe not, but is encouraged to consider it. But perhaps ESR could make more connections whether in paid associate or part-time work opportunities, just to hook up with devout seasoned pastors, to help train the young person. What do you say to someone who is dying? How do you handle a graveside service? One of the weaknesses of ESR when I was graduating is that people in the M.Div. track were going into their senior projects and faculty were saying, "That's not the right way," but none of the faculty had pastored.

~

ESR gave me space to grow in the ways that God was leading…in an affirming and challenging way.

~

Don't choose one branch of Friends over the other. ESR needs to stand in the paradox and be a meeting ground for Friends. I know that's hard and it's caused a lot of hurt, but I don't think ESR should go one way or the other.

~

That's the thing that was most profound in my experience, not encountering people as groups but representatives of groups, encountering individuals, studying with them, knocking each other around on the theological points in the classroom, eating together, playing together, worshiping together. That level of personal acquaintance, if sustained after the ESR experience over a number of years, can be pretty powerful. Part of what that means is that the environment needs to be one which is congenial and in which there is some basic level of courtesy and respect in all directions.

~

Curriculum

I've seen a recent catalogue and there is much, much more in that catalogue on what you might call practical theology than there was 30 years ago and I'm glad for that.

~

ESR should offer a course about Quaker business practice or a class that would begin to provide a sense of what a Quaker pastor looks like, since NWYM needs people who understand the Quaker business process and how to clerk and how that fits into clearness, discernment, etc.

~

Something I would love to see ESR do, for instance, is offer a course on evangelism; why not offer a course on human transformation, which is a little different from spiritual formation, that's sometimes a more developmental approach? Ask questions of transformation: How do people get changed by God? How does the devotional life develop life-changing vitality? And how do pastors and other leaders and anybody in the unprogrammed tradition as well, how do those people minister out of contact with a living God in ways that change people around them? If ESR can get its prayerful searching around those issues, it would be an amazingly exciting place, for all Quakers but also for people beyond Friends.

~

Can we afford [to look at new ideas] with the tight schedule that we've already got with our teachers and our curriculum and the regulations that we have to fulfill from the accrediting agencies? OR can we afford not to?

~

I don't know that the curriculum and the focus takes into account a whole lot of what folks in the pastoral Meetings of the evangelical sector are really seeking.

~

I would encourage ESR to risk launching some bold and innovative programs designed to equip the leaders of tomorrow with skills enabling them to address the needs and problems we confront in our Meetings and communities everywhere, even if this requires a departure from traditional core curriculum for theological education.

~

There's a problem with volunteer service, even within Yearly Meetings. People are too stretched for time to serve on committees. If there are so many groups needing volunteers, perhaps if ESR had service as part of the curriculum, then ESR students could be of help, for example, to the Meetings, to youth camps, the Quaker volunteer witness program, etc. There are lots of areas and places that need such help.

~

Faculty

The faculty when I was there [in the '70s] seemed very much to be a community of scholars with a common purpose, and that was to equip people for ministry.

~

I thank ESR faculty over the years for being willing to struggle with being faithful to the vision and divine leadings they individually and collectively have had.

~

It's very important to have some people who have pastoral experience among Quakers, as well as academic backgrounds, doing some of the courses.

~

Obviously, an appreciation for Quakerism among faculty is important. What would be ideal would be for someone to finance the development of Quaker academics at top institutions. We need the Elton Truebloods and the Rufus Joneses again. Somebody needs to take an interest. There needs to be a small group of philanthropists, for instance, who put up the money to educate our most promising Quaker individuals. We need to recruit more people to the Society of Friends from other areas who are going to end up being thoughtful leaders. It's a long complicated process, but the end result is that we should be finding the new Rufus Joneses and Elton Truebloods and others, and they ought to be serving on that faculty. The faculty is somewhat undistinguished at this point, is my impression.

~

Current leaders can't be blamed for all the decisions of the past, but the question of the conventional wisdom that an evangelical could never get hired at ESR in a faculty role at least needs to be named.

~

It just strikes me, though, for that [small] number of people to be able to offer a really competent, broadly based program, some of the faculty must be at the edge of their expertise, and I'm talking about technically, not out of a sense of knowledge.

~

I really can't speak very well to where the institution is these days. I don't know what it is capable of doing. Certainly the things that it did when I was there that would still be useful are these: It was a place where Friends from the different traditions met on common ground and in a relatively safe environment, and there was a lot of very useful learning that happened through people who were *liberals* talking to people who were *evangelicals* and seeing that there is some common spiritual ground in our Quaker tradition on which to meet and learn from one another. There was a genuine respect.

Now I don't know if all my Evangelical Friends would say the same thing, but I really felt like there was a major effort on the part of the faculty to truly respect and embrace different points of view. That was a real important piece of learning for me, as my scholarship in later years has continued to focus on the role of religion in American public life and on religious institutions. A lot of the research I've done in the last 10 years is with evangelical organizations. The ability to speak their language, to understand what they are talking about and to be comfortable with them and have them be comfortable with me, despite the fact I'm not in the conventional sense an evangelical, I relate this directly to the kind of experience I had at ESR.

~

Earlham needs to be more user-friendly for middle-of-the-road Friends and people that want to go into the pastoral ministry. I mean, they are moreso now significantly than five or 10 years ago. I know there's a change, and there's a change mainly because of one reason, that the two faculty members that were there are not there now and it has changed, really the atmosphere has changed some, but it can change more so the people who come from an evangelical background feel that it's really a place for them to be and be welcomed. I mean, they are welcomed but some have a hard time.

~

ESR needs a first-rate faculty—people with strong academic credentials and a background among Friends. We've had some spottiness in the quality. Some have been very strong; some have been good-hearted and well-meaning but not necessarily articulate and intellectually vigorous. ESR needs to make sure faculty have a high commitment to top-notch academic preparation as well as religious sensibilities.

~

I know ESR is small. But it should determine a viable size for the student body, and then support the number of faculty needed to do the mission—and go after that. If it's not possible, then look at being some other kind of institution. Sharing faculty with Earlham College is a wonderful opportunity to broaden academic strength.

~

There's a perception among the evangelicals that ESR is kind of a far-out place theologically. ESR has to do a better job of maybe bringing in an evangelical scholar just for that. Not a doctrinal evangelical but one from say Reedwood or with that kind of openness.

~

ESR, for its part, I don't think was as sensitive as it ought to have been in the '80s and the early '90s to how different culturally the Friends were out there in those small rural Meetings. There was a sense of superiority again that we know what we are doing, we know what's best. I think that came from a different kind of faculty than ESR had developed back when you had folk like Tom Mullen and Wil Cooper and those folks who had grown up in those communities, who had pastored Meetings, who had come up through those sorts of background.

~

[ESR should] re-examine whether the institution is gauging correctly and relating adequately to the state and prospects of the unprogrammed branch. To the extent that the handbasket prophecies represent its ethos, I believe it definitely is not; and I question whether your faculty represents the unprogrammed branch adequately, or is even much in touch with it.

In fact, I doubt it. My experiences over the past two decades suggests that ESR has been least visible in the space where the unprogrammed branch most displays its disheveled vigor: Friends General Conference, and in particular annual Gatherings.

~

I have been assured during recent weeks by several people in the ESR community that ESR intends to serve the *whole* Society of Friends and that it intends to be a seminary and not a Bible School. Am I optimistic that this can happen? Guardedly, and only if a concerted effort is made by the ESR community and friends of ESR to become versed in con-temporary Bible scholarship, to the end that liberal faith is seen as an adequate and legitimate expression of Christian faith, and to act on that premise.

~

…on the academic side, ESR can provide us with some courses and a very important mix in those courses, particularly with ESR being within the Religious Society of Friends, are courses in Quakerism. I think there ought to be a well-trained person there to do this, the history of Friends, all that goes along with that, and John Punshon would be an outstanding example of what can happen.

He's there now but I understand he's leaving and he has, just recently within the last year, done much to help us understand Evangelical Friends and where they're coming from. He's taken that on as a concern, so when he goes, I hope you can replace him. That's very important.

There needs to be someone on the staff like that who can understand the variety, the diversity among Friends, and can help interpret that to people. Ministry in some ways in an unprogrammed Meeting is different than ministry in a programmed Meeting, there are different characteristics to it. ESR can complement Pendle Hill with a deeper focus on the academic.

~

I'll mention again John Punshon and the role he has had there on the staff. He's leaving now. It would be a service to Friends if they had a strong Quaker history orientation. I would agree that they need to help us with some of the issues within the Society of Friends such as liberal, evangelical, same sex marriages…

~

ESR has a lot of students from denominations other than the Quaker and I think that is a very good thing. From what I hear, however, there is a desire to have those differences reflected in the teaching faculty. I am a bit more concerned about that. I would like all faculty to be Quaker because it is hard for Quakers to find a book to read about any aspect of what's ESR. It's vital to have teaching faculty who can talk about Quakerism, especially if people go there just for one year.

If you are trying to encourage someone to come to ESR for a year, why would you want to learn Old Testament from a Methodist. You might as well go to your own local seminary if that's your interest. It would be a big advantage to have Quakers, especially for the biblical, the New Testament, and the Old Testament.

~

The ESR faculty: they're *not* experienced in preaching and pastoring. Therefore, they teach from a *void*.

~

John Punshon has been a great asset to the school. He is just an amazing character in his own right and I'm glad it has worked out for him to be there because I think it's been a great thing for him as well.

~

There was a period of time when the perception was—and the perception may still be the case but you will have a better sense of that after having all these focus groups—that people were not being prepared well to do pastoral service. They didn't have good administrative skills and didn't have good preaching skills. Even though the language and commitment was of equipping ministry, people didn't really know how to equip people and draw people into service. I'm not sure that was entirely fair, it's kind of hard to judge. There are times when I thought, in fact, those areas were under-represented in terms of the strength of the faculty and the courses that were offered.

Actually, in recent years—again from perception—and I have told folks at ESR this, they are preparing people for pastoral ministry but virtually all of the faculty, save maybe one or two, had never been pastors, and/or were attending Clear Creek Meeting. It's hard to be persuasive that you are training people for pastoral ministry when virtually all the faculty attend a non-pastoral Meeting.

~

ESR needs to do what it takes to recruit excellence to its faculty. I really don't care where it comes from, what politics are involved, what YM has to be pleased, they have to recruit top-notch academics and thinkers. They need, instead of worrying whether they'll get a Quaker with credentials who may be marginal, to recruit the person who's best-suited to the job with the best academic credentials. What was impressive about the early crew at ESR was that they were exceptionally bright and highly motivated people.

~

ESR has to decide whether it's going to serve the academy or the church. People who serve at ESR can be good scholars, they can participate in the life of scholarship as it contributes to biblical studies or historical studies and other things…I am sure for the sake of evaluation and tenure and all those kinds of things that they are being evaluated on those things.

But I have seen in lots of places, colleges and seminaries alike, where the faculty basically are concerned that they have the approval and they give their energy towards having the academic seal of approval from other academics—many of whom don't give a rip about the church or religion or faith even though they are scholars in religion. I think it's a danger at ESR.

It's a danger for any of us in institutions of higher learning these days to keep our focus on who we serve first. I think ESR, like us at George Fox frankly, have to be very clear that the people we exist for and serve first is the church. And then whatever we do in the life of the academy gets arrayed around that primary purpose. I think that to evaluate how well people are serving the life of the institution needs to include how well they are serving the life of the church.

~

Board of Advisors
I'm not sure what the specific role is and what the boundaries are for the Board of Advisors.

~

I'm still finding a role on the Board. For me, that's not an uncomfortable place to be. I would much rather feel that there's some flexibility than be told what I have to believe or what I have to sell. I would not object to a quarterly newsletter in terms of just how the finances are going, this is what we are looking at in strengthening staff. That would be helpful to me because then I think I would be better equipped when I arrived in Richmond.

I do see the role as an advisory role, not as a major decision-making role. But if I had a dream, one of my dreams would be that in one of the Board Meetings we could just brainstorm what type of classes we thought would be useful at ESR, not that they would have to take all our advice but I do have personal questions about how that class system works. I'm not sure, for example, as I superficially look through the schedule, that there's enough New Testament in there. But probably someone who does pastoral things just doesn't think there's enough pastoral education in there. And I haven't been given the opportunity to discuss the thought behind why the schedule looks like it does.

~

If the Advisors meet in September, that means that the staff are very busy because they've got a new term starting. Does the Dean or does the faculty at the end of the academic year, which would be May say, pull itself together and do a detailed review of the year? If they do, should we not be getting that? I don't know what preparation they do for a Board of Advisors meeting because I don't think last year's Board of Advisors meeting was typical, because we had someone telling us about the potential consultation, and we had all the stuff around Jay Marshall's installation [as dean]. They have enough on their plates, but I would think that we need to know what happened and also perhaps be given a set of questions, both what could we have done last year that's better, and we're thinking of moving in this direction, what do you think about it, or do you have ideas as to what a five-year goal should be?

~

The advisory board and the Earlham board need to be able to see each other and even have a joint meeting for discussion about the future and direction of ESR. They only get that through the two or three people who are on the ESR board and that's not sufficient. The conclusion of the consultation might be a good opportunity to bind the two together.

~

They have people [on the Board of Advisors] who essentially can pick up the phone and contact most everyone across North American if they want them to do that.

~

It would be really important for ESR (the Board of Advisors) to have a long retreat, and to set some real goals based on the new century coming—about what's possible and what's needed; and also to draw people from the broader Society of Friends.

~

ESR leadership

Doug Bennett is taking over in a correct way. He insisted: Go out and talk to Quakers of this country, find out what they need in terms of leadership. God bless him and Jay Marshall; I hope they can stay the course.

~

I haven't met Jay Marshall, so that's one of the things I'm looking forward to doing is to getting to know Jay. But what I've read of him looks really good, and the fact that he has pastoral experience in Indiana YM is really a strong way to go. I'm very excited about Jay's leadership and hope it goes very well. Something I like about Doug Bennett is his pressing important questions and really helping getting people to talk about how to make a Quaker decision-making process function. I think he's right on in terms of determining which groups have responsibility for which particular issues, instead of assuming everything is everybody's business. That's one of the sloppy things that creeps into the Quaker egalitarian process. Doug's done a superb job of saying: This group decides these things, the Board is accountable for the institutions, these are the roles that the different decision-making bodies play, and let's do all of these well with the maximum amount of communication. That is really healthy and I think that's superb.

~

I do think that ESR has made a good choice in Jay Marshall as a well-respected pastor in FUM. I hope that that is not only a good choice of dean in its own right, but that it will open the channels in that direction better.

~

I see Jay Marshall having the blessing of being accepted as sincere, serious, deep, also a happy guy to be with.

~

[Some have wondered whether] Jay Marshall is interested in the international aspect of ESR, or whether he wants to focus only on national needs.

~

I look forward to Jay Marshall's leadership; that's a good move.

~

Doug Bennett seemed to be very easy with people. He seemed to be able to express things in a language that seemed acceptable to everybody.

~

My sense about Jay Marshall is that I want to know who he is. I still don't feel as though I know who he is. I need to probably get to know him second-hand and that's through what I'm hearing about ESR and how ESR is either changing or moving ahead or whatever. I'm not sure I need to know him personally. It would be really good if I heard that the staff morale was great—they have a new commitment to A, B or C. Or that Jay had identified that one of the things he loved was teaching, therefore, he was just teaching a short course or something. That there's energy and solidity behind it. That's what I would see as appropriate. I don't want to know what toothpaste he uses.

~

Relationship with Bethany Seminary

I had some hopes that when Bethany came it would be more a place of scholarship. I look at Bethany as the place that Christ went to when he wanted renewal. When he chased the money changers from the temple, he went to Bethany that night and to me that's a kind of thing where if you can combine the academic discipline, which I was hoping would be increased with a sister facility, it would mean a better library and all kinds of things. That renewal process is necessary, but I really see drifting at this point. I don't see the cohesive kinds of things that say, here I stand and let me pound my 95 queries to the door. Among Friends, queries has a special meaning, those are the questions that we ask ourselves not as rules but as guides for self-evaluation. [It may be too soon to tell if my hoped-for scholarship is emerging]…when I look at what the faculty is today, I really can't say that I want to passionately study under any of them.

~

ESR should help promote the historical Quaker experience while letting the Brethren, for example, teach the biblical experience. I can take a course in the New Testament from other schools and not go all the way to ESR for that.

~

The Brethren students seemed to be in a much more disciplined or structured path. The Quaker students—this is going to be an awful generalization—some of them were very worried about money or were having to be part-time students because they had to work part-time and were wondering how long it would take and would there really be a job for them at the end of this. The Brethren students seemed to be a lot more secure. My impression was that they were all fully granted and almost had a guaranteed position to go to. And that seemed to make a difference.

~

The connection with Bethany has strengthened the pastoral care kinds of curriculum. But that still leaves us with a call for a really clear model of what it is to be a Quaker pastor to be articulated. I would love to see that being the center of the tree flowing forth with the writing and the shaping as well as the curriculum. I think that's what we all hope for from them.

~

The merger with Bethany was wise, given the size of the faculty, but I'm not clear that this has been fully realized.

~

[My vision for ESR] is to do what you're doing right now which is begin to gather data, and it may be of only the broadest type and indicate the areas of concern. I'd be bringing people together to strategize for the next decade and I'd put together a real concrete strategy. Here's what we're going to do; here's what we're going to accomplish for the Religious Society of Friends for the next 10 years. It's a make it or break it thing. I'd pay attention to the merger they tried to effect with the Brethren seminary, which is an incomplete and poor merger and hasn't really served either institution very well. I don't think it was managed well. They have some potential to be the most exciting, powerful seminary in the United States, along the level of Princeton, Yale, Harvard, Union, and that's what they should be striving for.

~

ESR can serve leadership needs of a wide number of Friends and I'm glad for the ways in which it has done that. There are people in leadership among unprogrammed Friends, Yearly Meeting secretaries of various kinds, local Meeting service of various kinds who have been strengthened and grown in their period at ESR and are doing good work and I meet them as I travel here and there.

I don't travel as widely among unprogrammed Friends, but I still am glad for the things that they know and are doing. There are some good people. There are also some effective pastors out among Friends who trained at ESR. People may say, "Well they would be good regardless of where they went." Or, "Actually ESR helped." Well, okay, who knows. You can always second guess that, but there are some very fine folks who have ESR as part of their training and are very effective pastors, and I'm very pleased about that kind of leadership and in other roles and organizations and schools.

Training widely is important, integrity is important. Giving more attention still to depth of pastoral studies. Bethany's coming has helped by offering some greater richness in those offerings.

~

ESR has been successful in having, I assume, a good preaching and writing professorship, although that has to change now I guess. I don't know what the present arrangements are since Tom Mullen retired. I have mentioned the spirituality. I think that's key. I have been disappointed but again there's a financial issue that we don't have strong Quaker biblical instruction. We do have good, strong Brethren instruction and the woman remarked, when I was at ESR just a week ago, that she was getting a lot from her biblical instruction. She was a Quaker from Philadelphia area. I think you need a John Punshon, [someone with] that Quaker breadth that is very special.

~

Bethany has a clear purpose, but it's not so clear with ESR, so ESR could very easily become the weak sister that's controlled by the bigger sister. I think my perception of ESR in the past few years is that it's lost, doesn't know where it is, doesn't know where it's going, but that may be a reflection of the Religious Society of Friends, that we may not know who we are and where we're going. So Earlham has found itself caught up not only in the pool of diversity we have in Baltimore Yearly Meeting but the mess within the Religious Society of Friends in North America that ESR is trying to serve. How does it create the balance between a Baltimore Yearly Meeting and an Indiana YM or an Iowa YM?

~

I'm concerned that ESR is or is becoming a preacher factory. I've said it to Jay Marshall when I spoke with him in August. With the appointment of Jay as dean who comes from that tradition and is not familiar with unprogrammed Friends experientially. I'm concerned about it becoming a preacher factory and knowing that it's being pushed by some of the Yearly Meetings in its immediate area to produce more preachers. I did not perceive it as a preacher factory when I was there, maybe I was looking at it through rose-colored glasses. One of my greatest experiences at ESR was having lunch with two friends, one on one side from Pacific Yearly Meeting, very liberal unprogrammed Meeting, and on the other side was a person out of Evangelical Friends Eastern Region, and having that breadth of experience. Maybe it's because I don't know all that's going on now, but for me Bethany strengthens that push towards creating preachers, and that's the image I have right now.

~

During the process of discerning how to develop the connection with Bethany, they issue was how does ESR nurture and maintain its commitment to Quaker decision making and help Bethany folks understand that so that the cooperation could be smooth. I really don't know how well they've done with that.

~

Recommendations for ESR programs

ESR might offer a seminar on Friends social testimonies and action strategies in the current political scene. I'd like help understanding better how to deal with Congress, how to be influential in upcoming elections—a depth analysis of public issues—to help me understand strategies effective in the social and political sphere I want to work in. Also, ESR could help in my working with Friends Association for Higher Education—developing exciting sessions, dialogues, seminars at our conference of FAHE and regional conferences.

~

ESR should do research and development regarding the transition from Quaker discernment to *action.*

~

I don't know whether ESR could do things on the road. Pendle Hill does a certain amount of that. I know Woodbrooke does as well— weekends and short courses and conferences of various kinds that could be held under the auspices of the institution, but not on the premises, that bring that vision to people where they are that might not require travel to ESR.

~

ESR's position on gays would be important to us. Their graduates are either vague, soft, or accept homosexuality as normal. We don't.

~

It is cheaper to send one faculty member to California for a week than it is to bring 20 students from California to ESR for a year. I have a friend—and I don't know where her program is—but she is in a program in spiritual direction, and there are a number of them that I'm noticing around, where you go for twice a year for a week and then you have some kind of a correspondence study or something like that. It is important for ESR to really look at the idea that, yes, we have our paid pastors and our professional Quakers and that's some of what they are training, but what we've really abolished is the laity. And so it's a way of ESR training Friends who are not going to be professional Quakers but who want to develop their leadership skills just for their everyday member-ship in the Religious Society of Friends.

~

It would be interesting if ESR could develop creative forums for dialogue among Friends in North Carolina, in Indiana—imaginative ways of looking at divisive issues—maybe through drama, role-play, haiku, role reversal, whatever—so people could learn to see differently, more creatively. And I'd like to see seminars for leaders in Quaker colleges and schools.

~

ESR can and should provide training in speaking (homiletics); help in group leadership skills; help with skills in pastoral counseling. If ESR didn't do all that, I'd worry. If it worked only with the broad issues, it wouldn't serve the whole range of Meetings, and we would have abandoned our calling.

~

I'd like to encourage [ESR] to not only create a program or class that would be housed at ESR to address the concerns and development of leadership, but to *also* consider how ESR can be a resource to Yearly Meetings and local Meetings by providing consultants or seminar leaders who can address the issues on a local level. I can't send all my people to ESR. A few will be able to go. But have an entire Meeting, or YM-wide retreatants' experience. Some of the training or challenge that results from this consultation will make a big impact.

~

[ESR could solicit ideas from] graduates who have had real life experience in Quaker institutions and know what their needs are; pastors who have served in the trenches who can tell you what the needs are and what they're facing. I'd begin to explore new directions from that—Quaker urban ministry; establishing and planting Quaker churches and Meetings in urban areas; reaching out to a new constituency; developing a model for Quaker outreach and church planting that will work in both camps; how to solve the problem of placing leadership in unprogrammed Meetings. We could get a list of issues a mile long and ESR is one of the very few institutions in a position to address these.

~

I was reading about the trends in seminaries in terms of off-campus stuff and part-time tent-makers and not so much of just sitting in classroom type education. I think Earlham could set itself up as a place, a center of activism, where people come to get trained theologically as well as trained in being activist in the community, and they have a fairly-well developed field studies program, but if they could expand that so that the experiential part of a pastor's training would be away from the classroom and include actual experiences of say engaging the culture. So that maybe Houston and some of those other places say that for a quarter, we are going to send our students to Earlham for this great experience. They are not that far away from Chicago and Indianapolis and there is a lot of potential there for people to get that kind of experience.

~

As for what ESR may offer for realistic preparation of Friends leaders, I suggest the following:

1) an understanding of the bases for Quaker testimonies;
2) sound biblical study as a reliable source for ongoing guidance. The study may inspire a love for the scriptures, free from the fear-filled restraints of authoritarian, literalistic interpretations, and would avoid using the *gospel gun* to shoot down others who dare to differ;
3) nurture skills in seeking a balance between individual initiatives (leadings) and corporate responsibility to the Meetings;
4) sustain the thankful and humble recognition that we are beneficiaries of the spiritual GIFTS offered us by God's grace; help open the way for leaders to discover the joys of unselfish service and continuous learning.

~

In this day and age, it is my sense that we often fail to take the time necessary for what is most basic, particularly in the areas of discernment, prayer, what I am calling here *Quaker meditation*, and religious education. I would encourage Earlham to set up programs [that incorporate] leadership training and training the initial leaders in the following areas:

1) **Discernment:** Friends today use this term casually and inappropriately. Furthermore, the related term *leading* is used in my Meeting as a manipulative device. No one in the Meeting has the faintest idea of how to actually test a leading. A weekend workshop on discernment would be extremely helpful in building Monthly Meetings and teaching people how to be Friends.
2) **Prayer:** This is another term that gets bantered about in hurtful ways. Friends need to learn how to pray! We also need to learn how to lead others in our communities in prayer.
3) **Meeting for Worship:** There is a group of Tibetan missionaries moving into our community…I know that they will set up a class on Buddhist Meditation, I am thinking about setting up another class in Quaker Meditation. The purpose of such a class would be to teach

some basic skills such as preparation for Quaker Worship…I will use many of the activities from *Opening the Doors to Quaker Religious Education* as a text. The audience will be people in the community who are searching for inner peace—the same audience as the Buddhists…I believe that such a program on *Quaker Meditation* would be very popular in other communities and would help people define themselves—whether they want to commit to a Quaker, Buddhist, or new age combination type path. Use of silence is something that Friends can bring to the world.

4) **Religious Education:**…It is my suggestion that ESR work with the Earlham education department in designing a program to train leaders for a traveling teacher training program in religious education.

～

When I was at ESR I learned a word from a Mennonite professor: *acculturation.* I think it's important for a place like ESR to keep that reality in front, particularly whenever Quakers of different persuasions start getting excited about each other in a bad way.

If ESR can help people be faithful to the genius of Christian Quakerism but also recognize that every branch of Quakerism that I know, including my own conservative branch, is acculturated, and that the genius of the reality or the hope, lies in always being able to step back from our acculturation or have a sense of humor about it at least. And that changes the nature of the conversation a great deal.

The evangelical Protestant movement in general, various aspects of that have their acculturative aspects on pastoral Quakerism. American materialism in general affects all of us, but it is curious how it affects the pastoral Quaker in a different way than a liberal Quaker. Liberal Quakers tend to be acculturated in a more eastern intellectual way, one form of middle-class America, and then there is mid-America acculturation, and on and on—the intellectual and the individualistic bent of acculturation of liberal Quakers and a slightly different form of intellectual individualistic bent in various aspects of pastoral Quakerism and the whole individualistic, deep presuppositions of Western culture at the present time.

All of these are things that a good Quaker seminary should be holding up to its students and to its professors and to its board all the time.

～

When I thought about this question and what ESR's role should be or what it could be potentially, I think the seminary needs to train people to listen to God intently and to think critically. As far as what the role should be in developing leaders, because of what of I think of in my own life, it is a struggle to figure what it means to be a leader.

I keep coming back to the fact that I need to listen to God intently and I need to critically examine my own motives and my own sense of my decisions. Then the second part that I thought of in relation to this question—and I thought about it about George Fox—is more tentative because I don't know if it is going to work in the culture that we are moving towards…

I wonder if there is a role for a seminary to be a theological center that can build up the strong core, that can really articulate clearly and publish and promote and teach and do some of this hard work in figuring out what our message is and who we are and relating that with the culture in the world. That's different maybe than the role of the students, but that's kind of the model of a reach institution or something like that. I don't know if that will carry much weight in the world in the next 50 years but it might, and I think that might be another role for ESR.

~

…no other seminary that I have been a part of has the history of our movement and the difference we have made. I mean, they don't care about that, that's not their tradition. That's our tradition. So I see ESR being unique in that way. Then the next step is saying how do we enculturate? How do we allow our history to speak to culture today? I don't see anybody else doing that.

~

I have been very interested in the work that Marge Abbott's done in Northwest Yearly Meeting, North Pacific Yearly Meeting, and [others]. She's been creating these women's theological [groups]…and that has been a very interesting leadership-building process as well as building bridges. Maybe that's an area that Earlham could explore…women's theological issues. Getting people like Marge Abbott to be part of that would make this seem much more relevant to West Coast unprogrammed Friends.

~

…building new programs on past strengths—programs that renew skills in which Friends excelled in the past—now with new application for a very different society:

1) Discernment
2) Prayer
3) Quaker meditation
4) Religious education

~

What I would like to see ESR do is open their vision of what ministry is, beyond what I consider a hidebound traditional pastoral role or missionary role. There's not a lot of emphasis on what the traditional church calls tent-making ministries. There's a million ways to do ministry but we are teaching two, maybe: the traditional pastoral minister and then the religious administrator. Those are the kinds of things they are really encouraging people to do. I have talked to many students at ESR who, if they can't get paid for it, wouldn't consider doing it. Everybody has to eat, I can understand that. But there isn't any reason why the ministry has to feed us physically. That really limits the kind of ministry that gets done. If people can't pay for it, it means you have to have an organization and you have to put so much effort into funding. I think it's a backwards message.

~

I would like to see ESR get out in the field more. They've got to go out and serve the folk. So after they do the self-maintenance, and raise their funds, and do the consultation, and get through the navel-gazing period that they've been in for the last 10 years, they've got to get back out in the field. I think they've got to offer extension courses either in cooperation with Friends Center at Guilford or the new divinity school at Wake Forest or something else, but they must be perceived as serving the people. Serving the people has to be more than, "We will serve you if you come to us, if you pull up stakes and move your entire family and leave your job and leave your home and come up to Richmond." Some will have to do that, but ESR has to be out here in the field.

~

Can we match Luther's successors in a *disputation*, or converse with Jesuits about even our own place in religious and intellectual history? Can we talk about how religious concepts and experiences inform social, economic, political and technological developments? Or how they inform what and how we teach? Can we go head and toe with seminarians and teachers from other traditions? With colleagues from other disciplines?

~

Another approach would be to get together groups of pastoral ministers at ESR, but also away from ESR…like going to North Carolina and being with a group of pastoral ministers for a day or two, and make it a time of deep fellowship that enabled them to do what pastors often don't get a chance to do, but always with an emphasis on the equipping ministry, equipping ministers, so that nurturing groups could continue in their Meetings.

~

There should be a real emphasis on *nontraditional*—a better term can be found certainly—an emphasis on *creative* ministry in creating opportunities for ministry. Part of that can be done through internships. There can be an emphasis on satellite classes so that people can do independent study programs towards ministry degrees. Not everything has to happen in Richmond; actually not everything can happen in Richmond. And it really shouldn't.

ESR could do incredible things and be in a really unique position. But the difficulty is ESR has gotten caught up in the political bloodletting. I mean, ESR has gotten caught in the middle among Indiana Yearly Meeting and others. The right wing of the church and the left wing of the church have been screaming at each other over issues like abortion and gay rights and all of those things. Earlham has gotten caught in the middle as this hotbed of liberalism, like most seminaries because they are younger and a little more idealistic.

So what happens is a portion of the population sees ESR as the seat of the devil and is not willing to communicate with them much. The only way to change that is to bring Earlham to the people. You can't bring the people to Earlham. You have to do it the other way.

~

A few on-line courses in Friends history and certain aspects of Friends theology would be a welcome thing, depending on who's teaching them, of course, and how well they are done. But it would be very easy for students at those four institutions and elsewhere…it would be a great thing for the rising leaders in Burundi to be able to plug into. A course that had representation from all those places would be both a product and a catalyst for cooperation, and if people at ESR said, "Oh my gracious, I'm taking this course from Howard Macy and it's wonderful. This is just doing great things." Then they can't be quite so judgmental about evangelicals because he is one. And there's another one that may not pull up roots and go to ESR but drawing on him for certain kinds of teaching where he wouldn't have to leave his office to be the teacher. That would be so easy to do and wouldn't take much money.

~

Another issue that is coming up often is the issue of eldering, the relationship between the elder and the minister, helping train us to bring out the ministry of others. We're not going to learn how to be our own minister but we're going to learn how to recognize the gifts of each of the members of my community and to be a companion along the way. That's not uniquely Quaker but Quakers have a unique take on that relationship. And so the question is how to structure a program. It couldn't be a three-year program, and it couldn't be really expensive, but it could be an inexpensive way to develop those skills.

~

Prepare pastors more thoroughly for the pitfalls of ministry. Hire instructors with pastoral background. Focus more on the truths of - scripture, as if scripture was God's inspired Word rather than literature to be criticized. Be solidly evangelical so as to attract desirable pastoral candidates.

~

My wife has just enrolled in the Doctorate of Ministry program at Fuller and it was surprising that she went to Seattle to take a two-week course this summer. I don't know why, but that's the way they have set up their program. I suppose it makes it possible for them to draw from a much larger group. But why couldn't Earlham do that? Have its programs and classes in Seattle and Los Angeles? If the people on the West Coast wanted to get a degree some of them might be able to come here to study. It is even conceivable I might be interested in getting a master's degree in theology from Earlham if they had that kind of structure because I could go to Seattle or San Francisco much more easily than going out to Indiana.

~

I see ESR raising the issues to get people talking, bringing the important topics into general consciousness, providing fora that spur discussion. Could the school actively encourage the dissemination of the best and most provocative student papers (to *Friends Journal*, *Quaker Life*, Yearly

Meetings, advancement/outreach committees)? Could ESR ask Yearly Meetings which Friends among them have the gifts that Earlham is prepared to enhance?

Conversely, is it possible for ESR to be an institution that serves to acquaint students with the wider body of Quakerism, that gets them involved with the people who have leadings, and that encourages them to consider the tricky issues of identifying and supporting Meetings where there is special evidence of a need for their particular strengths? Can you as a seminary be less *free market* and rather view your purpose as being a matchmaker between students and Meetings, a perfecter of the skills and gifts needed within the community?

Can skills beyond those usually provided by a degree-granting educational institution be identified and addressed more explicitly than they already are as part of the school's life—skills such as peacemaking, centering/listening, healing, discernment of others' strengths and gifts? Can Friends among the faculty identify special gifts of the students and let these be known not only to the students, but to Friends far and wide? How can a feedback loop be developed between ESR and the wider Quaker community, and the wider Quaker community and ESR?

I assume your faculty and staff are overworked and underpaid already. I also know that a good teacher does much of the above within whatever institutional framework s/he teaches. Yet there may be ways for the entire school to acquire these skills. Certainly, through taking the time for staff-wide or even school-wide Meetings for Worship with a concern for this business, ESR could further move in a direction that gives Quakerism *more* than just our own seminary. We could have a center for energizing, for reflection on the wider picture of Quakerism today, and for a spiritually informed support network to the initiatives coming out of our Meetings. And we could have a place where discernment of the Spirit's leadings for our movement are a priority, and an inspiration to us all.

~

I suspect that the Earlham School of Religion provides a focus on these matters of leadership at the present time. Yet, it may be that a collaborative mode of working together—faculty, prospective "students" and others, might be useful to you. I have a couple of things in mind about walking the talk, putting these ideas into some sort of action.

~

Some of the persons who are going to be trained in our Yearly Meeting will be trained at Western Evangelical Seminary but maybe they can take a term at ESR, or maybe there could be some reciprocal kinds of student exchanges, which would be useful, even from electronic classes…I think that to get into that circuit is important for ESR, probably more important than trying to do a balancing act that may be almost impossible for them to achieve.

~

To my way of thinking, leadership in the Religious Society of Friends can only be as well prepared as the Society as a whole is prepared. ESR should work to develop a program of studies that is academically and spiritually challenging, that may or may not lead to a degree. I know that Indiana and Western YM are two significant players in the ESR student body, so some attention needs to be given to pastoral study. But significant opportunities could be created to develop leaders who are not going to be pastors, or not even directly involved with a local Meeting.

~

ESR is committed to preparing pastors for local Meetings. Is a full-time residential program still the best way to accomplish this? That's a very important question because so many of the people who are turning to theological education are people who have already had a career and have found in their 30s or their 40s, or even older, that what they have been doing with their lives is not fulfilling. I wonder if it's possible to provide the kind of experience that ESR wants to provide without having people on campus all the time.

~

Earlham School of Religion might consider:

1) Research on why we are failing in our outreach, and programs based on that research to train Meeting leaders.
2) Conducting seminars (possibly on-line) on Quaker theology within the context of unprogrammed Meetings.
3) An on-line selection of courses (we are quite wired out here), possibly in cooperation with George Fox University, so that a greater number of our leaders can participate in well-designed and targeted programs without the cost of taking a year or more off.
4) Take a leadership role in organizing Friends-related Internet resources which, while expanding, are becoming more difficult to identify. Help Meeting libraries to access those offerings. Put more

of Earlham's own extensive library resources on-line and cooperate with other Friends institutions (Haverford, Woodbrooke, etc.) in maximizing access and avoiding replication. These steps would be especially useful in serving isolated worship groups and Meetings as well as Friends connected only through FWCC.

ESR may well be already doing some of these things but I am not seeing it from out here. *(Pacific Yearly Meeting)*

~

I encourage ESR to consider ways of linking with Pendle Hill, Quaker Hill, even Ben Lomond. Bringing Earlham faculty out and really developing a specialty on this question of leadership. What is the role of leadership across the spectrum? What is leadership in an evangelical context? What is leadership in an FUM context? What is leadership is an unprogrammed context? And then to develop that as a specialty and leading the Religious Society of Friends over the next 10 to 20 years to really look at our relationship to leadership. Not just doing it in terms of, "You have to come to ESR in order to take a full course." But to come out to us because unless we get ourselves straight on this issue in some way, we'll stop sending people to ESR. Coming out in ways like doing workshops around the country will be a way of seeding future students.

~

ESR could perhaps develop an internship program for their students to work at Quaker camps for credit towards their degree. ESR might also help with maintaining contact between camps across the country. Because the structures are so different between the east and west/mid-west, it's more difficult to be in contact, but perhaps ESR could help to bridge the gap, such as they did when they hosted that first meeting of camp directors.

~

Some of the things ESR has done in terms of having people from different aspects of the Society of Friends gather around particular issues and really try to explore what are the best things that we know from our heritage on certain points. A number of years they did consultations in connection with Quaker Hill Conference Center on worship and membership and service…probably 15 conferences over the years. Representatives were invited from all around the country. I participated in a couple of them and observed some. I think that was quite fruitful, though it did not directly engage current students very much. I think they have discontinued those a couple of years ago and they may have good reason for doing so, but one way or another to engage specific issues would be useful, to allow communication in a respectful environment. There might even be some things they could do electronically that might be interesting.

~

Other advice and recommendations

In terms of the contributions ESR has already made, certainly there are a lot of very fine Friends pastors that I have met over the years who were trained at ESR and who have gone on to very fruitful ministries as pastors, sometimes shifting into other things as well. Quite a number of important leaders are here in the east among unprogrammed Friends whose training at ESR was a strong imprint on them, and the momentum of those years seems to continue to carry them forward. That fellowship among ESR graduates has formed a network that has been a good network of shared understanding and visions for the future of Quakerism. I think it has been a good thing in both pastoral and unprogrammed Quakerism. ESR, I hope, will continue to play that kind of role.

~

When ESR was established, one of the nagging questions that haunted us was, "Can the Society of Friends utilize, that is, provide a niche for the leaders ESR produces?" No one could answer that question. About 12 years ago a young and distraught couple, both recent graduates of ESR came to see me. They were serving a Friends Meeting with limited membership and financial resources. The young husband and wife were carrying a combined educational debt of $30,000 and they were in the process of coming to terms with the fact that on their current salary, they could never even hope to retire their debt. The Meeting had been declining in strength for many years. It needed young, able and vigorous leadership but it could not afford to pay for it. While this is illustrative of a dilemma ESR cannot solve, it is a reality of which ESR needs to be aware.

~

Locals could be the adjuncts who mentor us!

~

It's very important for the administrators and faculty to visit broadly, so they can stay attuned to concerns and needs. We shouldn't ever have a monolithic group. ESR can create dialogue so people can understand the root values and concerns.

~

There's a large mailing list for ESR; we could expand it. It would take someone to do a spreadsheet, a database, some questionnaires and inquiries, a systematic networking to see who's coming along, even teenagers.

~

I would not like to see ESR being overwhelmed by people who are just drifting through and doing a couple of courses. But my sense would be that the Theological Reflection Year (TRY) program, may be a good program. I couldn't have done that because I was only there for one term and I'm not sure how flexible that is. But it would be interesting to me if a contract or covenant could be signed by students who aren't clearly on the degree track, making a commitment to do a number of courses and to speak with advisors and to accept advice as to whether this is the right place for them. I'm not aware that that sort of personal input is available. I could see that with the careful description of the experience and the careful selection of the people, this could perhaps enhance the experience of the degree candidate.

~

…if ESR could take a lead in talking about who we are as Friends in the 21st century and if they wouldn't shy away from talking about what it means to bring those two poles back together, the Christ-centered emphasis and the social justice emphasis. I think that the FUM leadership is trying to do that. But that, again, doesn't impact us in Northwest very much because we are not part of FUM. Whereas ESR is a group that's outside of any specific alliance and so might be able to provide that role. So, just that whole issue of the role that Christ plays in Quakerism and the role that social justice and the outward journey plays in that, I think, is real critical.

~

We were talking about this 10 years ago, 20 years ago: no leadership in Friends. At some point we either have to fish or cut bait and do something about it. Now how that gets done is up to the people in leadership, but specifically as to ESR, when people see that there's a real authentic desire to go in some positive directions, people will make a decision for themselves to get on board.

~

Have ESR faculty mentor upcoming young Friends.

~

A sense of the special quality of Quaker history must infuse things
at ESR…

~

ESR should consider distance education programs. Can we participate
in classes from Pittsburgh?

~

Another thing I would love to see would be a really strong active program inviting people, say like me, or like Bill Taber, who is semi-retired
now, to go to ESR for a term, not as a teacher but as a fellow student.
I don't think that it would need to be fully funded but it would bring
more Quaker leadership into the student body and it might broaden
those of us who haven't been to seminary. Pendle Hill, which is a study
center, for example, has Friends in residence and they don't usually
teach. They are like an extra pair of hands. People like that could be a
very good maturing element and literally an extra pair of hands because
I know the staff must be overworked. To have Bill Taber on campus for
a term would be a real gift to both students and faculty. I think that
would be a gift to Bill himself.

~

Be the *best* things to *most* people. ESR can't satisfy everyone, and
shouldn't try. Some people will be disappointed. But ESR mustn't
be a chameleon.

~

I have been told that ESR must train preachers or die. Some who say
that also want to select administration and faculty who would make of
ESR little more than a *trade school* improving the skills of the *mechanics
at their trade.* It has even been insinuated that when there are differences
between church and seminary, the church should prevail. This is a sure-
fire formula for a return to theological Dark Ages.

It has been suggested too that ESR give more attention to the
Richmond Declaration of 1887. This document essentially laid the dead
hand of the past on Orthodox Friends. It is a fundamentalist document
including statements on the creation and the fall, the virgin birth of
Jesus, the authority of scripture, atonement through the blood of Jesus,
and the resurrection to heaven or hell. New Testament scholarship
had rendered the Richmond Declaration untenable at the time it was

written. Any reputable seminary should deal with it as they would with Nicaea and Chalcedon—as relics of the past.

~

Of the ESR grads I know, many *have* gone into pastoral ministry in programmed YMs. But there doesn't seem to be much possibility of real partnership between the seminary and the YMs they go into. ESR needs to develop that partnership.

~

I think the *interpersonal* stuff of ESR is *more* central. The theological regular stuff can be gotten elsewhere. Don't learn about Quakerism—DO Quakerism.

~

To make leaders, *be a leader*, ESR!

~

I'd hope that ESR could serve both ends. It will always be awkward, but that shouldn't stop them. Perhaps ESR does need to fine-tune its attractiveness to pastors. They're the majority.

~

What's wrong with ESR making its OWN cutting edge?

~

1) What is the wisdom ESR has to share? How are you sharing it? Do students come? Do they become passionate?
2) Where is the authentic voice of Jesus at ESR? Is Christ recognized in fact as well as in the mission statement?
3) My assumption is that the skills of leadership can be learned, but leadership is truly a gift from other persons. How do ESR students practice leading?

~

As a long-term proposition, it is very hazardous for Friends to have all or most of our professionals trained at one institution, no matter how worthy.

~

1) Go find *big name* professors with broad appeal. Get people who can articulate Quakerism.
2) *Train pastors*. Don't ignore that part of the mission.
3) Be connected with churches. Help them function better or to have a prophetic approach.

~

…how well people are serving the life of the institution needs to include how well they are serving the life of the church.

~

ESR's *defect* here is not what it does, but its splendid isolation; the fact that no place else is doing it. Thus, I believe it is time for ESR to assist in the creation of alternative avenues through which such persons can emerge.

~

1) Relate ESR more fully and sympathetically to the liberal unprogrammed branch;
2) Produce some quality scholars and thinkers taking on the many Quaker issues and concerns before us; and
3) Head off the perilous tendency toward an ESR alumni/ae hegemony among Friends.

~

I hope there are ways in which ESR can build up its credibility and its attractiveness to a variety of pastoral Friends. I don't see that lack of credibility and attractiveness as necessarily ESR's fault. People have not given them a fair shake regarding the success of ESR in drawing unprogrammed Friends. There are many pastoral Friends who will say, "Well I'm not going to a place that obviously must be too friendly with those unprogrammed Quakers." There's that mentality of fearfulness of bumping into other varieties of Quakers which works to ESR's disadvantage at times in some of the sectors to which it really wants to reach out. And that's not ESR's fault. That's the risk that you take doing the right thing sometimes.

~

Here in Northwest we don't think about ESR a lot and so [perhaps they could find] ways that they could communicate more with us who they are and what they have to offer, more than just sending us flyers or catalogues, but maybe sending us people, maybe giving a workshop at our Yearly Meeting sessions, or if they have people to offer us for any of our young adult retreats. We do several each year. If they have great resource speakers that they could make available to us, that would begin to build a relationship.

~

Produce some polemicists ("old Friends" someone else said), some tough people. Friends who are able to argue with people from other traditions, who have spent their lives reflecting on the consistency of the gospel, what the gospel message is, what is Truth. That is very much what we are, and yet that's been the hardest thing to do. That was part of what the Catholics would call the founding charisma of ESR and it seems the most difficult to sustain.

~

…this week's *Christian Century* talked about an organization or group that sets as its mission the designing of dialog. If I remember the specific illustration, they brought together the full spectrum to talk about the issue of abortion. In other words, they discuss issues that divide the church.

The thing that I was intrigued with is they found that one of their missions in that whole process was to define fairly carefully the ground rules of how this was going to take place. The one that they elaborated on was that they insisted that people attending from the broad spectrum had to agree to respect the integrity of the other side, and not to attribute motives or anything else.

I was trying to think of what would happen if Earlham were to do some dialogs setting forth some fairly clear ground rules in advance, because one of the things I think Earlham is called to do is to attempt to help the Society of Friends articulate their vision, but at the same time to help the Gurneyite Friends articulate their vision, maybe in the hopes that when they get those articulated, they'll realize that they're much closer than they think they are.

But until that's done I think we talk at cross purposes. I would recommend to you this week's *Christian Century*, that article on how you go about this dialog; maybe that's what ESR is called to do.

~

Two suggestions: for ESR to be clear about its mission and to articulate that clearly, because I don't think that ESR can be all things to all Quakers. Secondly, look at some way of developing *ESR on the road*. We've heard here about the number of people in Baltimore YM looking for some kind of *seminary experience*. We all want that, and we have a hunger for both the intellectual and experiential development of ourselves. Is there a way to have a John Punshon come out for three or four long weekends in a semester? Some of us may want to get credit for getting that kind of Quaker background; get someone from ESR with a Quaker understanding of the New Testament to give courses out in the countryside.

~

As a visiting lecturer, I would suggest Doug Gwyn. *Words in Time*, a group of his essays is worth checking out. He has been invited by FUM and FGC to give major addresses, also by Woodbrooke to be on the staff there and he's now writer-in-residence at Pendle Hill. He's writing on the growing edge and dealing with some of these issues because he's had the experience of being in various branches of Friends, plus being a pastor, and I find him very helpful to my own thinking.

~

Provide, and facilitate others to provide, internships and other professional growth opportunities so that when people leave ESR, there are places for them to go for professional opportunities that are natural extensions of their studies.

~

ESR should use web sites like Pendle Hill does.

~

ESR can start pulling together the graduates from the unpro-grammed tradition and strategizing about solving the problems and the riddles before us. We need to do that before the Religious Society of Friends disappears.

~

The *center* of Quakerism needs to be served by ESR.

~

Don't just come to speak. Come to worship and to hear and to experience us. Get out here and *feel* what we're about.

~

ESR needs to be more user friendly for middle-of-the-road Friends and people that want to go into the pastoral ministry.

~

ESR needs to emphasize performance and they need to get serious about being the *best*, not just the best Quaker seminary. Since it's the only one, that's not a problem. They need to compete head to head with the top seminaries in the United States and they need to settle for nothing less. The problem is that the vision among Quakers is so small. If we've got the best religion in the world, let's start acting like it. Let's go for the gold and not settle for an academically second-rate institution. And that goes for the students they recruit as well.

~

One thing ESR could do is to make use of leadership outside of its own immediate ranks of faculty and graduates and people close to the institution. I think people could be brought in from various sectors that would make it more clear to people, and through the involvement of Quaker leaders outside the usual ESR orbit, that would help make them exponents of ESR to their constituency. My sense has been that ESR has relied on its own richness of knowledge and creativity which is not lacking in own right but it's not good at making nurturing connections.

~

Advice to ESR:

1) Clearly delineate.
2) Focus on the *center* and go for that.

~

I'm also glad for ESR to serve other Friends groups who need good leadership and need informed and theologically grounded leadership.

~

Be clear about who ESR is; state it up front. Get away from the fear of *training leaders. Say* it. Take the role of training pastoral leaders more seriously. Use a lot of experienced Friends (in Western Indiana) as resources.

~

As ESR now tries to respond—and do what should have been done years ago—don't lose the progress already made with eastern Friends.

~

ESR could help people catch a vision for ministry in the city—help young people make that vision a choice. Cities have grown out to many formerly rural places; the world is fast becoming urban.

~

ESR has wonderful resources, great academic standards, a nice campus, the college. But they've been caught in the dynamics of the Society of Friends. They need to join the quest in which all of us work toward unity, to move the Society forward in unity.

~

We need to be visited by ESR in the spirit of ministry and not in the purpose of fund raising.

~

Advice to ESR: Don't give up! We *need* you. We want teachers, not sales people. *Teach* us to be Quakers.

~

QUAKER ORGANIZATIONS

I have the instinct that the Religious Society of Friends is so good at developing organizations that we've about reached or exceeded the carrying capacity for specifically Quaker things. The institutions that reach out beyond the Society of Friends, like the schools and colleges or AFSC have much more possibility of flourishing and continuing to attract support than the more specifically Quaker entities such as FWCC and Yearly Meetings. ESR is in an interesting place because to the extent that it's a theological college for the Society of Friends, it faces that same challenge, but to the extent that it reaches out beyond the Society of Friends, it may find greater financial help, but then it may not be as attractive to some parts of the Society of Friends as a training ground. That's a tough set of dilemmas that ESR faces.

~

FUM and ESR are so important. They represent the middle road, historically. The polarity is even greater now; the extremes are farther apart. People on the edges try to get the middle to break up. We need a new vision for what it means to be in the middle. We need to claim it and bring unity. Some of that will have to start with kids. Most revivals have started with young people.

~

There's an organization in Philadelphia which was set up about five years ago, the Friends Board Training and Support Project, which has been helpful to Quaker organizations in addressing governance and other institutional issues.

~

The intention at Pendle Hill is to be a resource for a wider variety of Friends than actually show up at our door.

~

Adults need some type of support, some type of nurturing system to keep them going as well. One thing that keeps coming back, that stands out to me when I look at the Quaker community, is resources that are there and we're not tapping them. We need to try to figure out how to tap these resources to provide that support. How can we tap Earlham's resources other than being students at Earlham? The same thing goes with other Quaker institutions, other Quaker schools, as well as organizations that depend on them.

~

…here at Guilford and when I was at Earlham, time and time again I saw students who said, "I was a minority in my high school. I lived in fear of getting up every morning and going to school. But here I'm accepted. Here they are like-minded people. Here I don't have to apologize for who I am. I'm accepted for who I am because of those basic Quaker theological and social values." And then people are introduced slowly but surely to the value of silence, of consensus, of nonviolent resolution of conflict, equality, global understandings, justice issues and before long they are saying, "this is okay." I see that happen over and over again. So I think our Quaker higher education, our colleges, have a real vital role to play in the maintenance of the Society of Friends, both in maintaining a culture for our Quaker students and children and as a mission field from which the next generation of Friends are going to come.

~

My feeling is—and this isn't necessarily shared by other Evangelical Friends Yearly Meetings—that we should be supportive of FUM because I believe that FUM is moving in a positive direction, and if that continues I can see a re-merging of FUM with Evangelical Friends in time. I don't think that would ever happen until FUM gets far enough down the road that somebody splits the sheets and decides that they are going to be totally and thoroughly Christ-centered and then you have to make a decision. But as long as FUM is moving in that direction I think we should be tremendously supportive.

~

[FGC] is a good source of publications and is developing something on traveling ministry and nurturing and things of that sort. Those are important. I don't know much about FUM's activity. I like what I see in the publication *Quaker Life*. I think FCNL is a very important source of Quaker work in trying to translate the spirituality into practicality and I like the way they go about it.

~

I would say George Fox, Earlham, and Guilford are about the only schools that have maintained a strong sense of being a Quaker school with a strong Quaker presence, and a strong Quaker culture on campus where young Friends can find a ready-made community and subculture in which they can be authentically Quaker. Only Guilford of those three actually can then do the next part which is to be challenged by the diversity of Friends in a supportive environment. Students can come to not only deepen themselves and their sense of their own particular tradition of Friends but also to be awakened to the variety, diversity, and strength of the other types of Friends around. That is something that Guilford has going for them that others don't and it is something that ESR has going for it that none of the other seminaries have: that mix of diverse elements of Quakerism.

~

FCNL is a group that articulates concerns that are very close to our group's heart to Washington which we don't feel very close to. We see these as people doing a wonderful ministry in a place that we would be but we have not a clue how to do on our own.

~

If it weren't for Quaker educational institutions I think the Society of Friends itself would be a mere shadow of its former self. That's one of the advantages we have over the U.K. The U.K. has no Quaker universities. They have eight Quaker boarding schools and only Woodbrooke has an equivalent of anything like Earlham School of Religion. They are very envious of what we have here in the States.

~

FGC's mission: A gateway for refugees, without anyone standing at the door with a checklist. Come in, listen in the quiet for nudges of the divine, and begin to heal. But there's more: the deep Quaker tradition of inner work. Come in further. Here's what we do.

~

ESR needs more people like Johan Maurer who actually can communicate with all of the various armed camps and help them to unarm. ESR really needs people who are willing to step out of the battlefront and begin to help local Meetings and groups of people and organizations at all levels begin to look for creative solutions.

~

As an unprogrammed Friend, it feels very important to me that ESR maintain its sense of invitation to Evangelical Friends, because it would be very easy for ESR to be overtaken by liberal Friends and become a liberal institution exclusively, and we would all suffer from that. We would be less well-off as a result if we divided ourselves into evangelical seminary in California and the liberal seminary in Indiana. Liberal Friends need some good, solid education in how to be in a relationship with Evangelical Friends. Too often there are all Friends conferences that get flooded by liberals who feel like they want to be in relationship with evangelicals but we come in and we act in a way that drives the evangelicals away from those events. It is inhospitable, the messages can be as much as insulting. As a result, there will be 30 people including two evangelicals. It's a terribly hard job but somehow we must try and create those environments that are inviting. We liberals need some help in knowing how to enter into those environments, and maybe FWCC can give some guidance on how to do that.

~

I have had some concern that since there are such great poles in Quakerism, ESR tries to stand somewhere in the middle and tries to speak to both wings as best they can. Therefore the evangelical wing is more comfortable with places like Western Evangelical Seminary, but more of our students here even before it was part of George Fox went to WS or down to Fuller or someplace like that. Someplace that they recognized as evangelical without the baggage of the kind of a fear around here of unprogrammed Friends. I served nine years on the ESR board and I have less of that fear than I did before. But my fears reflect the fear that a lot of other people had. That's why some kind of connection between ESR and the other educational institutions might provide for some convergence or otherwise it will be divergent. With an electronic age and e-mail there are many things that ESR might be able to do that would not be competitive but would be complementary with what other institutions are doing.

~

ESR has been absent from FAHE by and large and that's too bad because even though they are mostly undergraduate people, ESR could benefit a lot by that fellowship. ESR is a very different kind of entity and the people from there need to show up at meetings.

~

I've worked with Guilford's Friends Center—a marvelous program, Quaker leadership scholars. Outreach to Quaker Meetings in the region, cooperation with ESR, may make this a site for educational opportunities for ESR credit as a fledgling project.

~

ESR has got to recognize that they are a middle way. They are not a secular kind of liberal institution the way Swarthmore has become, nor are they a Bible college the way Barclay College has become. They have got to be an apologist for an authentic Quakerism that takes seriously the various roots out of which Quakerism arose, for the fact that we do have a vital unprogrammed tradition and a vital programmed tradition, but that a Quakerism that is going to be equipped to sustain itself and make a contribution of the 21st century has got to shake itself finally clear of the excesses of Holiness and fundamentalist theology that has cast a long shadow over much of pastoral Quakerism.

~

What is the situation with regard to Quaker leadership and are we finding leaders we need? The answer is no. There are at least two elements of that that need comment. One is if you look at Quaker organizations such as American Friends Service Committee, Friends World Committee, Friends Committee on National Legislation, Friends General Conference, Friends United Meeting, Evangelical Friends International, in some of those bodies the leadership is nearly wholly female. In others it is exclusively male. What's going on there? Why aren't liberal Friends finding male leadership? Why is it necessary for a woman in Evangelical Friends who wants to be a pastor to have to go to another Yearly Meeting other than her own? These are serious questions and have a lot to do with the kind of developments one would hope to see in a school training Quaker leadership.

~

I'd like to see ESR's people sponsor a retreat and talk to the heads of Quaker organizations about what they see regarding the profile of students, the future of the Society of Friends. Doug Bennett and I and some others could put together a great weekend. It would draw us together, help us be supportive of one another as we try to give service to the world and also nurture this precious religious society.

~

FCNL doesn't speak for all Friends, but it tries to reach out and, as a national Quaker organization, we really value the involvement of Friends across the spectrum.

~

I think that FCNL is extremely well respected I think in part because we really stand by our principles and don't cave in. But also because the way it works as a Quaker lobby group, as an education organization, is a little bit different than the secular peace and justice community. This results from the Quaker belief that we can reach and speak to and hear from that of God in every person. The way we do lobby work is a little different. We really believe that it's a dialog and that relationships are important, so that even if we don't agree with a legislator on his or her position, that doesn't mean we can't talk. We don't go around beating people over the head with our viewpoint, so to speak—it's a kinder, gentler way of lobbying…Our faith gives us a long-term view, a stick-to-it-iveness.

~

EFI and FUM Meetings a lot of times have fallen on hard times and they decline in numbers and get real discouraged.

~

Our leadership is short-sighted and confused and so we don't have goals beyond evangelism. Evangelism is an extremely important goal and we want to play it down though. But we don't have a plan to bring the kingdom about here on earth. Jesus said I am the presence of God, returned again to the temple. And the kingdom is now here on earth. It's among you. And here is how He'll identify it. He said nothing about getting into heaven, almost nothing.

But He talked about the changed people changing the culture. He talked about being Light and soul. Living it by an entirely radically different way than the culture he gave to the Jews, and learn to live it in a half a millennium since the exile. That's where we are falling short in leadership…we don't know what to do except to convert different people. So we look around at different models and see who is growing the fastest—who can convert the most people and get them in our churches. (I know this is a way over-simplification.)

We need to do that but I think we also need to say: You are a disciple so you must model a whole different way of living—a way of peace, a way of honesty. One reason people are bored with leadership and bored with the Friends Church is there is really nothing to do. Once you are converted, you serve on the nominating committee, then what? You've experienced hell and heaven both! There are no people leading us to do anything, really. Places like our own School of Religion and other educational institutions ought to think about paradigms for flushing out the faith, for setting up ministry experiences, and ways of engaging the culture around the seminary work.

~

I think and hope that more of the Evangelical Friends read *Quaker Life* than might have at one time. I think it has rightly seen itself as a publication for a broad range of Friends, not just those who are tied to FUM.

~

We talked some years ago of Guilford, George Fox, William Penn House, and ESR jointly putting together a program for a master's degree online and it petered out. The resonance was out here but ESR was not comfortable with that; their experience is on campus, an academic enclosure.

~

Friends United Meeting has taken some hard knocks in the last 10 to 15 years trying to be a similar kind of meeting place and it is institutionally pretty weakened by the struggles that have taken place, but I still have some hopes that FUM will continue to be a place where those exchanges can happen as well.

~

FWCC has set a goal this year: a percentage of Friends who could have face-to-face meetings with Friends across boundaries.

~

We worship every day together [at Pendle Hill] and there's an intensity and intentionality of living out a Quaker faith and practice here that is at a higher level of intensity than most Friends are able to find in the life of their local Meeting. So possibilities of kind of intensified learning and personal spiritual growth are high here. I think, though I've never been really a part of the ESR community, that many of those pieces are present in the dynamics.

~

FWCC deals with the diversity of Friends—gets us to talk to each other.

~

…the terrible truth is that there is not one Quaker institution or organization equipped to address this sad situation at the leadership development level unless it is ESR.

~

INTERNATIONAL PERSPECTIVES

The trend has been that EFI has very much internationalized itself.
I think FUM and FGC haven't quite figured out how to do that. But
EFI recognizes that the majority of their contingency is non-American
and they've set up structures with regions in different parts of the world
and given them positions and leadership and tried to simply coordinate
with them and put North America alongside them, not on top of them.

~

[ESR] is not well known and there are many reservations about it,
particularly because it has been seen as the most liberal school. There
are many reservations in relation to that. The fact that you are conducting this consultation, and the fact that ESR is thinking more about this
aspect, is very important. I know that ESR has conducted study groups
that go to Latin America. I believe that in one or two cases they were
also trying to learn Spanish, or something like that. But in some of
these cases, ESR went to a country, like Mexico for instance, and made
no attempt to meet with Friends. Some people went to grassroots-level
religious communities and learned Spanish, but there was not a conscious effort to contact Friends, and know what Friends are doing, what
Friends' concerns are in a given country. It will be important to do that.

~

I would suggest that, in terms of international students, ESR needs one
staff member who has some sensitivity to different educational levels
that may be equivalent but roots that have been different. Also, for
people other than say Canadians and British, some cultural sensitivity
is necessary. I'm not sure that's present. I'm not saying it isn't, but
I'm not aware of it. I don't think that necessarily means an extra staff
member. It means identifying a staff person who has those awarenesses
because some of us know that the Midwest is pretty insular.

~

Some Canadians would feel quite strongly and say we are not the
51st state. ESR and other Quaker groups need to be clear whether

they've got a national mandate or an international mandate or the third option, whether they have a national mandate, and a smaller part of their vision is to include international people. I haven't heard that expressed clearly. It's like a *both/and.*

~

I realize that which I respond to is called a National Consultation and therefore as a Friend from Ireland I do not really have any right to respond…I have visited the USA on two occasions to be with and among Friends and from what I found in general, Quakers are similar the world over. There are the evangelical, the liberals, the universalists, the pastoral, the conservative, and as you know the list could go on. From what I read of ESR's concern, categories do not come into the matter simply the challenge: What are the potential contributions that the Earlham School of Religion can make to the preparation of leaders?

~

We need to analyze local histories to find more about each one's strengths and weaknesses. For me the two areas of main concern that continue to be top priorities for most of these groups, regardless of local and foreign efforts, are in leadership training and Quaker literature in Spanish. With very few exceptions, many of the Friends who are pastors were trained in non-Quaker schools or seminaries dealing with different theologies and traditions.

It has been in the last two decades that many of these Friends groups are looking for more specific and deeper understanding of our own Quaker faith, particularly because we are a minority within the minority. Still, during the last two decades there have been several individual efforts to translate Quaker literature into Spanish. But in most cases these efforts have responded more to someone's concerns to translate and make available what that person felt was needed, rather than responding to specific requests from those who need the literature.

I would say the leadership of these groups—perhaps a few exceptions would be El Salvador, Mexico, Cuba and to a degree Guatemala and Bolivia—have a higher level of education. The rest of Friends on the whole come from rural areas and have little preparation so we're talking about another factor that needs to be taken into account when thinking about translating Quaker literature into Spanish, for example. So it's basically those two challenges that we face.

~

My own experiences among Friends in other parts of the world said to me: We need to listen very, very carefully to them.

~

I see also, at least in terms of what I heard last year, that Earlham was talking about becoming global. I know of other efforts Earlham, and ESR especially, has had with sending people to Fiji and other places, intercultural exchanges and things like that. Within that frame, I believe it will be important first for ESR to serve Friends outside the USA.

I see it on two levels. One will be to offer opportunities for those Friends who would like to be trained in the ministry at the residential level, which we need still because there are not many Quaker options in Latin America. And the other one, perhaps thinking more in terms of what we can start doing now. Perhaps in the same way ESR offers winter courses, for instance, ESR could offer summer or winter courses for Latin American Friends in Spanish, or perhaps some in English, but these would be fewer, that will lead to a diploma in Quaker studies with emphasis on history of Friends and early Quaker thinkings or Friends testimonies. Perhaps ESR could also consider sending teachers to already established seminaries or Bible schools where courses of the same tenor could be offered. Also perhaps consider offering fellowships with interdenominational seminaries such as the Latin America Seminary…a University in Costa Rica, or places like Cuba or Mexico, where Friends could develop a program on Quakerism.

~

It's wonderful to see more Friends in Africa than in the U.S. That has led some evangelical/conservative Friends and Meetings in FUM to want to place emphasis on evangelism. There are some quandaries about what that means in Quakerism. There has been a strong testimony not to proselytize but to let people follow their own leadings. But we want people to know. So the challenge is how to reach out, to find ways to invite people to participate?

~

Perhaps create possibilities for residential training at ESR for those interested in a project that could lead to production of Quaker literature in Spanish or self-writing, and making these available to local centers that ESR could create in the long run in Latin America; facilitate the possibility of people in the Earlham College department of Spanish taking up the translations that we need [in Latin America] as part of their academic work. And perhaps looking at possibilities of facilitating the training of Latin American Friends or Friends who are bilingual as translators in the college, whose work also would be to translate Quaker writings, excerpts or small leaflets or pamphlets that would be more suitable for the kind of work we are trying to do. That is, in addition to the possibility of having major works reprinted or translated, George Fox's Journal and John Woolman's Journal, for instance.

~

What ESR hasn't done as well is preparing people for pastoral ministry among Quakers. And this is nothing new. People talk about how to do that better all the time. But the fact is two-thirds of Quakers in America are pastoral Friends and four-fifths of Quakers around the world are pastoral Friends, and if ESR is going to have a national and global mission in preparing leadership, they have to take that very seriously. And so far, pastoral studies has been perceived to have received less meaningful support than some of the other programs.

~

ESR and Earlham and the other Quaker schools need to be very careful when they use statements as in the announcement that I have in front of me: Leadership in the Religious Society of Friends: A National Consultation. Do they mean a national consultation? Then the other statement I have is Call for a National Consultation. I'm not clear if they have really worked out whether they are national or international. I don't have problems with either decision. The group has to work that out for themselves. But currently they are talking about a national consultation.

~

One of the reasons [I'm involved] is to perhaps try and see if there are ways of enabling foreign students to get a more positive welcome. I fully respect that ESR needs to be accredited and that other degrees from foreign countries may not fit into the U.S. system, but when you are dealing with people who, within the Quaker tradition, are considered to be *weighty* Friends, you don't just tell them: "You're not qualified." There needs to be some other track and some other much more caring way of talking to people.

~

My experience with Friends in Britain is they are totally confused [about ESR]. They don't understand that ESR is essentially a Quaker seminary. They think of ESR and Woodbrooke and Pendle Hill as being three similar institutions. But I do know that the British Friends who've come over have known what they are getting into. I also know, or know by hearsay, that there have been some historic tensions with students who have come from Kenya.

~

As persons—I'm not speaking as a Society in general—in every controversial situation there have been wonderful Quakers as pioneers trying to help in, let's say, negotiations in Sarajevo, in Palestine with Israelis, and elsewhere. I value that and I know wherever I go, one or two of the outstanding people that are contributing to build up a certain project or philosophy on an issue are Quakers, struggling with an issue. Quakers are doing a lot. And they have a good reputation. But it's not enough to live on that reputation. If we take the Quaker bodies in general, let's say you take all the different Quaker bodies—and we have many of them—they are not in the lead, and the issues that the Quakers have been in the lead with, many other churches have adopted and are doing much more with.

~

As long as we hang on to the superior or inferior model, then it's real hard for us to learn from people elsewhere who certainly do have an awful lot to teach us. Yet they themselves would be the first to say that they have not been as effective in sharing messages of reconciliation in their cultures as they would like to be.

~

A lot of those non-American Friends were the product of missionary work and they tended to, a lot of times just say, "Well let's emphasize the gospel and don't do the other stuff." But the exciting thing for me to work with Burundi Friends is that they say the so-called "other stuff" is really *the* stuff. In other words, peacemaking is maybe the one thing that validates the gospel in that setting. The so-called "good" church members that have been killing each other for these decades have missed it, and the ones who are sick of that are only going to respond with enthusiasm to people that say, "Yes we want to tell you about Christ, but we also want to make it clear that Christ calls us to peace and to leave our killing behind."

~

To what extent should ESR's reach extend beyond the United States to address needs in other countries? I don't think ESR is well equipped to deal with students from [places] other than the developed world.

I've had several friends of mine from the developing world who attended either ESR briefly or over a period of time. The experience separated them from their own culture when they went back. It seems to me that this is one of the most difficult things to do, to try to provide the riches that you have in spiritual and intellectual ways without dumping a whole lot of the cultural value system on them too. So I think that's one to move pretty cautiously on. I don't know a Friends organization that does it well.

We in the North, we in the developed world, tend to see ourselves as the givers, not the learners, from people from other parts of the world. I think that's an area to move into with great care and great sensitivity and lots of advice from people who are wiser than I am.

~

There is another thing that I have seen in Latin America that is of great concern to Latin American Friends because as I said we are a minority within a minority. All the development of the neo-Pentecostal groups, all of these are subsidized by North American organizations and you can find very large numbers of people in these congregations. We are talking about in capital cities, for instance. We are talking about having congregations of 5,000 people. This is a phenomenon. It is happening particularly after societies have gone through a long period of war. To me, that speaks about the eagerness, the real need for people to really come back to the spiritual roots of their life. And it is a great opportunity for Friends, or for anyone, at least to offer what we believe is the answer.

~

I would really encourage ESR to try to make itself more known in Europe. ESR is the only seminary that is available to Quakers all over the world. One need relates to the fact that international students aren't allowed to work in the United States, so we really need to find ways to fund international students.

~

There is only one visible form of Quakerism in the United Kingdom and that's unprogrammed non-pastoral silent Friends. Now the Friends who worship in those Meetings will cover the whole spectrum theologically, from very Christocentric to absolutely Universalist, pagan, atheist, and everything in between.

~

Presbyterians, Methodists, all of them sometimes, and many seminaries in the United States, bring some of their students once a year to come and speak to some of the Christians in Palestine or the Middle East. This is how they get exposed to the situation here. Many of them come with their professors. I know, I have spoken to many of these groups.

Sometimes an Earlham group comes but I don't know if they are Earlham School of Religion students.

~

One of the discussions we had in the general Board when we were doing a mock "what will it be like when these consultations get into the field" session was: Is ESR's goal of raising up Quaker leadership happening? My response then and now is it isn't happening in Canadian Yearly Meeting. I'm not blaming ESR for it. My sense is that Canadian Yearly Meeting will not be sending many students to ESR because we are not discerning gifts and calling and ministry. If you start off with 1,000 people and you don't do that, nothing is going to go through the pipeline.

~

[New members need to know] more about our Quaker roots. Many of these groups have developed their own literature. Not in many cases, but I would say in two cases at least. But they will not really tell you, and more and more they say, "You see we have been using someone else's literature." When it comes to basic points like the sacraments, for instance, we either skip it or we don't talk about it. This is the kind of thing people are facing every day. As one Friend said to me, "When you live in a society where in terms of religion 99% of the population or 99% of the other groups practice the sacraments outwardly, and you are the only tiny little group that doesn't, then what are we? What do you think our people or the newcomers feel like? How do you help them, to really grasp the Quaker understanding of the gospel in such an environment?"

One of the greatest challenges is understanding our history, both for British Friends and for American Friends. British Friends are trying to recapture the understanding of the Christian roots and various streams have fed into that interpretation of Christianity by the early Friends. American Quakers, especially in the programmed and evangelical wings, have just about lost a sense of the Quaker history. They see themselves as maintaining the biblical base, the Christian witness, but don't have a very deep appreciation of the distinctively Quaker flavor of that Christianity or that interpretation of the Bible.

~

I will put it this way—and very humbly I say this—I think that in many ways Quakers in the United States, or many Friends in the United States, have changed the center of their lives so it is no longer depending on the Spirit but it is more depending on one's own thinking, rather than having a life centered in Christ or in the Spirit. The other thing that I would say is that this is not only true for Friends, the numbers are not only diminishing among Friends. I think this is true for any religious group in more developed societies than it is in our countries. I think that it's a totally different thing to be in the United States where you have all your needs met—and this is also a broad generalization—than being in places in Latin America where you don't, and really have to depend literally on God for many of the things in your life.

~

[Friends in the United Kingdom] are at a point now where about 80% of the attendance at their Meetings—400 to 500 Meetings in the U.K.—are convinced Friends, and many of those are fairly recently convinced Friends so they are wondering who's going to equip these folk with what it means to be a Quaker.

Who's going to translate Quaker faith and practice to them, or are we just going to make it up as we go along? There is a lot of concern about that. There's a good deal of introspection about how far away from the roots of Quakerism Friends have moved. There's very little of the original Christian language left in contemporary British Quakerism and those who are more Christocentric feel they are on the periphery.

Some others who are refugees from the spiritual malpractice of other denominations have found a home among Friends and are affronted by too much religious language and so they are still wrestling through that stuff. I think Friends are healthy in the U.K. I was surprised by how dynamic some of these discussions are and how dynamic many of the Meetings are. You get the impression, if you listen to some circles of American Quakerism, that British Friends are dying and they are all gray and grizzled and they are one foot in the grave. But that's not the case. They are quite lively.

~

In Latin America, the voice of Friends has not been heard in terms of the peace testimony and the biblical basis of the peace testimony. I think it's very important and I don't think it's sufficient just to say that other people are doing peace work. I think Friends, if they are serious about what is happening in places such as Latin America, this is a great avenue and there are many other people—even at the World Council of Churches, Conrad Racer, for instance once said not too long ago in Ireland, that the so-called third way that the historical peace churches we are talking about are offering, as part of their tradition, was not any longer a third way but *the* way to answer to the need for peace in many of these places.

~

The Latin American program of the World Committee is trying [to develop on-site training]. They are holding leadership training seminars in Central America and that's what Latin American Friends have been asking for—ever since they first came to the Wichita Meeting in I guess it was 1977 of Friends from all over the Americas. They know they need leadership training. But it has to be in their cultural context. This is 22 years later and it has taken this long to get if off the ground and the people who are doing it and organizing it are very optimistic. They feel very good about the plans, but only the beginnings have been held and so I can't judge.

~

I'm not so sure that this is unique to Latin American Friends, but a very important aspect of our life is depending on prayer for all the things we do in life and an open way of testifying, whether in the Meeting or in other places, about how one feels God's presence in one's own life.

It isn't only a weekly thing in Meeting for worship, but it's important to express those things in our daily life. This creates a stronger sense of belonging, a stronger sense of community for many of these groups. We really are involved with each other: I care about you, I pray about your son who is sick, you pray for my looking for a job, etc. This is very, very important.

Most of the groups in Latin America are trying to share this good news with other people. You don't do this only in front of someone who doesn't know you, but you testify with your daily life, in your work. You take all opportunities to share this.

~

Internationally, Quakerism of an evangelical and recent sort is growing rapidly and taking new forms in South America, in Peru, and in Bolivia. Quaker work with longer antecedents in Central America has some very interesting and promising aspects and it remains to be seen how those Quaker communities will develop over time, but they're lively and growing. In east Africa, particularly in Kenya, FUM—which has held the mission relationship over time—has been working very hard in recent times, and it's not easy, to change the relationship to a more mutual than a dependent one.

~

RESPONSES TO THE
NATIONAL CONSULTATION

I think it's actually really good for Quakers to have someone else look at us because we look at ourselves all the time, so we have certain biases. On the one hand, we think: We're so different they'll never understand us. But the idea that someone can look with fresh eyes is really important.

~

This consultation will have been successful if we have a far greater shared conversation about the future of Friends.

~

I have done this sort of work that you are doing on a smaller scale and I know it's difficult, pulling it together and getting the right balance, especially when you don't know the people you've spoken to.

~

There's an underlying sense that this is a defining moment for ESR, that after all this is said and done, will there be more done than said in terms of the response to this consultation?

~

These are questions [being raised in this consultation] I have wished somebody would have asked me over the years. You don't ever feel like anybody cares what your opinion is, of course.

~

I had never been trained to be a corporate listener, nobody had even spoken to me about what it was like emotionally and through body language and spiritually in terms of rebellion to let myself be a receiver corporately. In a sense, it's a question of are we empowering the person who is anointed to lead at that point in time, or are we sending them out to just tough it out and let's see how it goes? There's so much responsibility on the other side of the interaction there. I feel that so keenly for myself. But we have no training. We never talk about this. I mean, this is the first discussion I have ever had with anyone about that.

~

I want to express a somewhat different sentiment of appreciation for whoever made the selection of the persons invited to this meeting because I think it's an extraordinary gathering and I have learned a great deal from listening to you. I have particularly appreciated the sincerity and the lack of posturing and willingness to listen to one another, and the sharing of information without oppositional kinds of feelings… some have been very rich and good, and very thoughtful.

~

The fact that they are conducting this study in the way they are is one of the most hopeful and interesting things I have seen them do in a long, long time. What may come out of this is potentially enormously interesting and important to the wider Society of Friends. If one of the things that might come out of this is the opportunity for ESR to stage some kind of day-long symposium or conference in a number of different places around the country, where what's being learned in this process could be shared and become a topic for discussion in different Quaker centers, whether in Philadelphia or Whittier or Richmond or wherever, that alone might be a very significant contribution for the School to make to the larger Society of Friends.

…questions earlier about leadership and how do we make it possible to nurture and support people in leadership roles are topics that those of us not in leadership roles should get serious about. Certainly in this Yearly Meeting there are lots of people who would be interested, at least potentially, in spending a day focusing on that question and thinking about what we could be doing here to bring not just young people along, but particularly young people, and to prepare them to help us grow and move forward as a religious community.

~

Thank you for the chance to talk about developing religious leaders with a group of diverse Quakers who haven't always talked to each other.

~

It's good that someone is doing this consultation, listening to a wide variety of voices. This is a good time for self-study.

~

Even though I don't get there much these days, the institution is still dear to my heart and I take hope in it. So thank you for your work in this. I hope it will glean some helpful insights from a variety of people and make the next steps more clear.

~

I hope this consultation raises people's interest and awareness. I'd hope the feedback will push ESR to be stronger and be who the mission statement says they are, and to move forward with it. I was disappointed in some of my teachers at ESR, because they didn't seem secure enough in who *they* were. The average student age there is around 40—that's a lot of life experience. We need professors who are comfortable with who they are and what they're doing.

~

It will be very important to pay attention to the messages that come back from places that have been critical or disdainful or alienated in the past, where there probably isn't immediate likelihood of a lot of crossover.

~

The danger of a study is that you raise hopes and, if not fulfilled, then it's worse than not doing it. My advice is to look closely, listen closely, to what people have said and figure out a short list of things that can be done.

~

My experience with something like this consultation, which I think gets a bit expensive, but it's worth it in the sense of credibility is, where possible send a paper copy summary to everyone you've specifically spoken to. I think it's really important to have a little slip saying, "Thank you, just thought you'd like to hear how your insights fit into the group." It's very demoralizing to open up and then see something in a newspaper.

Seriously, I think it's very important. I found that in doing clean-up after some focus groups, there was a real sense of being unfinished by the participants because they did their stuff and then they really never heard anything else. Just the courtesy of saying thank you, here's a summary, and if you want more information, write to this person. I think it needs to be part of the process because my sense is that the people who are being spoken to are potentially the ones who are going to find you students and are potentially some of the donors.

~

I want to express our gratitude for what turned out to be a tremendously energizing conversation among Chicago Friends. You would be surprised at the immediate and promising changes that have resulted from the consultation…the ESR consultation brought Chicago Friends real gifts! We hope it may have relevance beyond Chicago.

~

Doug Bennett is a bright guy, and I don't know Jay Marshall. It's very smart of them to be taking another look and doing these interviews.

~

I think the consultation is a great idea. Just to be able to say to somebody that I really think ESR is missing the boat…and Earlham, too I mean, the whole thing…missing the boat in terms of not being more active out in the communities, inviting or offering their expertise and inviting other people's expertise and involvement. For a number of years I made it a real practice of visiting other Meetings. I don't do that as much any more because I need to make a living, but in every Meeting I met wonderful, brilliant Spirit-led people who nobody ever talks to. ESR can't be the center of the universe, but it can be very active in the universe, helping people find the center. This was a real privilege.

~

This consultation will have been successful if it helps us identify who we really are as Friends.

~

QUAKER STORIES

I conduct workshops all over the country and one of the things I ask people to do is to just see what they can do in the workplace. I'm getting an amazing amount of feedback from people telling me stories, for example, about "this terrible, horrible person who was incorrigible and was making our lives miserable...I just did what you said and loved him every day and it's all changed and the person is transformed." I think that if anything, I have underestimated the power that we have, the power that everybody has...I don't mean that parochially. I have always given much space for free will and everybody's choices, but the power of love is very persuasive, very persuasive indeed.

~

I was on jury duty and was put in a jury pool for a murder case. I had the experience of being in a room for two-and-a-half days with 50 strangers talking about our beliefs about guns and violence. I was not selected because the prosecution liked my views on the things I was expressing, but I've been thinking about that and about the goal that Friends have of being able to articulate a way of thinking that is not vengeful or polarized and of simply "walking the talk."

I think this is the most powerful piece of what we do. I have no idea if my not very well-expressed thoughts and feelings in response to questions from lawyers made any difference, but there was one guy, for example, who was at the bus stop with me and we discussed gun control and the issue of violence in society. I don't know what kind of influence all of these small things have. I work in the public sector, where a lot of the people I work with are not Quakers, not pacifists, so what they know about Quakers is the way I do my job. It can be a small thing, not expressing theology, but expressing things like work ethics and being responsible to other people you work with, caring in that way. That's where you have—if you're not in a leadership role in the Society of Friends—the real opportunity, in those day-to-day things to express what it means to be a person of faith, acting your faith in your life.

When I was working for Friends it was a lot easier because there were baseline assumptions. I sometimes envy the Amish because there are a lot of questions that don't come up when you are not dealing with the world. I've been thinking about this, particularly the experience of being on jury duty…and I think that's where there's an important opportunity for living your testimonies—in just the day-to-day witness.

~

The very proper answer [regarding the source of financial support for our Meeting] is that it comes from God. The more realistic answer is we don't have a clue where it comes from. We don't have any capital expenses; we are not buying a building…we've done various things to help pay overhead (heat, light, those kinds of things); we have shared space with other churches…We shared space with a school for a while. Our people do donate, but the donations tend to be fairly small. We've actually never had any money. Somehow the needs always get met. We don't take a collection, and the reason is that most of these people are very leery of religious organizations asking for money. We very consciously don't ask for money. We put a basket out there and if people feel led to give, they give. The reality is we've never been unable to pay the overhead…it's pretty special. It works for us. I don't know that it would work for anybody else, but it works for us.

~

My Dad's been burned a lot by Christians and we still argue a lot about what the faith means. He is far from being a convinced Friend. But one thing stuck with me. We were arguing about pacifism or something— I was so frustrated—and I said, "Why do you go to our church? Why do you keep going here? Why don't you just find somewhere that fits you better?" He had been upset about something in our worship order. He stopped and said, "Because I see in you and in the people in that church people who are real…who live out what they say they want to live. In all my life I have not had close relationships with people who can do that." That really floored me. I think that was a sign of how God's working in his life.

~

Was anyone else here present in the [FWCC] Meeting for Worship at the Hilton today? Well that's what I would hold up. Let me describe it briefly. It was a silent Meeting for Worship. There were translators available whenever a message was given. If it was given in English, it would be translated into Spanish immediately, and although I don't know Spanish, the sense of gravity and presence of the translator led me to believe that he was doing a remarkable job of staying in the power of the message.

The messages came from all kinds of Friends including Latin Friends. One woman stood and spoke. She is a member of an unprogrammed Meeting. She said that she had in her own personal journey discovered the saving grace of Jesus Christ, but that she could not feel free among the members of her Meeting to speak honestly about that because members of her Meeting, many of them refugees from bad experiences with Christianity, had an allergic reaction to such language that she wanted to use.

She broke down in tears and was ministered to by those around her. There was a sense of gatheredness and grace throughout the entire hour…a sense of loving one another across the divisions, of welcoming one another, treasuring one another. I'm moved to speak about it now and I was very moved this morning. One of the things I wrote in the statement that we all filled out was the hope that in the very act of building bridges across the divisions, we find once again the core of the center of the heart which we all really hold a piece of. That's where our vitality and our strength lies and our future. I was greatly encouraged and uplifted by the entire experience.

~

…my experiences of finding God in human experience usually have to do with a decision-making process. It has to do with letting go— a willingness for people to voice their own opinions with no question… but at some point there is the letting go. The first time I discovered this was in a Service Committee Meeting where we were trying to make a decision about a new program about employment discrimination. We had done an enormous amount of research. We came to a meeting in which the committee was half Friends, half not Friends, and we suddenly realized that we really couldn't do any more research. We had done the research, and we had to make some decisions, and really put forth ideas with the willingness to really listen to one another.

At the end of the meeting we came out with an idea that nobody had at the start. Everyone was surprised and people came up to me and said, "That's what you mean by Quaker process? That's really something." Whatever it was, we didn't name it that. But whatever it was, everyone recognized that God had been acting in that room, and we came out with a very exciting program.

I need that kind of experience about once every five to 10 years. It is enormously dramatic…to really viscerally feel God act by allowing people to work in certain ways and it may be a loving way, a letting go of what other people have said. It is interesting how it all adds up.

~

About a month-and-a-half ago I sat down with a college student who I have done a lot of ministry with here. She had just been in a church where women were not allowed to teach, not allowed to be elders, not allowed to do a lot of things. She has grown up among Friends and has really been transformed by her experience of worship.

I heard her telling her story about an argument with her roommate about women's roles and the struggles she had with her boyfriend. I just heard her all throughout say, "I tried to really pray and listen to God as I was speaking, I tried to speak the truth in love." I saw her really feeling passionate about things she never felt passionate about before, and wanting to make a difference here at George Fox in some of the ways that women are treated and spoken about. That's a process that's continuing with her. I see those little things as being evidence of how God is transforming people in a real way. Watching her trying to let God be a part of these fierce emotions and channeling them in a way that is productive—the way that God is working and leading her life.

~

At the close of a particular session of FCNL's annual meeting last November, someone remarked, "This is really Quaker process at its best." We were doing business, but it was worship *and* business, as our Monthly Meeting presumably is. Certainly FCNL's constituencies represent a wide range of viewpoints and categories of Quakers, but to see that group frequently move through this process, one really gets a sense of what it means to be a Quaker…being led by the Spirit, respect for diversity, the social issues with which we're involving ourselves. It's a marvelous experience.

~

[This story is about] a mother who lived in this area for a while. I won't tell all of her story, but she was a very needy person, that was very obvious. She had two children. She told us she was hiding from an abusive husband. We learned several months later that, in fact, she was a fugitive from the court system which had awarded custody of those children to her estranged husband. We also learned that she was an alcoholic and when the system discovered her and began to work on her case, the children were returned to the father.

With the church's help she entered a rehabilitation program and eventually moved to another state. She's been there now two years, but she called to say she's been attending an unprogrammed Friends Meeting there. She called to say, "I finally get it, I finally know what you are talking about" in terms of hearing Christ and being in a relationship with Christ. She was thoroughly excited about that, and has been sober now two years, and is in touch with her children and with her ex-husband. He's a Christian, and though that home has not been mended, they are at least in communication. She is sober and she is in touch with Christ. I think that's powerful.

~

When we were young and newly married, my wife had miscarriages, and we were discouraged. She was ill. A recorded Friends minister out of the blue came to see us and he said, "I've been concerned and will pray for you." So he laid hands on my wife and prayed for her healing. That's an example that stuck with me of the power. It meant a great deal to us. She was healed.

There are other times he prayed for people that weren't healed. I mean, this came out of his own discernment. I don't know that he had any empirical knowledge that would separate him from other people about this. But here he was, sensitive—in the old sense of the minister's sensitive—to the need of a young couple. Maybe he could read it on our faces. But that struck me as an early example of real power. Spiritual power. It was good for my rational mind because I tend to be skeptical of miracle claims.

Being philosophically oriented, I still have questions. But here is an example of spiritual discernment and the power, and it came out of an ordinary person who wasn't necessarily a major leader. He was a recorded minister. I don't know that he was even active as a pastor at that time. But that discernment served me well....that comes to mind as an example of discernment and power.

~

A few months ago a young man, probably in his forties, walked into our building for a Sunday morning worship service. I met him as he was coming in and saw him at the end of the service. He was sitting there weeping. I learned that this was the first time he had been in a church building as an adult. He really had no church background as a child either. But he just felt this need to go to church, and he walked in here and what he was weeping about was…[his] sense of the presence of God. I think that is a powerful witness to the reality of worship. It was also, I felt, "conviction." I wondered about myself, and for many of the rest of us, how much we take for granted the experience we call worship.

This man was just overwhelmed by this sense of the mystery of Meeting God in the midst of a group of people in a building.

~

...the most profound example of power related to Friends was an experience I had over a period of six years in this small, dusty town in Kansas of 800 people. I saw 26 oil field workers—violent, angry, immoral, evil, dishonest, corrupt, uneducated—just appalling people. Those people changed from those characteristics to men and women who believed in God and believed that God would lead them. They began to treat each other with dignity and respect and equality and gave up the ways of violence. They even put to shame almost immediately the testimonies of the Friends Church they became a part of, because of their lack of concern for the oppressed and the downtrodden. They actually became leaders.

One of these people came to Portland, Oregon and walked the streets of Skid Row and recruited alcoholics to help homeless teenagers. He asked, "What's your big fancy church doing with these homeless people." I said, "Nothing." He said, "Well I'd better get out here." So he left his house and packed up everything to come and minister to these poor homeless kids when there were five or six Friends churches surrounding that same Skid Row for I don't know how many years, and they hadn't done a thing about it.

That just convinced me of the Friends testimony that once convinced to follow God, it is not necessarily an emotional one-time experience, but it is a convincement of the wisdom of Christ's teaching and how that wisdom is practical in its outreach. It's an allegiance to Christ's teaching that is different than...I don't even know what words to put on it. It's an adoption of a whole new way of thinking, a whole new paradigm, and for these 26 people at least it was a Quaker paradigm. It was one that they took very seriously. The women began to exert spiritual leadership, and the men began to give up violence without any prompting except learning the ways of Quaker spirituality, listening to God individually and corporately. It was an incredible thing.

~

I have an adult handicapped daughter...she was very frail and small and was picked on and beat up every single day of her years until high school. The big question that we had was, "Do Friends testimonies of loving the enemy work if you're helpless? Or is that only for the people who are strong? And do you as a parent then make a choice to live that out in the life of the child who gets beat up every day?"

An autistic boy in her class would beat her with his belt buckle every day and she was seven, she was a little tyke. So each day she would come home crying, and I would take her in my lap and we would pray for—I forget what his name was—but we will call him Joey. We would talk about what would make him so unhappy that he would be beating his little colleagues every day. This went on for some time. I talked to the teacher and did all the normal kinds of things. One day I got a phone call from the teacher and she said, "You are never going to believe what happened. This morning Joey came in and—whoosh—off with his belt ready to hit [my daughter] and this day she did something different. She put her hands on her hips—as only she could have done—and she looked him in the face and she said: Joey, if you will stop hitting me, I will talk to you and I will be your friend."

He not only ceased hitting her, but he spoke for the very first time and began his healing process from being a non-speaking, autistic child. So there was the immediate thing that Jesus said: Love the enemy. He didn't say good things will happen but we believe that to be true.... That experience has been a touchstone miracle in my daughter's life that has given her power. Now in her mid-thirties, she thinks of herself as a God person who can do anything. She doesn't think of herself as a handicapped person who's a victim of the world. And it's because she was obedient in her incredible weakness to this radical notion that God means what God says. Pretty good stuff.

～

I was pastoring a church in a town with a large Hispanic population. It seemed to me there was a good deal of oppression in the community. There were no Hispanic families in the church. I got to know the local Catholic priest pretty well. He was Hispanic, and we both knew this was a problem that we didn't know what to do about.

So praying about it, one of the opportunities not afforded to Hispanic kids was to play soccer at the school. It was another way, really, that the white-controlling interest refused the soccer program for the Hispanic kids. Football was the mainstay in town. So in praying about it, I felt I would like to start an after-school soccer program in the elementary school where guns and knives had already been brought in by kids. There was a lot of racial tension in this little grade school. It was really sad.

So we started this after-school soccer program and it was glorious. The first time we were out there the police came, but it was just really amazing. We played for months and for the first time, Anglo kids and

Hispanic kids were playing together and having a good time. Before long we actually had a couple of Hispanic kids coming to our Wednesday after-school program. We had 100 white kids coming every week and after a little bit we had four or five Hispanic kids coming too. It was a huge breakthrough.

There was a particular family in the church that was adamantly opposed to the peace testimony. I was told that by the father. But he was also a very good friend of mine and he got involved in the soccer program with me. God really began to teach him something through that. Towards the end of the program, his son was beaten up by a group of Hispanic kids and the boy was asking how he should respond. Could he gather his friends and retaliate? His father was the one who sat him down and talked to him about the love of Christ and how we respond to our enemies. Violence wasn't the alternative. It was *really* powerful. It changed that man's whole view of Friends.

I was just back there a few weeks ago; he's an elder in the church now and he wouldn't even have been a member prior to that. It was God working in very powerful ways through simple kinds of actions.

~

I can tell you an FWCC story. This relates to the Friends for Lesbian and Gay Concerns. A number of years ago FWCC had their tri-annual gathering in three countries: Honduras, Kenya and the Netherlands. It was quite a challenge for the Hondurans to sponsor that gathering. They were a minority faith within a quite conservative country and probably risked their viability within that country to sponsor this meeting. In the end, one of the struggles was whether gay and lesbian Quakers would be allowed to come or what communication would be given to gay and lesbian Quakers at this gathering. It really endangered Honduran Friends to sponsor people and have gays and lesbians walking around openly in a country that didn't understand and wouldn't approve.

…Friends for Lesbian and Gay Concerns [were basically told], "You can come but you can't be open and honest about who you are when you come to this gathering." Kind of like telling a Christian that you can come but you can't bring the Bible, or you can't have what your essence is out in public. I was present in the gathering when Friends for Lesbian and Gay Concerns tried to find God's leading…and they spent a year in reflection about how, as a community, to respond to this request. Some wanted to be violent, some wanted to quit, to leave… but they stayed together in prayer and wrote one of the most moving pieces I have ever heard.

It was summed up by asking members of FLGC to seek a deep leading as to whether they were supposed to go and if they were to be living witness of the wholeness of their life and the love that was at the center of their experience. The whole community organized in circles of support around individuals who were called. It was a year of prayer and deep searching, the rejection of the initial anger, hatred, violence—that whole reaction—and the engagement and love that there were no perfect, good, clear answers. There was no obvious—this is what you are supposed to do, but honest searching and the continual return to love as the response and the hope that if one acts with truth, that that will be answered in some way. It was a powerful example for me about how I am to engage in life on small and large matters.

~

What inspires me is the stories of Friends who follow their leadings, who have taken some risks, and have been faithful to where God is guiding them. That's what got me involved with the Society of Friends. I could have been a Presbyterian or Methodist or something else, but I didn't see these people stepping out in faith in other churches the way I did amongst Friends. It's affected my life in a couple of ways.

In my own work, I was led to help the youth in Southern California to start a youth group doing service projects. I didn't want to do that. I fought God. I thought, "This is scary, I don't want to take this risk." But I was empowered by the example of other Friends who had similarly taken risks and followed the Spirit, so I said, "I'm going to try to do what God leads me to do." It's that part of the Quaker experience that has been very attractive to me. It empowers people to trust in inner leadings and to go out to the world and take some risks. I hope that Quaker institutions' education can help young people getting started to really trust that they can change the world, that they can change themselves… through the power of the Spirit.

~

[…we were dealing in my Meeting with] that issue again: homosexuality…and there was a pastor really in favor of rights for gay and lesbian people…and, of course, I think probably the majority of people, the majority of the rural Meetings…are against that. So there was one side pitted against another and we went over and over this whole issue. There were two particular people who were on opposite sides and they used to go at each other all the time in personal confrontations sometimes and in Meetings expressing their viewpoint.

One time they worked together on a Habitat for Humanity house and they had to work really close, hammering nails and doing other tasks. At the next Yearly Meeting, we had a session on this issue that was really getting acrimonious. The clerk called for a period of silence—and out of that came a reconciliation between those two people, with one apologizing and asking forgiveness of the other who was in favor of the gay community. There were hugs and tears and everything else during this time.

It showed how working together on a common project can sometimes overcome what seem to be irreconcilable differences, how having a common goal can sometimes really help because we have a tendency to stereotype, to put labels on people, and working together sometimes can help get rid of those labels.

~

…a [spiritual formation] program was designed around bringing people together from different congregations,…each community that was part of the program had its root in a particular congregation. I've heard numerous times about the effect of those meetings in terms of people becoming stronger and deeper in their own spiritual life, and in their willingness to hear their calling and get involved in service. The program was essentially an academic year-long type. It began in the fall with a retreat that brought people together from different congregations—usually there were between three and five congregations. Those people would come together for an opening weekend retreat.

They made a commitment to meet once a month in their congregational groupings to worship, to break bread together, to have fellowship, and to discuss some piece of spiritual reading. They also made another commitment to be part of a small group of usually two or three people, sometimes as many as four or five, drawn out of the membership of those congregational groups. Those groups met for support and for discipline, and each member of this program selected and agreed to try to stay with and practice a particular spiritual discipline of their choice for the full year.

In May, the entire group came back together with a closing retreat which gave them a chance to both re-establish that network and to focus on the discernment of spiritual gifts and vocation. It was clear this was not just about making oneself feel good about the spiritual…but as one grew deeper into one's faith journey dealing with what was one called to do. I think one of the things that has kept that program going is that it provides a network and a web of connections and supports that cross congregational lines. It is also rooted in local congregations. Each congregation can adapt it to their own interests…

~

As a pastor, I've been thrilled to see how someone in the Meeting has been able to apply one of our Quaker concepts. For example, I was standing with an assistant district attorney of [this] county watching his son play soccer, and he was new to Friends. He said, "Tell me about this idea of the Inner Light that we discussed in our Sunday School class." I said, "Well, it is when you look at someone else and realize there is the Spirit of Christ in that person." We continued our discussion, but didn't talk about it again for a while.

We were on the soccer field again months later and I asked, "I want to know, as a prosecutor how you can justify that with your Quaker faith, particularly if a person may be innocent?" He said, "When I look at everyone whom I face in the courtroom, I look first for that Spirit of Christ within them." And I thought that makes all the difference in the world. It was exciting to me to see how in my pastoral ministry a faith concept had been internalized by a professional and used in his ministry.

~

I'm very conscious of a dramatic experience [related to] an interim pastor at a small church here about three or four years ago. On her first day in a church of 25 people, the father in one family shot his wife and three daughters. On the first day! The amazing part of that story is that the pastor ended up staying with that church for two years, and over the two years that church which is more of a community church because it's the only church in a small town—dealing with loggers and people out in a rural area—pulled together around this whole question and grew. Two years later that church that had been 25 when she came, 21 on her second day, grew to 90 people.

Those people were understanding the peace testimony in a different way because the family was not calling for vengeance but trying to work through these very real, very personal, very hard questions, and trying to work through personal healing. This is the kind of thing that can tear apart a community where everybody carries guns in their cars and that kind of thing.

This small, rural community is now supporting the pastor in doing retreats and talks on domestic violence, and it has a real concern for other people in the area and around the state. They understand what domestic violence is all about and are trying to stop it, to break some of those patterns. They have gone from a potentially devastating, destructive event, the worst of all evils, that has somehow pulled the community together and helped them to be able to reach out and try and help others out of their experience. It is a really amazing kind of story.

~

…a lot of different situations come to mind, but one relates to ESR, so it is probably a good one to use. When I was there, I wrote a sermon on free will in which I essentially said that free will was not God's plan. My feeling was that humans essentially had been created to be close to the will of God and much more open to understanding the will of God. So we would try to live out God's will without thinking about it much. Part of the fall, in a sense, was the emergence of free will, being given a choice to actually do things that were not good for us and not good for other people especially.

This idea is really contrary to my contemporary Christian under-standing, which is that free will is a gift and perhaps the greatest gift from God. My theology professor was really offended, to say the least, by my notion. He just did not like it at all, but he took my sermon away and he read it and he came back and he said, "Well, as much as I detest this idea that you have come up with, it is logical and it is scripturally based, and I can see how you can come to that conclusion."

So he encouraged me to write an article for publication on that. I was really struck by that, how he hated my idea but at the same time he was able to encourage me to go ahead and investigate it and to write about it and bring it out there for other people to hear. Actually, I had a lot of experiences like that at ESR. It was truly a place where, it seemed to me, that self-interest was put aside in the interest of a higher principle.

~

Appendices

This profile provides information about the Friends who were selected to participate in the focus groups. They cannot be presumed to represent the Religious Society of Friends as a whole.

Age

18–24	1%
25–39	17%
40–54	38%
55–69	29%
70 and above	15%

Gender

male	56%
female	44%

Race

White/Caucasian	99%
African-American	1%
Latino/Latina	1%

Which of these words best describes your membership?

by convincement	62%
birthright	43%
programmed	51%
unprogrammed	46%
other (e.g., semi-programmed, conservative, sojourning)	6%

When did you become involved with the Religious Society of Friends?

in the home where I grew up	56%
in high school	12%
in college	5%
as an adult	27%

Who first introduced you to Friends?

parents or other close relatives	58%
found Friends myself	19%
Quaker friends or colleagues	11%
Quaker educators	5%
other (e.g., spouse, pastor, the Spirit)	7%

I have been active with the following groups:

Friends United Meeting	61%
Friends General Conference	34%
Evangelical Friends International	14%
American Friends Service Committee	45%
Friends World Committee for Consultation	44%
Friends Committee on National Legislation	37%

I've attended the following Quaker educational institutions:

elementary school	7%
middle school	7%
high school	16%
college	38%
seminary	27%
other (e.g., Pendle Hill, Woodbrooke)	10%

Please indicate any current or previous connection you've had with Earlham School of Religion:

ESR graduate	17%
ESR Board of Advisors	13%
other (e.g., contributor, alumni council, in-law of graduate)	10%
ESR alumnus/alumna, non-graduate	8%
Earlham trustee	5%
parent of alumnus/alumna	3%
spouse of alumnus/alumna	3%
former faculty	2%
former administrator or staff	1%

Date	Yearly Meeting/Group	Location
12/15/98– 12/16/98	Faculty and staff Students Alumni/ae Board of Advisors Earlham trustees FUM staff	Richmond, IN
12/15	Indiana/Ohio Valley YM	Richmond, IN
12/16	Wilmington YM	Wilmington, OH
1/10/99	Iowa (FUM)	Oskaloosa, IA
1/31	Baltimore YM	Baltimore, MD
2/16	Indiana/Ohio Valley YM	Richmond, IN
2/17	Indiana YM	Marion, IN
2/18	Western YM	Plainfield, IN
2/19	Western YM	Kokomo, IN
2/22	New York YM	New York, NY
2/23	New England YM	Wellesley, MA
2/24	Iowa (FUM)/Iowa (Conservative)	Marshalltown, IA
2/25	Mid-America/Nebraska YM	Wichita, KS
3/2	North Carolina (FUM)	Asheboro, NC
3/3	North Carolina (FUM)	Oak Ridge, NC
3/3	Alumni/ae	High Point, NC
3/4	Illinois/Western/Ohio YM	Chicago, IL
3/9	Philadelphia YM	Wallingford, PA
3/9	Philadelphia YM	Philadelphia, PA

Date	Yearly Meeting/Group	Location
3/10	Alumni/ae	Gwynedd, PA
3/18	Lake Erie YM	Pittsburgh, PA
3/19	Northwest YM	Newberg, OR
3/20	North Pacific YM	Portland, OR
3/20	Alumni/ae	Portland, OR
3/21	Western Assoc./Southwest/Pacific YM	Whittier, CA

FOCUS GROUP PARTICIPANTS' WRITTEN RESPONSES TO THREE QUESTIONS

Participants in 22 of the focus groups conducted during the national consultation filled out a two-sided questionnaire constructed both to help determine the representativeness and diversity of the sample, and to collect spontaneous written opinions before the discussion began. This section provides the participants' responses to the following three questions on the survey instrument:

> 1) *Twenty years from now, given current trends and conditions, I see the Religious Society of Friends as…*
>
> 2) *My ideal vision for the Religious Society of Friends over the next 20 years would be…*
>
> 3) *Earlham School of Religion's best role in that vision would be…*

Twenty years from now, given current trends and conditions, I see the Religious Society of Friends as…

ASHEBORO, NC

If not close to ceasing to exist, in the last stages of trying to maintain survival.

Even more fragmented, splintered, and divided than we already are.

Further divided between Quakerly and institutional.

Changing, learning to "tolerate and accept" differences, experiencing a spiritual transformation.

Continuing to explore "who" we are.

Opening doors, developing memberships, revitalizing old Meetings, and serving our communities.

Hopefully a stronger body of worshipers with a greater vision of mission.

Functioning as several different branches. This will happen whether there is an actual "split" or not. I can see these different branches flourishing in their own right but having less in common as they follow their predominant vision.

Seekers who move from faith to action, probably still small and fragmented.

BALTIMORE, MD

Growing, maybe. Serving.

A vibrant, living organization (spirit-filled) that calls and encourages (nurtures) individuals to respond to God's call on their lives.

Fragmented, struggling (internally). At odds with the rest of the world; that is to say those Friends who have not blended with the world by compromising testimonies and Quaker values.

More like a family.

Publicly represented overwhelmingly by Friends and Friends practice in Africa and in Central and South America. The most vital parts of Friends Meetings in North America and Europe would be concerned with mission and discernment. There will probably be a long history of skirmishes about identity of different bodies of "Friends" and further scattering.

CHICAGO, IL

Getting smaller and smaller; moving toward being laid down.

Much the same—quietly seeking the Light with spiritual and social concerns.

Smaller in numbers than now.

A theologically diverse but culturally (in North America, at any rate) homogeneous group divided by historical disagreements.

Scattered and unfocused with several visions.

Twenty years from now I see the RSF as…

What I think the Society should be now: a gentle, but firm voice in national discourse, showing by example what we have always practiced as Quakers—peace, testimony, equality, and justice for everyone, especially the unempowered.

Diminishing in the U.S. When I go to national meetings of Quaker groups I see a plethora of gray-haired people.

GWYNEDD, PA

Largely ineffective and dwindling even more.

Confused and contentious as it is today.

Growing and vital within each Monthly Meeting with more interconnection between Yearly Meetings.

Limping along, trying not to get anyone mad at them.

Struggling, mired in power struggles.

HIGH POINT, NC

Fragmented.

Continuing to grow apart from theological differences; reorganization as some groups wax and wane.

A group continuing to struggle in finding leadership. I see smaller Meetings possibly closing and some continued generational struggles. But I see a REAL NEED for Quaker presence and witness.

Hopefully having grown.

Continuing to decline and having little impact.

No more necessary than it is now for God's work to be done—but, it is to be hoped we can find ways to continue to do justice and love kindness and walk humbly with God and reflect that in a hungry world.

KOKOMO, IN

Diminished and struggling for survival.

An association of nursing facilities and cemeteries.

Split irreconcilably between explicitly Christian, highly restrictive of the morality of leaders, ministers, and members vs. attenders, and completely free and open in moral and theological categories; gathering together with no common principle.

Strong delineation of FUM from FGC (not mutual identity as "Society"). Fracturing of FUM and alignment around new identity as clearly Christian and distinctly Quaker.

Programmed Friends in the USA growing smaller in size. Kenyan Friends maturing some. Because unprogrammed Friends need smaller budgets and appeal to certain groups of people, some of their Meetings and Yearly Meetings are growing.

Two possibilities: 1) dead or dying. Friends in FUM have lost their zeal and their focus on the living Christ. Spend too much time arguing about social problems, etc...that are only symptoms of our lack of focus. 2) vibrant. Friends in many EFI and some FUM Meetings are regaining their clarity of vision. Pockets of growth can help encourage the rest of Friends if we let them. Christ desires there to be revival and spiritual transformation. It will happen if we let it.

Depleted, with only a few strong Meetings surviving—both programmed and unprogrammed.

Still making an impact on society.

Very small but vital.

MARION, IN

Smaller, hopefully with still some strong leadership and good examples, as Woolman/slavery and lifestyle.

Leaven within the body of Christ, more of a movement than a denomination OR ruptured.

I hope to see it growing, becoming more focused on encouraging spiritual development and outreach. It seems like the headquarters also has this goal in mind.

Smaller and more evangelical.

Even more fragmented.

Twenty years from now I see the RSF as…

About the way it is now. I don't know of much effort among Friends to make master plans and long-range goals and visions (ESR is to be commended for this effort!), so it will continue to run by the inertia of its history and tradition as well as being tossed here and there by the winds of cultural fad.

Trying to hang on and doing about like they are right now: struggling, but taking their stand in the world.

MARSHALLTOWN, IA

Having the potential to become much more known and bringing Gospel Truth to bear in various cultural areas especially having to do with international relations, peace, human justice. Hopefully all this bounded in the Love of Christ.

Continuing as it is, but struggling to teach in real ways what Quakerism is. The challenges will be for younger Friends to rise in leadership and ministry as older seasoned Friends step back.

Spiritually viable.

Dying out if current trends and attitudes aren't changed.

Maintaining their place in society.

Dying slowly except for a few growing programmed and unprogrammed Meetings.

Maintaining present status.

Decreasing to a few.

NEWBERG, OR

Needing to make some decisions about who they/we are and how they/we might work/be present in the world. We are in need of some good leadership. Individuals rooted in the tradition of an openness to how God is calling the community into the future. If this doesn't happen I could easily see many programmed Friends becoming part of the larger "evangelical tradition."

Not a unified picture! Every time I speak of Friends I begin with some sort of disclaimer as to which part of Quakers will be the subject.

I imagine more fragmentation than less, and potentially serious divisions within and among Evangelical Friends as issues of sexual orientation and other lifestyle questions come to the fore.

Continuing to struggle with the same issues of power, theology, mission, and direction with which we struggle now. On the positive side, I see us with a strong potential to actually get out and effect some positive changes in overt, public ways and not always behind the scenes.

Predominately Latino/African on the world scene, with a dwindling of membership elsewhere unless there is a renewal of Christ-centered faith and spirit-filled leadership.

Recapturing the spirit and vision which empowered the earliest Quakers.

Smaller, weaker, less effective.

In three broad camps: 1) generically evangelical, without distinguishing characteristics from the evangelical mainstream; 2) generically "spiritual," with little distinctly Christian or Christ-centered; and 3) programmed and unprogrammed Friends who are effectively engaging a post-modern culture by being Christ-centered and spirit-led to demonstrate real relationships with God that transform lives personally and move society in just and peaceful ways.

Either smaller and frailer/irrelevant or salt of the earth/fruitful.

Losing her "middle-sized" congregations. Large, healthy groups will continue to attract new members; small groups with close family or ideological ties will continue (if independent of buildings); but many groups will no longer be able to afford buildings and/or "released" leadership.

Increasingly fractured between evangelical/non-evangelical. Weakened leadership. Watered down Quaker identity among Evangelical Friends. More and more part-time pastors due to declining numbers.

Still divided, but with a more widespread vision of Jesus Christ as savior, leader, teacher.

NEW YORK CITY, NY

Having fewer people.

Both coming together—Hicksite, Orthodox, Evangelical—as well as pulling apart.

Twenty years from now I see the RSF as…

Holding on, with Friends involved in many good things but neither on fire nor leading the world community in living a God-centered life despite its consequences.

Becoming more like a standard Protestant denomination unless special efforts to combat the trends are undertaken.

The denomination, people throughout the world will be asking advice on peace and social concerns.

We will probably be one percent per year fewer in number. Our focus will be more maintaining our strongest institutions and laying down our financially weaker ones.

About the same.

A third smaller numbers in Northeast U.S. with fewer to *no* "Christian" Friends.

Becoming increasingly polarized between Christocentric and humanist/universalist Friends, with the humanist body becoming more and more secularized.

OAK RIDGE, NC

Growing, becoming more influential (but not necessarily through local Monthly Meetings) but through all sorts of ad hoc Friends organizations; formal and informal events; social action; spiritual growth groups; and impact of individual Quakers.

About where we are now. We are small in numbers and content with the *status quo* in most areas of involvement. We struggle with contemporary issues but are content with the accomplishments of the past.

Either (1) a source of spiritual renewal for the vast group of the spiritually hungry in our society or (2) completely dead because of our inability to identify and offer our unique gifts for that same group of people.

Smaller, more polarized, yet containing subgroups that preserve most interpretations of the Society.

Continuing to provide a different choice as to form of worship and decision-making process. I am concerned about the apparent decrease in tolerance of different views.

Continuing to be divided between 1) evangelical Christ-centered and 2) mystical/socially concerned/spirit-led.

Looking like it does now. Attracting some convinced Friends and losing others. Remaining a small group, important for those it touches and keeps…and for some it touches and loses.

Continuing to make a profound impact on individuals with whom they come in contact. And making the world a better place in which to live.

Further divided by doctrinal differences.

PHILADELPHIA, PA

Potentially divided among all the various forms. Also ideals absorbed by like-minded individual who are not joiners. Move toward personal search for spirituality rather than corporate.

Having become three (or more) independent denominations.

[The unprogrammed segment of RSF as] diverse theologically, not much larger than today.

Probably not basically different from what it is today. Doing its several things with good and earnest intentions, but still with lots of room to grow in grace.

A small but significant religious denomination which, in the U.S. and Europe, will continue to suggest and model alternate spiritual and social concerns moralities.

Not in existence. Friends in the east, especially unprogrammed Friends, take their existence for granted because they were here from the beginning. They worship the history and culture of the society and can be very closed to new attenders and ideas at times.

PITTSBURGH, PA

Possibly an anachronism in the religious community and in society as a whole. I view this, though, as an opportunity for Friends, the quiet people, to get on with what we have stood for for 3.5 centuries. Perhaps we are in another Quietude period that may be ending if we get going.

A continued source of inspiration and challenges for our society.

Twenty years from now I see the RSF as...

Absent a revival, dissolved into a feel good/feel concerned club focused on a cluster of social concerns, unaware of, and vaguely embarrassed by its Christian history.

A necessary belief system that needs to broaden and grow if our current society is to continue.

Small and vital.

Composed of individuals who are so totally over-programmed by their commitments to the outside world and the structure and organization of the Religious Society of Friends that little is left for the journey of the Spirit.

A continuing strong voice of social activism and religious acceptance, and openness.

PLAINFIELD, IN

Struggling, if things do not change.

Splintered. Sometimes effective and authentic on a local level, but generally silent outside the Religious Society of Friends.

At the same level we are now.

Struggling to exist.

Similar in size as today or even smaller. We as a Society of Friends are not providing enough leadership types.

Status quo.

Continuing in the same state or declining in programs and participation partly because of two-income families. This consumes time for Meeting involvement.

Needing to continue to seek to combine the ideals of "new" Friends with testimonies, actions, and reflections of long-time Friends. Still politically active, seeking to find Christ as the center.

A continuing and meaningful influence on a social activist level, and let us hope, a reinvigorated church (Meeting) on the local level.

Not sure.

Probably still struggling with problems of diversity.

Being a place of diffuse and watered-down spirituality; members losing more and more touch with the roots of Quakerism and the power of the original message, being uninformed about the Bible and Christianity and uninterested in contact with other branches of Quakerism; members are burned out with guilt from not doing enough to save the world.

I hope, growing; I hope less divided within itself—and I hope ESR will be contributing to that.

About where it is now: quietly influential and providing a base from which individual Friends may be led to public action. Unprogrammed Friends Meetings will continue to provide a refuge for those who have found other denominations to be too narrow. This is both a strength and a challenge. There is a need to keep a strong pool of people who are grounded in faith and practice.

I think there will continue to be those who would work to bring different strands of Friends tradition together but they will remain in a minority.

Split into many groups, many of which do not know about the others, or do not care if they do. Many focused inward and a few outward, being relatively effective locally but without a sense of the whole.

Increasingly active in Africa, primarily pastoral Friends; continuing to be primarily Caucasian in the U.S. and Britain; less active on social issues on the Meeting/Yearly Meeting level, leaving the work to the likes of AFSC, FWCC; increasingly diverse in terms of beliefs within the Society; and remaining roughly the same in numbers with small increases in Africa.

Moving towards being two separate bodies worldwide, one under EFI, one affiliated with FWCC (a pessimistic view) who have little to do with each other. Particularly in matters of theology we are already at a point where differences will be incredibly difficult to reconcile, but there at least seems to be an openness to work at this and stretch among some people. The efforts to understand our roots and mutual tradition I see as positive and providing possibilities for speaking out and acting strongly and with integrity in the world.

Twenty years from now I see the RSF as…

Yet more diverse and inclusive. The general membership may well be comprised of convinced Friends who found the Society as adults. There may be greater polarization between the liberal, universalist, and Christ-centered groups and individuals.

Much as it is today but hopefully with an increasing awareness of and appreciation for diversity within the Society of Friends and in the whole of human experience.

RICHMOND, IN

A small group of Christians who honor God in their daily lives and who reach out to the world around them with the hope of God's forgiveness of sin, His love and peace and care.

Training laity to be leaders, training Quaker pastors (prison ministry, the peace testimony, gay ministry, peace justice studies, women's studies, current events) and how Friends view their personal world.

Diminishing in size due to slowly losing younger families. Those involved in Society of Friends will be thoughtful Christians, attempting to continue bridges within the community, and Yearly Meeting. At present, we lack some tools for communicating who we are. I see this impacting our Meeting.

A small religious body, but still witnessing and working effectively (hopefully) guided by the distinctives of our faith in its wholistic applications.

My hopes and fears are so far apart on this that I cannot give an honest answer. I am very concerned about radical departures by all branches of Society from the essential historic Quaker norm (which I believe comes closer than any other tradition to God's Truth) and to the widening gulf between Christ-centered and non-Christ-centered Friends.

Very small and difficult to distinguish from mainstream America.

Similar to the way it is now—but spread more widely in urban areas.

Continuing to decline and lose strength (given current trends). The trend can be reversed and we could become a growing and increasingly visible organization with higher impact.

Small and vital. A significant voice of truth/Truth. An avenue for a varied, unique and individualized spiritual journey.

Important as a witness to Christian simplicity (using the word as Wilmer Cooper uses it).

More relevant than ever in speaking to the world's problems, but seriously handicapped by lack of leadership.

Vibrant and filled with a push/pull of folks who are content with religion that requires little and many who crave and work for a depth of spirituality that transforms. These factors will continue to create tensions of "ownership" of the RSF.

Their message is very much needed. We should not hide our Light. It could be a vital force.

Struggling to have its youth understand its history and live its truths.

Losing our important source of spiritual strength for those unwashed.

Increasingly polarized, unfortunately, with the main growth at the evangelical and universalist wings, with decline in the center.

Fragmenting, unless we focus on the spiritual life which strengthens and undergirds us and sustains our work.

WELLESLEY, MA

Either dying, aging, nobody but baby-boomers, or revived by healing, evangelism, service.

More fractured than now, with universalists and Christ-centered more militant about how the other is ruining the world, especially the Quaker world. Unprogrammed will hold their own numerically, middle of the road will continue to decline, and near-fundamentalists will expand some. In Northwest Yearly Meeting there will be an amazing revival.

Experiencing pockets of revival and renewal but overall remaining the same in numbers and impact.

Still vital and central in my life.

Twenty years from now I see the RSF as...

Struggling to deal with the spiritual crises of humanity as we deal with a sudden end to our ability to maintain a growth economy and an increasing population.

Growing stronger and larger where Friends practices and testimonies are taught and encouraged and where all are recognized as ministers. Growing more generic, becoming just another community church or Unitarian Universalist Group where Friends practices are not taught.

Hopefully a part of a larger ecumenical grouping faithful to the basic Quaker testimony.

Spiritual home for many.

WHITTIER, CA

Continuing its decline in membership and vitality.

An even older group than we are now and still *very* divided between evangelical and liberal Friends.

Struggling to mediate in the "culture wars" between liberal progressives and orthodox conservatives. Can we be a model of peacemaking and ecumenical dialogue? Can we find common ground? These are the questions we will continue to struggle with.

A vital force to meet the needs of individuals through a personal relationship with Jesus Christ.

A pivotal force in societal change.

Declining in numbers unless we can clearly state what we believe in ways that are understood by those who are seeking.

Holding its own, but just barely.

Growth in evangelical Meetings; more mission-oriented.

Maintaining current membership numbers. Some small Meetings closing or joining larger Meetings (pastoral Meetings) depending on leadership to some degree.

Transformed.

Evangelical Friends are growing rapidly, while liberal, unprogrammed Friends and programmed Friends (FUM) seem to be holding steady or in some areas, declining. I suspect that these trends will continue, with resulting demographic shifts in membership.

WICHITA, KS

Continuing to grow and flourish in some areas, but struggling to serve in others. The world needs the Friends message and we need to strategize spirit-led methods to get it out.

More and more diverse and out of touch with one another…rural churches continuing to decline, many closing, with urban churches and Meetings growing.

Smaller and weaker than I would wish it were unless we are able to have and implement a larger, more unified, more fully Christ-like vision.

Having little or no significance in some areas or regions. In other places I see it being a very vital part of the life of society.

An organization of religious activity in form, but not experiencing Christ's power, having become what the early leaders rejected in the 1600s.

Few in number, concentrated in a few vital centers.

Continuing, in each future generation, to define and redefine itself through consultation, and efforts at community—the goal is continued growth and coming closer to maturity in Christ.

My ideal vision for the Religious Society of Friends over the next 20 years would be…

Movement toward re-establishment of Quaker procedures and testimonies.

Christ-centered, mission and service oriented body. Working together in harmony in spirit of differences.

Bigger, bolder, more present in the local communities it serves.

A vibrant active group with programs for all age groups and a great bond of love among the seekers.

For Friends to experience a passionate, embracing of Christ-centered, Biblical Quakerism. To be a model of blending social concern and gospel teaching and evangelism.

A movement, not so much denominational in structure—more united, less fractured.

An increase in spiritual maturity and outreach with 20% more members and new Meetings established in regions in the U.S. and around the world.

To see a new wholeness in the Quaker movement where we would hold the "journey inward" and the "journey outward" in balance; where we would be both active on cutting-edge social issues and Christ-centered; where prayer and service would be seen as important. We need to put the pieces of original Quakerism back together once more.

Growing, definitely. Serving, sharing our experience of God, mutually, with others, modeling Quaker testimony and process, educating, mentoring, nurturing.

All branches of our Society accepting each other and uniting on some level to promote Friends' goals, concerns, ideals.

The Society of Friends could be a "movement" neither Protestant or Catholic, but a *third* witness.

A body with the discipline necessary to sustain public testimonies.

To be strongly persecuted.

A re-invigorated Society of Friends with liberal/FGC Friends establishing new Meetings.

That more young people (children) are drawn to Quaker Meetings and that their interest continues into adulthood. Young people brought up knowing Quaker "traditions" will become our next generation of leaders.

A worldwide body growing ever more united in commitment to the everlasting gospel of Christ as the foundation.

All branches of Friends understand and respect each other so that even though they disagree, they can work together to enrich lives and solve social problems. Each member does individual study and disciplined prayer and those who visit the Meeting for Worship and Meeting functions "catch the Spirit" and either stay with the Meeting or take "Spirit" back to their own church.

A struggling group working to humbly hear how we can all *together* come to what God wants of us.

What I think the Society should be now: a gentle, but firm voice in national discourse, showing by example what we have always practiced as Quakers—peace testimony, equality, and justice for everyone, especially the un-empowered.

Increased membership, more grounded in Quaker faith and practice, alive with the spirit, and more unified in our diversity.

To be leaders in peace, social justice, and human rights issues and situations.

Growing cooperation between the various groupings of Friends—FGC, FUM and Evangelical. Less drawing of absolute lines dividing Quakers.

My ideal vision for the RSF over the next 20 years would be…

Friends return to spiritual roots, return to speaking with spiritual authority among ourselves and to the wider world.

To move to and beyond tolerance of our variations.

Growing and vital with members who are aware of their spirituality in everyday life.

To mend its quarrels with other branches of Friends and busily living our faith within our Society and in the world.

Discernment about issues of power and accountability. Providing Quaker education to Quaker children more cognizant of other branches of Quakerism. Socially active on many levels.

HIGH POINT, NC

To recapture the centrality of Christ as one and the same with the historical Jesus. To recover a sense of Biblical authority.

Capture hearts for Christ. Worship groups and fellowships grow stronger, outreach and evangelism become strong, outgrowth of renewed fellowships.

A growing group, developing leadership, outreach and transforming lives.

To be a strong force in showing our social testimonies.

That Meetings might begin to make inroads into their communities. My ideal vision is that the message of Friends might be heard in a new way.

Find ways to continue to do justice and love kindness and walk humbly with God and reflect that in a hungry world.

KOKOMO, IN

For Friends United Meeting to be more able to grow. I think we have a message for people who want to be Christian but have had negative experiences with more authoritarian groups. Also we may appeal to persons who experience God but need to maintain their intellectual integrity.

That a deeper vision is shared with a wider and more varied audience.

Growing and recognized beyond our own circles because of participation and contributions to society in various fields.

A vibrant, diverse, Christ-centered people, attractive, bearing witness to the love and justice of God to society as well as the other members of Christ's church.

A recovery of our identity—differentiating ourselves from the religious culture to which we have comfortably adapted—differentiating ourselves from the civic culture which excuses us. This is not just being "counter-culture" but rediscovering the source of our corner on the western mystical Christian tradition and living into that identity fully.

Vibrant. Regaining our relationship with God through experiencing Christ daily. Letting go of out-moded traditions. Getting back to our focus on Jesus Christ as the One who speaks to our condition. Jesus' ministry was almost entirely devoted to relationship (with God) over religious systems.

A return to spiritual vitality that would revive declining churches, provide a context out of which strong leadership would be raised, and unite Friends around a common purpose. This would necessitate a willingness to let go of some of our Quaker "traditions" in order to participate with God in today's world.

"Christ-centered" "liberal Friends" separating from "post-modernist" "liberal Friends" and re-engaging Gurneyite Friends, re-engaging Christian pastoral and Christian unprogrammed Friends, together engaging in the work of living out and sharing our experience of God's love *and* sovereignty.

Strong delineation of FUM from FGC (not mutual identity as a "Society"). Fracturing of FUM and alignment around new identity as clearly Christian and distinctly Quaker.

MARION, IN

Gospel believing, spirit-filled; evangelistic; church-planting; inner-city; multi-racial, cross cultural, cross-generational; non-isolated; fully participating in the Great Commission.

My ideal vision for the RSF over the next 20 years would be…

I hope to see it growing, becoming more focused on encouraging spiritual development and outreach. It seems like the headquarters also has this goal in mind.

Continued growth and renewal.

A united and clearly articulated direction. A unification of at least the programmed Friends. That Friends clearly proclaim their strengths and distinct doctrines in a relevant way.

That major elements among Friends (like ESR) would articulate clear identity within the diversity of the Society.

Remain true to its heritage and make necessary adaptations to be meaningful.

More congeniality.

MARSHALLTOWN, IA

Have more ministers and working to encourage Friends to grow.

To—(and I hate this word, it's too clichéd) have some revitalization— rebirth—renewing—and forget part of history—(the people and we've done it this way forever attitude) and work with today and tomorrow. Get off our laurels and be evangelical again.

See more people introduced to "Friends." In many small rural Meetings, growth is limited. It would be great to see an influx of convinced Friends come to these Meetings to bring new "blood" if you will as well as fresh ideas and new insights.

To build community, to strengthen and deepen our Quaker values— for unprogrammed Friends to become clearer that Quakerism does not mean anything goes, yet to remain inclusive. To work on diversity, to center ourselves in the Spirit.

To see the Christ lifted among our relationships with culture and our communities.

Clear about who we are as Christians, Quakers. Clear witnesses to Quaker testimonies and as a result we are a growing, vital, vibrant, prophetic denomination.

Revitalized within the Society.

1) For Friends to unite around a commitment to engage our culture at points of need, oppression, waste, consumerism, nationalism, etc.
2) For Friends to recognize the need to build quality leadership expectations, positions, and practice.
3) For Friends to use our distinctives as tools to engage culture not quaint differences, etc.

A growing sense of unity; a faith and practice which truly reflects the heart of Christ; the re-connection of "evangelical concern" with social concern; the emerging of a distinguishable people (marked not by plain clothes or language) but by a Christ-centered character and spirit of service/ministry.

That it be larger, stronger, more effective.

Programmed and unprogrammed Friends who are effectively engaging a post-modern culture by being Christ-centered and spirit-led to demonstrate real relationships with God that transform lives personally and move society in just and peaceful ways. I think the next 20 years will be critical in determining how large or small that group will be.

For us to renew the experience of the early Christians and early Friends. Sometimes I wish there were a church that taught the gospel so strongly that it was not at all attractive to any who did not fully subscribe to Jesus' radical teaching. For example, the early church and early Quakers totally rejected war and the attitudes that promote it. However, I also want to be inclusive and accept variety and understanding of Christ's teaching.

That programmed and unprogrammed folks would become more aware of one another. That Friends might be able to spend more time focusing on their similarities instead of their differences.

I envision an intentional, creative reach of communication throughout the spectrum of Friends that could recover some sense of cooperation and understanding. I imagine the varieties of Friends offering their strengths to one another and seeing the history and tradition of Quakerism in a fuller sense. I imagine feeling safe and heard in more Quaker places on that spectrum.

My ideal vision for the RSF over the next 20 years would be…

Leading a rejuvenation of the soul of the U.S.A. We are a hungry nation seeking for categories and language to describe the truthful reality of the Spirit within us. Quakers can offer ways to discuss, deal with, and foster this inward life and its outward actions.

To be forthrightly the Friends Church with flexibility of worship modes and strong recorded ministerial leadership.

To live fully into the pieces of truth that are ours. To be alive and vibrant in the integration of God's presence in all endeavors.

Renewed confidence in our "offerings" as Friends to the larger Christian community. We have something to give and teach the church; we need to boldly do so.

N E W   Y O R K   C I T Y ,   N Y

To see it grow and attract many more people from many different walks of life and many different racial groups.

Continue to provide a model—practical one—of journey inward—centered leading to a journey outward into the world.

For Friends to begin grappling with the hard inconsistencies of living the average American Life and following the teachings of Christ. What does Jubilee mean for us? How can we break away from our culture of fear (lawsuits, need for insurance against everything, putting away for old age, prison building…) into God's culture of love? Can we help each other listen to our hearts and follow these leadings despite worldly arguments to the contrary?

Growth in numbers and commitment to basic Quaker concepts of experiential religion; gather economic and ethnic diversity of membership in U.S.

To do church planting in big cities. Have both programmed and unprogrammed Meetings. Involved in more outreach programs.

A diverse body of young/old, new/experienced, with Meetings in many states where there are currently few Meetings.

Better informed about one another.

A single identity of Friends with enough room to cover a wide balance of people who identify themselves as "Friends" who continue to seek and learn and are familiar with Christian and non-Christian language. This would require planned educational programming from elementary school to older adults and solid Meetings spiritually and financially.

A multi-racial and multi-cultural religious body in which the lines between "programmed" and "unprogrammed" Friends are blurred, and doing the work of God is at the center of all activities.

OAK RIDGE, NC

The various branches seeking their common threads and providing unified leadership in prison reform- and education-work with consensus decision making and other service work as they are led. Interiorly, I would like to see the movement reclaim an integrated approach to the spiritual journey—integration of body, mind, spirit. We have strayed up into the head far too often. Reclaiming the concept of abolishing the laity within all branches of Friends which does not remove the need for training and preparing folk for pastoral ministry.

Probably more and more decentralized—less stress on national connecting but development of impact groups.

To see the number of Meetings greatly increased, good attendance at worship services, good financial support, and Friends reaching out in all areas to a hurting world.

For more and more Friends to become knowledgeable about the history and practice of Quaker principles—for the traditional testimonies to be the focus—and for a large percentage of Friends to practice the semi-programmed format of worship.

The worship-centered community that includes wide variety of views among those who share an appreciation for a common form of worship and are appreciative of the roles of a religious society in the larger community.

To see the division described above become less (much less) antagonistic and to see an acceptance of our diversity and an appreciation of the value therein.

My ideal vision for the RSF over the next 20 years would be...

A group that grows, one at a time, until it becomes a spiritual and social force in the lives of more and more people.

Having members who are committed to living in the Light whose lives inspire and give leadership to a greater valuing and appreciation of diversity and contribute to a loving, just society and work for peaceful reconciliation of differences.

That [we] learn to be more understanding of each other.

PHILADELPHIA, PA

A loving family exhibiting the varied charisma of a fecund God.

[For the unprogrammed RSF] Strong commitment to nurturing spiritual life of members and attenders regardless of theological orientation. Double our size, with 1,000 Meetings and worship groups, knit together by traveling seasoned Friends, attendance at regional and national gatherings, by print and electronic communication. *Deep spiritual life, strong community life.*

More multi-racial. More known to others as a living religion. New ways of being corporate and a community. Providing education and support for those on a spiritual quest.

More educated about the various parts and more open to a broad and inclusive vision of God's work among us—more concerned with answering God's call and less introspective.

To be more visible and accessible and, hopefully, more informed among its parts/branches about each other and more respectful of their differences as well as their similarities.

An organization which responds compassionately to the needs of others, takes the leadership in social justice issues and is centered in the spirit of Christ whose example members try to follow.

PITTSBURGH, PA

Dynamic growth in new members while maintaining and deepening our spiritual core.

A vibrant religious organization; bring real spirituality, even Christian spirituality, to those who don't need or can't tolerate the liturgy and organizational bigness of conventional religions.

That more people would encounter our visions and see, experience, and feel us.

As diverse as it is today, I do not long for unity. But I would welcome better grounding in our history. I see the Society as a leader—raising questions which enable others to see the best in themselves and others.

A community in which individuals prioritize their spiritual journeys, committing time and energy to them with great deliberation. A culture which supports and encourages this aspect of the human within the society.

Easily accessible and strong channels for causes that support our testimonies. Perhaps a more vigorous drawing of new members.

To be a spiritual community living out our testimonies and affecting the world; a community that has developed, through continuing revelation, a message that speaks to the condition of our world (e.g. multi-ethnic, multi-faith with life models ranging from "experience," to "scientific" to "the market"). Innovative concepts will have moved us to new forms of expression, moving beyond our historic concepts of witness.

A concerned, trusting, group of Friends Meetings warming toward similar goals, seeking to find directions that encourage growth, social concerns.

A group, "internally" ecumenical, that will quietly grow in its influence in American society, particularly in secular matters as business, industry, finance, in addition to mainstream life. And, our outreach will grow in similar ways to Quaker outreach following WWI and WWII, and similar desperate needs.

PLAINFIELD, IN

More active leadership by non-paid Friends. A great deal of respectful cross-communication between branches. Friends speaking with a strong, united, prophetic voice.

A rediscovery and revitalization of our Christ-centered principles.

My ideal vision for the RSF over the next 20 years would be...

Expanded urban outreach; shift from rural to urban, suburban; aware of Quaker distinctives and testimonies.

To provide opportunities for each member to find a ministry in which to be involved and to share our unique Christian witness with the larger church. Also to understand that we can evangelize without demeaning others.

Stop talking about how great we think Quakers are and start acting like we believe Quakerism is important and seek new "converts."

That we would be increasing in number rather than declining; that we would be a vital force in society in general; that we would actually have a vision for ourselves.

Developing ways Friends can reach out to unconvinced Friends. I feel the general population feels Friends are not open to "outsiders."

Friends seeking recognition in our changing society. Actively looking at the younger generations for leadership. Continuing to respect our testimonies—teach history, and seek to realize those ideals in society—continue to share the message that Christ is the center for each individual.

To recapture the original vision of Friends—i.e., a return to the connection that Christ Himself is here to teach and lead His people.

A Christian Religious Society dealing pragmatically with all of the issues of life—religious, social, and economic.

A committed religious community dedicated to religious and social justice growth among individuals and in the public forum.

That people in modern society would "discover" the authenticity of the Quaker Christian message and turn away from the materialism/shallowness of the present toward a strong and faithful service-oriented life.

For the small town and rural Meetings to consolidate into groups large enough to have the resources for ministry to Friends and an outreach to the community. Friends to quit worrying about being so Protestantly competitive and instead focus on the values and testimonies that made us so "attractive" in the first years of the movement.

A revealing place for God, with a deep connection to the living Christ, where faith provides an abundance of love towards all groups of Friends and marginalized groups, and that love inspires and gives energy to become involved in showing the human potential, showing how to live a life of love, for all humanity, witnessing a life of justice and mercy.

A voice of reconciliation. An alternative to restrictive fundamentalism. A place where faith is deep but not narrow. A witness to a faith-based social conscience.

A vibrant international society of people who strive to respond actively in their lives to divine guidance, loving and respecting one another and God, working in pro-active ways for peace, justice, and community.

A Society which welcomes and contains a wealth of diversity in ethnicity, race and spectrum of belief; a Society where the rifts between different types of Friends have healed; local and regional involvement in expressing faith in action; more of us, and more of us united across those pastoral/non-pastoral differences; and a wider awareness of what Friends do and are like around the globe.

To see acceptance among Friends of our different branches as being the equivalent of different monastic orders—able to accept each other as holding valid perspectives on our faith and willing to interact and challenge (in a positive way) each other to be more faithful to a broader vision than any may hold of what it means to call oneself a Friend, and willing to convey that more clearly to the rest of the world.

While this is hard to answer without a long opportunity for reflection, I would hope for a larger number of small, cohesive worshiping communities in the unprogrammed tradition. I would hope for systematic instruction in living disciplined, religious lives. These I take to be the ground for effective social witness.

Providing a safe, nourishing community for spiritual growth and development, affirming both its roots in Christian experience as well as the truth and wisdom of other traditions.

My ideal vision for the RSF over the next 20 years would be…

That we reach out within our own communities; that we walk our talk and that we are active in the larger community—the world. I hope we are comfortable with all Quakers.

RICHMOND, IN

Help members, attenders to feel as if their meetinghouse is a light-house, a place of refuge. To empower Friends that trusting the good news of God's love is an ever present aspect of daily life, e.g., with anxiety and business so prevalent in our lives, prayer and meditation are needed habits.

A strong vibrant group of believers who believe in God as a one true God; a faithful companion in everyday life; a restorer of hope and a giver of love to all…A faith community that reaches out to all, drawing those to our God, His Son Christ Jesus through the work of the Holy Spirit.

A broad spectrum of classes, as it is now—not dominated by Christ-centered Friends. Open to the Spirit of God leading people's lives. A strong theological school with many viewpoints.

The words above plus a deeper, broader faith and living witness in the "world."

Growth in numbers, growth in visibility, growth in ministries, growth in vision for change, growth in impact in people's lives.

Diverse but inclusive. [The worst thing we can do is splinter and quarrel within.] I was picturing the ideal when I wrote in the previous question: Spiritually vital!

A movement that has returned to its roots of mobility not so wed to the traditional meetinghouse bound place of ministry but perhaps returning to more "home" churches/Meetings.

Regaining the early Quaker vision to win the entire world to the gospel of Jesus Christ and to radical Christian discipleship in the Quaker movement, empowered by His Spirit at work within and without— yes, that is exactly what I mean.

As a vital, religious community in which people are able to identify their spiritual gifts and be supported in using those gifts in the service of God.

To refine and strengthen its testimony on simplicity.

With more service programs keyed to high school and college age, and expanded training though internships and ESR, a new and dynamic wave of young leaders giving vital life to the Society of Friends.

Similar to the above, with the added overlay of continual dialog on the issues of difference—both in terms of style and substance.

Growth, greater impact on the world, greater influence on policies/politics (e.g. peace, reconciliation, against addictions such as consumerism, gambling, quick-fix "happiness." Healthy love for each other along the theological and cultural spectrum). Growth as a church that is meeting the spiritual hunger of many people.

Their message is very much needed. We should not hide our Light. It could be a vital force.

Resourceful young leaders and followers that will know how to reach a diversified group and functioning well together.

Grow in depth and strength.

Strengthened, growing Meetings; deep inspiring times of worship; a renewed corporate vision and commitment; continued work in conflict resolution throughout the world, but with more prominent *Quaker* identification.

WELLESLEY, MA

Hopefully a part of a larger ecumenical grouping faithful to the basic Quaker testimony.

Spiritual home for many.

To articulate an understanding and practice of Christianity that is relevant to many seekers today and of which they are unaware. To provide a model of decision making that expands into political process.

To pay greater attention to the needs for pastoral care—and to do a better job attending to eldering and guiding membership. Also, for Friends to return to social action not as a "concern" but rather as an expression and outpouring of their Living Faith. I continue to be

My ideal vision for the RSF over the next 20 years would be…

concerned that the foundation and prophetic message of our faith is watered down with "hazy" theology and "whatever you profess/believe is okay with us" approach!

All branches of Friends will be in close communication with each other and the offering to the world of these practices and testimonies of Friends will continue to draw in those who need that aspect of Christian practice.

Revived by: healing, evangelism, service and…expanding, offering a witness to the world, developing leaders.

I would see a revival from both a Jesus-focused and environmental/peace focus where our take on these two religious concerns would be lifted up, made more coherent, and would energize our congregations as a source of life and hope in their communities.

WHITTIER, CA

A vital, *inclusive* society able to welcome religious seekers and committed Christians/universalists into dialogue and service. A place where *young people* and *young adults* will find not only welcome but be energized and inspired.

To continue the vision of a great people to be gathered—because there is one "Christ Jesus" who still speaks to individuals today.

To be more visible in our local community. To be more influential nationally. To live our faith so clearly our beliefs would be easily identifiable and recognizable by all.

Overcome our reticence to state what we believe and stand for clearly.

I'd like to see unprogrammed Friends strong enough to be a visible force in their communities. So many of our Meetings seem to be struggling to maintain a *status quo.*

Revitalization of the Quaker Christian testimonies among all groups of Friends (evangelicals to rediscover the Quaker roots and some unprogrammed—the Christian message.) [Of course this is over-simplified and too generalized!]—Continued significant growth in attendance and membership.

A re-commitment to a practice of discernment; a ministry of truth; a grounding in love; an opening to transformation; a unity which surpasses understanding.

The exploration of common spiritual roads and bridges across Quaker divisions, may hold out hope for a strengthening of The Society of Friends in the future. Ideally, Friends will continue to be represented far beyond their proportion of the population in activities of healing, reconciliation and service. May the center grow brighter, and the outreach extend.

Increased growth by remaining true to our testimonies yet also adapting those to changing times. It seems to me this means that we have to let our communities and society in general know who Quakers are and what we are about. In other words, be clear about our identity.

To attract more younger members, and to reach acceptance for each other among all kinds of Quakers. We are a small denomination that has had tremendous impact on the world but we could be even more effective if we could spend less energy on our differences.

Growth—outreach programs—both domestic and foreign.

WICHITA, KS

To increase membership in *all* parts of the world-maintaining a balance of spiritual and social concerns.

Re-energized by a renewed vision of Christ's call, moving beyond a comfortable *status quo* to a place of connection with the poor.

For us to take seriously Jesus' visions in His inaugural mission as He stated it in Luke in the Nazareth's synagogue and really walk with Him in that.

A beacon to the world of how we can live together and how we can follow our own leadings to make the world a sharper focused place.

A Christ-centered force for spiritual and social change, moving toward the work of God in the world in redemptive strategy.

My ideal vision for the RSF over the next 20 years would be…

Everyone would think of us as undeniably and strongly Christian, but would also recognize us as advocates of our historic Christian testimonies of peace, simplicity, equality and truth.

A broader acceptance of the distinctness of the various segments of Friends with greater stimulus to good work/action.

[Continuing, in each future generation, to define and redefine itself through consultation, and efforts at community—the goal is continued growth and coming closer to maturity in Christ].

Continue to be a national and international force for spiritual, social and political good.

Earlham School of Religion's best role in that vision would be…

ASHEBORO, NC

Emphasis upon the lives of individuals and work of agencies that demonstrates the Quaker way of life. Consideration of quiet worship, Quaker Business Meetings by sense of meeting under the Spirit, the testimony against war, universal compassion, that of God in every person, etc., especially the function of the clerk as the agent of the Meeting to carry out Quakerly concerns.

Providing some of the people and intellectual resources to develop leadership and spiritual growth.

Train and help provide leadership.

To equip students to be biblically trained to share and live out the gospel as Friends.

Leadership development. Help with the struggle for identity in the 21st Century. Who are we?

Equipping men and women to serve the Society of Friends—providing strong leadership in local Meetings and Yearly Meetings.

To provide mature and trained leaders as pastors primarily as well as other leaders, and roles for those not led to be a pastor.

To make its primary focus on producing visionary spiritual leadership for our local Meetings. To communicate a vision of wholeness that could bring us together again.

Education/understanding of all Friends faith ways. Networking.

Academic training—Bible, Quakerism, testimonies.

A place with resources and leisure to reflect on the integrity of Friends practice and speak "truth" in dialogue within and without the church.

Facilitating, networking, maintaining connection among current and prospective Quaker leaders.* Nurturing, educating Quaker leaders and followers; not just educating, but providing and facilitating others to create internships and other professional growth opportunities. (*not limited to young people, but leaders emerging at any age.)

Provide (at least a part of) a vision for this entire Religious Society of Friends, while providing a vision for Gurneyite Friends.

Education to appreciate different perspectives on the essentials of Quakerism.

A place for Friends to become better grounded in Quaker traditions and spirituality.

Supportive-relationship with local Meetings: ties, friendship, assist in the development of the next generation of leaders.

Have two different programs: on-campus and get off campus to where the Quakers are. Recognize who are potential leaders, pastoral and others, and nurture/develop them. We need youth leaders and pastors as well as lay ministers. Develop on-line courses/lectures lay Friends can take as they have the time available. The outreach aspect is crucial.

As a place where Quaker leadership can be equipped and encouraged, coming into a sincere understanding of the Christian basis of the faith, and then turning out into the world to continue that vision.

ESR's best role in that vision would be…

Teaching the whole Quaker tradition, practice, history, etc.—and while doing so, do it *across* traditions. Bring in faculty from all these places.

Providing training for potential leaders, who may or may not be students of Earlham, providing outreach throughout the Quaker community.

Educating leaders, educating Meetings in faith and practice, Quaker scholarship, a gathering place for important discussions among and beyond Friends.

GWYNEDD, PA

To commit to being a top-notch Quaker theological seminary whose purpose is to train and develop Friends ministers.

Keep trying to help us get to know each other.

A resource for all Yearly Meetings.

To continue to try to get more EFI students, to continue to sharpen its vision of who/what it is, and to joyfully broadcast its mission throughout the Quaker world.

Education in local Meetings. Clarification of leadership. Creative offerings for education within Friends circles but not necessarily in Richmond.

HIGH POINT, NC

To make its MAIN focus training pastoral leaders for FUM. To move in a more decidedly evangelical direction.

Continue pastoral equipping, become more intentional in areas of Christian education, youth and children's ministries; continue spiritual and scholarly challenges.

To equip, prepare, develop leadership—specifically pastoral leadership.

Prepare students for leadership both at Yearly Meeting and international levels and particularly the local Meetings.

Training leadership, particularly training individuals interested in pastoral leadership. ESR needs to concentrate on leading the way in communicating the messages of Friends and helping others to articulate the message.

Providing options to what other seminaries and Bible colleges offer in theology, etc.

Providing leadership, preparing leaders, stimulating and articulating an authentic Friends vision, nurturing and training pastors for the challenges and opportunities of ministry in local Meetings.

A resource beyond the preparation of professional leadership—a community of thought and creativity that would challenge us—as part of us—not a remote academic institution.

Provide leadership and education that prepares persons for ministry in local congregations and for the Society of Friends.

Providing trained leadership to articulate the message to a new generation.

To concentrate more on solid pastoral preparation with greater acceptance of evangelicals and work with non-evangelicals toward greater acceptance and less ridicule of others. Aiding visibility in significant ways through publicity, etc., would be helpful.

Teaching toward students who believe in God's sovereignty and human need of God's intervention in our lives and giving up catering to self-centered religion and self-defined theology. Offering distance learning, non-degree programs, extension courses for all "kinds" of Friends— pastors, prospective pastors, "elders," Sunday School teachers, prospective missionaries, etc.

Defining and training leaders. Clarifying the core affirmations and distinctives of Friends.

Teaching and encouraging "ministers-in-training." Teaching them to "rightly divide the truth (scriptures)." Encouraging them in their faith. Encouraging them to stand firm in the faith. Also, it would help if some more "practical" classes could be offered. Hands-on training so to speak. Perhaps it would be good to reach out beyond the campus. Make use of some of the technology to offer classes at satellite locations.

Be positioned to support and equip a "new brand" of Quaker leadership unlike any in our recent past.

ESR's best role in that vision would be…

MARION, IN

Teach reconciliation among Friends and tolerance. FWCC tries to an extent.

Teaching/developing pastors/leaders and promoting Christian Quaker works and growth.

I honestly cannot picture ESR involved in this kind of mission. What is sorely lacking in Indiana is a Bible school which honors the Friends positions. I don't think ESR can "get there from here."

To adopt more Biblically based standards yet also help us to have an understanding of other world views.

Education of leaders and laity.

To clearly state their objectives and directions. To develop people into strong and effective leaders who will take Friends toward an ideal vision. For programmed Friends, ESR could play a strong role in the training of pastoral leaders if they (ESR) articulated and instructed people in programmed structures and theologies.

To be a major source of such an identity [for RSF] and the thought and work that goes into it. Not that other Friends are denied their Quakerness, but that here at least is one clear strong identity of Quakerism.

Prepare leaders to assist.

MARSHALLTOWN, IA

Help publicize who Friends are and what they are all about. I'm continually surprised at how many people have never heard about Friends/Quakers.

Send ministers who would [prevent] Quakerism from seeming ingrown, but show that Quakers have something that others want to be a part.

Get in touch with local issues and trends of multiculturalism even in rural areas (Iowa) where it traditionally has not been an issue.

To train, inspire, educate Friends. To continue to challenge the society to recognize Quaker ministry. To do writing/teaching/training in various ways.

Model revitalization.

Encourage local Meetings to support ESR and to make use of leaders trained by ESR whether it be as pastors or lay leaders or Meeting general secretaries.

To offer education for those of us who cannot move to Richmond. To provide a center of Quaker thought and leadership. To offer spiritual direction and mentoring. People yearn for searching and sometimes do not feel able to ask for that.

NEWBERG, OR

Equipping people to serve in a variety of ministerial/leadership positions across the spectrum of Friends. Youth pastors, spiritual directors, pastoral counselors, etc.

1) To train for leadership not just ministry. To work with Yearly Meetings nationwide to upgrade leadership skills.
2) To raise "bar" for leadership qualifications. To recruit our "best and brightest" for leadership. To help Friends to see advantage of leaders who make a living wage, etc.
3) To model for our society examples of engaging culture through writing, teaching activism, etc.

Resist the trend toward "unitarian Quakerism"; affirm Christ-centered theology and practice. Cooperate with other Quaker educational centers such as George Fox, Azusa, Houston.

A center of Friends thought, integration, training. A model of intellectual and spiritual authenticity. A meeting place for the family of Friends.

To be as Christ-centered as possible and as academically strong as possible. Continue to emphasize the history of Friends as fundamental to us today. Be a center that would attract Friends students in other schools toward special short- or long-term missions or projects.

By educating and training servant leadership which helps enable Friends to live out their transforming faith in society.

I doubt seriously whether ESR or any other Friends institution will be able to significantly affect the future direction of the Friends Church.

ESR's best role in that vision would be…

To model, train, and teach leaders how to listen to God intently and to think critically. I'm not sure if our post-modern culture would accept this, but it may be that Earlham could become a sort of Quaker theological center, which could articulate and publish our faith in an academically credible way which would bear fruit spiritually.

Training the people who might have the immediate experience of bridging Quaker differences (and differences with other denominations and faith traditions), so that they might model and lead into creative communication. ESR would continue to support and enrich each person's call and ministry to honor, ultimately, *God's* vision for Friends and the world through the particularity of specific lives.

Training and equipping *leaders* (people with a clear understanding of their role in working with others to bring about change—personal and corporate).

By preparing the spectrum of Friends to minister to a hungry, spiritual world. Both major branches have strengths which are needed as we move ahead and offer the truth of the Light of Christ within each person. ESR can also, by its presence, create spaces for discussion where there may not have been before.

NEW YORK CITY, NY

If there could be an ESR on-the-road program, ESR could function as an advancement/outreach tool for Quakerism.

To be radical! Challenge young Friends and help them find the tools to challenge others without causing despair in the difficulties of discerning one's path and the means to follow it. ESR, if it could become a place where Friends meet to engage in worship, Socratic dialogue, testing and renewal—as well as formal learning—could play an important role in the spiritual renewal of this country. I see a need for a non- (or barely there) institutional center to stimulate and nurture the souls of seekers, to provide a forum for real dialogue among Friends.

To train people for mission fields as pastors/Christian workers.

As an R&D institution.

Training for teachers of children and adults.

1) Facilitate formation and maintenance of support groups for "Friends" employees/staff/outreach, etc. through face-to-face contacts and electronic connection.

2) Educate in fund raising, planned giving, grant writing, and ways to provide and or maintain solid financial base.

3) Training for elders/M&O/M&C committee members.

To encourage universalist Friends to send students to Earlham, and to find as many ways as possible to build God-centered bridges between FGC and FUM Friends.

Equipper—bringing/offering ways to bringing dreams and visions into reality. Providing a safe place whether in Richmond or satellites where Friends can seek, explore, and question their relationship with God/Jesus/divine, and deepen and lengthen it.

OAK RIDGE, NC

Continuing its fine academic intellectual work but bringing in "other ways" of knowing. Having more coursework on the mystical traditions and elements of our historic foundation and on those that currently are being experienced. Refreshing the ways of past Friends into use and service within our Meeting structures, such as eldering (in a positive sense) oversight and clearness committees.

Vital. Primarily for the spiritual nurture of Friends both with and without intent of formal employment with Friends.

To equip people for ministry, leadership, and outreach.

To provide nurture and education for the wide spectrum that is modern Quakerism, both helping to train pastors (by establishing a stronger connection to Quaker strongholds, i.e. North Carolina) by making an alliance with another seminary, i.e. the new Wake Forest divinity school; and providing training which will prepare Quaker students for less traditional forms of ministry, i.e. concern for ecology, peace work, etc.

To train QUAKERS in QUAKERISM. Don't try any fancy stuff, just train Quakers to be Quakers. Everything else will work out. All the Society needs is to be more Quakerly. That is about all we can expect from a non-institutional, institutional religion. ESR can serve us best by being more purely Quaker.

ESR's best role in that vision would be…

Training people to aid Friends in developing individual ministries and to facilitate community building within the Society, especially within a Monthly Meeting.

As a place where Friends of varying points of view can learn to accept each other and to learn from each other. Is it logistically feasible for ESR to do outreach type of education programs? A sort of extension program or distance learning?

To prepare pastors able to bridge the kinds of gaps represented in our Meeting.

Development of leadership skills in the general membership so that every member can develop their calling to be a minister.

To provide distance learning and continuing education for Friends.

P H I L A D E L P H I A ,   P A

Being a center of *intellectual* life of Friends—of all stripes. And more…informing and equipping Friends—as *Quaker Life* says. Equipping to live in the real world and healing it.

Helping us find a common religious language, or at least understand each other. Provide educated leadership grounded in Quaker faith and practice.

To provide solid, rigorous instruction in a variety of religious studies— to enhance religious leadership to Quakers from *all* Quaker branches and to allow great spiritual growth to a wide variety of Friends and non-Quakers.

To train catalysts with knowledge of Quakerism and Christianity and filled with the experience of the Spirit who would travel about in Pacific Yearly Meeting's Meetings and listen for what needs to be done. Those ministries would then find ways to organize Friends to do what they are led to do. Training in pastoral care would also assist overseers in Meetings to care for their members.

To nurture individual and corporate gifts or charisma and to educate the Religious Society of Friends about our history and tradition.

Prepare Friends for ministries to support [my ideal vision for Friends]— without expectation of common theology, but with deep expectation of experiencing God, the Spirit. Prepare Friends to work and travel in listening, nurturing, and teaching ministries—but not in judgmental roles.

PITTSBURGH, PA

To be a community, a catalyst for spiritual education, an integrator of life concepts in order to visualize God's continuing revelation, a force to engage in dialogue throughout the world, a living organization with a real-time presence throughout the world.

To train individuals who can serve as resources and as anchors in our spiritual seeking.

A repository of Quaker history; a fertile, bubbling source of contemporary spiritual and intellectual energy.

Identify young Friends who have the capacity (personality/intelligence) to lead. Allow them to experience a process which they can then model, take to other settings. The process? Raising questions which evokes "that of God" in others.

To train individuals who are able to encourage others in their spiritual seeking.

Incorporates many traditions into an enlightened program that supports both structured and unstructured Meetings.

The three major points in the announcement of the national consultation—these should be examined by the School and Monthly/Yearly Meetings and from that dialogue, direction(s) will emerge.

PLAINFIELD, IN

Train facilitators of change, rich in scripture-based teaching and effective in leading others toward a life of faith and love.

Provide stimulus for the renewed focus in the previous question [ideal vision for Friends]—a vision for Friends, not Lutheran, Baptist, etc. Provide pastoral leadership in sympathy with the above focus. Provide inspiration to young Friends that will generate their interest in the value and importance of local Meeting/church ministry.

Strong pastoral leadership. Teaching Christian materials. Bible teaching to know how Quakers have come to the beliefs we currently practice, etc.

ESR's best role in that vision would be…

Enable, empower pastors to minister to both programmed and unprogrammed Friends.

Perhaps through pastoral conferences on a regular basis; perhaps also to create internet connections, classes, seminars, conferences to strengthen and encourage Friends at large.

To train leadership and shape the vision of the Society.

Equipping leaders, both professionals and laity, to *feed* the two-pronged mission of individual and corporate development of self and of service to society.

To provide a place for individual Friends to respond to and prepare for (and perhaps test) authentic calls to ministry and service.

A center for communication and exploration of views. The prime institution for training leaders and pastors.

Education of pastors and creating regional centers for education and spiritual growth.

To make sure it keeps in touch with the *real* and *felt* needs of Friends directly, particularly pastoral Friends.

Be prepared to train leaders and I hope we send them people to train as leaders.

Preparing leaders who can be responsive to the needs of Quakers; who can be change agents. People who have vision themselves and who can communicate that vision to others.

PORTLAND, OR

To invite Friends worldwide with leadership potential to ESR, but also take classes "on the road" to Meetings, educating on the Biblical and historical roots of Quakerism. To be a place where Quakerism is learned (since one cannot read church dogma to learn), where love of liberal and evangelical approaches to the Quaker message is fostered, where one learns to discern God's call and how it manifests itself in one's own life and in the lives of others.

To train ministers in pastoral Meetings and those who minister within programmed Meetings. Catholics talk about "formation." I think they mean forming whole persons who can then serve. I hope ESR reaches for that *plus* good grounding in Quaker history and practice. And *of course* good Bible study.

I think the Society of Friends needs people who are well grounded in Friends history but also able to articulate a vision of the future.

Providing education for: a common basis of Friends history and theology; training for Friends workers, both pastoral (for both programmed and unprogrammed Meetings) and for social action.

Assisting Friends who are led to ESR in developing their strengths, and a greater sense of what it means to be Quaker, historically and in present times; helping them establish ties with Friends around the world. ESR could (and does, I believe) also tailor some programs to the needs of Friends who do not need a three-year program, but would rather have a year of study, or an opportunity to work with Friends in other parts of the world.

To help build the foundation of those who understand the radical interpretation of the gospel message as central to who Friends are— (neither a quaint distinctive nor an anachronism) and provide a place to explore what this means in our practices in our local Meetings and churches and also what this means in a interfaith world. A place where people can explore the theology of our business and church governance practice, for instance, and how to apply it more widely and make it accessible to others.

Short-term residence courses would make the school more accessible to working adults. Instruction which requires up to three years residency takes leaders out of their worshiping communities and does not send them back, to everybody's loss. Our religious life begins and ends in community and as such is a witness against the strong individualism of our time and place.

Equipping leaders who appreciate the specifics of Quaker thought and experience but who also can relate it to a much broader array of thought and experience—connecting the specific and the universal.

ESR's best role in that vision would be...

Continue to provide a Quaker distinctive environment for studying Bible, Quaker studies, Quaker approach to pastoral care, etc. Emphasis should be on Quaker perspective and not just merge things into a general Christian approach.

RICHMOND, IN

Provide a broad education for pastors. Expand teaching the meaning of "lay ministry" for both programmed and unprogrammed. Help provide leadership regarding acceptance of diversity, dealing with competitiveness, seeing that of God in each.

To help us break out of the mold of meetinghouse worship, and equip ministries to gather seekers with Christian community, but are not bound by walls.

A radical reorientation and a return to the purposes for which the School of Religion was created.

ESR isn't large enough to be everything to everybody, so they should prioritize, should train Christ-centered pastors in sync with the majority of Friends Meetings in this area (IYM).

To equip leaders with the theological training and listening, consensus building, speaking and writing skills needed to create these supportive Quaker communities at local, regional, and national levels. This training should include a strong background in Quaker faith and practice.

To train and inspire leadership, both professional and lay leaders to express the vision of where Friends may be going.

Train/educate pastors. Inspire members of Meetings to take on more leadership and ministry responsibilities. Be a model to Quakers everywhere.

Preparation of pastors and leaders whose faith has been tried, tested, and challenged intellectually, spiritually, and faithfully. Exposing potential leaders to a world view of Truth and our responsibility to demonstrate God's love to that world. Express a faith that is "real" both intellectually and spiritually. Church planting, missions, evangelism.

Not a Bible-based school. A liberal institution that can accommodate many viewpoints and welcomes students of varying backgrounds. I'd also like to see a non-degree program of continuing education, classes at night, speakers and lecturers to appeal to working persons in the area.

Preparing diverse leaders—some for pastoral work, some for social justice, some evangelical, some others.... Also being a place where people can come who are called for spiritual credentialing and renewal.

WALLINGFORD, PA

Giving quality training to fill the pastorates of programmed Meetings as well as leadership to Quakers service bodies that need spiritual leadership as well as efficient administrators.

To nurture folks to join into the structures that exist at many levels— not just as the top leader—so that they can have the ideals of Friends and help these organizations to struggle with the ongoing question of, "What does it mean to be a Friends school, hospital, retirement home, Meeting, etc."

Educate potential leadership—good theological grounding. Encourage respect and listening among Friends. Don't get identified too much with one narrow faction. Offer quality satellite programs in places with concentrations of Quakers (Jamaica, Kenya). Develop distance learning D.Min. with summer school.

Training of leaders who are prepared for long-term commitment and vision for the Religious Society of Friends over the long haul—leaders who can deal with pressure and discomfort. Training in Quakerism (including history, theology, testimonies), Bible, Christianity, and practical skills.

To train people to go back to their communities and be leaders.

To give its students appropriate background and practice in being Friends.

Leadership training and development.

Illustrate and educate in the spirit of *Christian* simplicity.

WELLESLEY, MA

Working with those who are preparing in a deeper way, having made a commitment to a life of ministry.

ESR's best role in that vision would be…

Pull in non-scholars from time to time. Get out more. (Not get all worked up about their own internal problems—the community there can get quite insular…). Participate more in Yearly Meetings and international conferences.

Providing spiritual nurture for "leaders," members, and seekers. Providing content—historical understanding and practical application of the spiritual life in the "work" world and providing a focus for life issues.

Grounding students and future leaders in the Bible and gospel message as understood by Friends historically. Inculcating the integrity of living one's whole life within a spiritual framework.

To *educate*, *train*, and *support* Friends of any/all traditions for leadership—and to pay attention to nurturing those Friends who are already active in their call to ministry.

To help people called to ministry to mature in their understanding of the basic Quaker testimonies of the Inner Light (Light of Christ), simplicity, and harmony.

Bringing people of various branches of Friends together to share and learn what they have in common and what historically has made the various branches different. Training for those who would serve in pastoral roles and youth work.

WHITTIER, CA

Continue to be a center for training people to serve in all areas of Quaker Christian leadership, but especially in training those for pastoral ministry—at ESR in Richmond and by courses and/or classes via video and the Internet to reach those unable to attend at Richmond—to reach Friends around the world. Also to be able to assist Meetings in special ways—especially—the nurture and care of their pastors!

A unique gathering place, of interest for perhaps different reasons to Friends from our diverse traditions, where we can meet each other in the spirit of loving truth. Explore honestly the economics of Quaker ministry and leadership in the 21st century. Train individuals for skillful leadership/ministry; gather Quaker leaders/ministers/elders in conferences/workshops. Are you open to adding a degree in spirit-led organizational management?

Hold to the tradition of Quaker integrity; do not abandon Quakerism for a homogenized, trendy Protestantism. Strengthen the appeal of ESR to *all* branches of Quakerism by making explicit its value to each. Specifically (for example) show FGC-type Friends the value for their own spiritual practice of ESR involvement.

To prepare leaders (especially leaders who can fill the pastoral role) who can speak to the theological needs and demonstrate the similarities among Friends and be able to break down the barriers.

Train and *encourage* leaders in pastoral care and for work with youth.

I'm not sure. You could probably best help western *liberal* Friends by providing them with a better grounding in the Biblical and historic roots of Quakerism. We also need more programs for *young people*.

To train students to be ministers, missionaries and church planters in order to make an eternal difference for Jesus Christ through leadership ministry.

To train pastoral leaders. To train and educate members of local Meetings. To help local Meetings define their identity.

More visible in local Meetings, more often to assist local Meetings in creating belief statements that are giving the same or very similar message across Quakerism.

To seek out those who are interested and called to ministry and provide paradigms in leadership that are in line with Quaker principles. In the pastoral tradition, it would mean providing a means to sort out different leadership styles that would fit into Quaker theology.

WICHITA, KS

The preparation of leaders (and followers) to fulfill our mission.

As a cheerleader for a new emergent Quakerism that is less self-indulgent, more willing to sacrifice respectability.

To help students catch the "fire" of the 17th century Quakers and, like them, let Jesus "teach His people Himself" and follow Him.

ESR's best role in that vision would be…

To train people who can help people learn what their true calling is; to encourage them in carrying that out; to train people in relationship building, clear communication, understanding and upholding one another.

To participate in the definition [of ESR]; to implement its mission statement; to offer expertise in all leadership efforts; to let us know through the Internet what's happening; to develop class offerings by correspondence and the Internet.

To train leaders among Friends with a missional focus reflecting the life-changing heart of Christ.

Leadership/modeling in bringing groups/ideas together.